HITLER'S BANKER

HITLER'S BANKER

HJALMAR HORACE GREELEY
SCHACHT

John Weitz

LITTLE, BROWN AND COMPANY

Boston   New York   Toronto   London

First Edition

Illustrations 4–19 courtesy of UPI/Corbis-Bettmann.

Library of Congress Cataloging-in-Publication Data

Weitz, John.
    Hitler's banker : Hjalmar Horace Greeley Schacht / John Weitz.
      p.   cm.
    Includes bibliographical references and index.
    ISBN 0-316-92916-6
      1. Schacht, Hjalmar Horace Greeley, 1877–1970. 2. Bankers — Germany —
Biography.   3. Banks and banking — Germany.   4. Inflation (Finance) — Germany.
5. Germany — Economic conditions — 1918–45.   I. Title.
HG1552.S33W45   1997
332.1'092 — dc21
[B]   97-7832

10 9 8 7 6 5 4 3 2 1

MV-NY

Book design by Julia Sedykh

Published simultaneously in Canada by Little, Brown & Company (Canada) Limited
Printed in the United States of America

For Susan and the children

CONTENTS

Illustrations/photographs
appear on pages 171–79.

ACKNOWLEGMENTS

I would like to express my warm thanks to the following:

> Kurt Viermetz
> Baroness Christina von Vietinghoff-Scheel
> Joyce Hoven
> Dr. Hans Huber
> Frau Manci Schacht
> Mark Lynton
> Herlinde Koelbl
> Tom Wolfe
> Michael M. Thomas
> Morley Safer
> Michael Mertes
> Hans Jürgen and Victoria von Goerne
> Countess Aline de Romanones
> Paul Volcker
> Joachim Stresemann
> Karola Noetel
> Jonathan Kranz

My special thanks to Roger Donald, who has shepherded the likes of Shirer and Manchester and, eventually, me, and to Ned Chase, who had the idea.

INTRODUCTION

THE TIME OF Adolf Hitler continues to fascinate and to horrify. The events he unleashed baffle and bewilder even those of us who lived in the midst of them. How could they have happened in Germany, that bastion of ethics, logic, and enlightenment, with its high rate of literacy and education?

Even though some were well born, most of Hitler's paladins began as vagabonds and failures. Their worship of National Socialism and its high priest was comparatively easy to explain. But what of those with secure backgrounds and worldly success who decided to throw in their lot with Hitler? What could persuade a prominent industrialist, landowner, banker, lawyer, physician, or academic to join a mixture of vulgar working-class brawlers and hate-filled upper-class misfits?

The internationally famous German banker Hjalmar Horace Greeley Schacht was one of these anomalies. His place at Hitler's side seemed as incongruous as his mélange of names. Schacht's early endorsement and subsequent know-how legitimized Adolf Hitler and eventually helped him fulfill his many promises to the German people.

Schacht, a seasoned banker, first became world-famous in 1923. As the democratic Reich's tough new currency commissioner, he throttled the fledgling republic's ruinous runaway inflation, restored a semblance of financial order, and probably saved his nation from anarchy. That same year, Adolf Hitler, an upstart agitator and political loudmouth, tried to overthrow the government of Bavaria as a first step toward national revolution. He landed in prison.

Ten years later, Adolf Hitler, now the Nazi chancellor of Germany, recruited the famous Hjalmar Schacht into the newly structured Nazi hierarchy.

This is Schacht's story.

HITLER'S BANKER

NUREMBERG,
OCTOBER 1, 1946

HJALMAR HORACE GREELEY SCHACHT, sixty-nine, a tall, forbidding, gray-haired figure dressed in a rumpled business suit, his reptilian neck rising from an incongruously informal sport shirt worn with a tie, stood on a small platform in Nuremberg's Palace of Justice. He was flanked by a white-helmeted American Military Policeman. They faced a vast courtroom crowded with people. For a year, day after day, he had shared the dock just below the platform with twenty-one other men, all defendants, all accused of war crimes. His assigned seat was at the far right of the front row facing the dock. Their defense attorney sat just below them.

Photographs of the fallen and disheveled deities of the Nazi firmament, crowded onto two long wooden benches like superannuated schoolboys, had appeared in magazines and newspapers all over the world.

Schacht, one of the world's most famous bankers, Germany's senior representative during two decades of international conferences, the Nazis' former minister of economics and president of the Reichsbank and member of Hitler's cabinet, calmly faced the judges and their decision. The verdict was pronounced by the dapper former attorney general of the United States Francis Biddle, the American member of the International Military Tribunal.

Speaking in English, Biddle said that the accused Hjalmar Schacht was acquitted of the charges against him. He was free.

Through Schacht's earphones, a tinny, mechanical voice needlessly and redundantly repeated the court's sentence in German. Schacht, who spoke excellent English, had no need for interpreters. His hawk-nosed, leathery face showed neither relief nor joy. He almost shrugged his shoulders, as if regretting the waste of time — the court's as well as his own. Like the easy winner of a drawing-room debate, he accepted the verdict as a foregone conclusion. For him, there had never been one moment of doubt. He knew that he would be acquitted. Nor did he feel a single second of guilt. The harsh testimony and brutal evidence about the mass murders of civilian and military prisoners, and the horrifying films from the freed extermination camps, had crushed many of his fellow accused, but he knew the judges would find him innocent of any complicity with this beastliness. As for "conspiracy to prepare for war" and "conspiracy to commit war," the crimes with which he was charged, he had indeed helped rebuild Germany's military strength, but for the sake of peace, not for the conduct of war. If he had erred, it was on the side of patriotism. Like most of the world, he too had been deceived and betrayed by Adolf Hitler, and he had even been sent to Dachau. Surely, the verdict proved what he had been claiming all along.

He made a small, courteous bow and left the platform.

The ten men who had stood to hear their sentence before him earlier that day were no longer in the courtroom. They had been sentenced to hang the next morning.

THE FRISIANS

THE SCHACHTS CAME FROM the narrow strip of land between the two seas that connects Germany and Denmark, which is named Schleswig-Holstein. Anyone who loves the Hamptons on the South Fork of New York's Long Island would feel affection for the flat, salt-sprayed fields of Schleswig-Holstein, which reach west toward the North Sea and its offshore islands. As in the Hamptons, the area's seaside resorts of today began as fishing villages. The locals — Frisians — are tall, unsmiling, reserved people; many are light blond and blue-eyed. Frisians seem as placid as the famous cattle they breed. Like most people who live within reach of northern oceans, they are rarely impulsive. They usually think long and carefully, laying their course before setting out to sea. They are not given to shows of affection, and as they will tell you, they live long lives, "if they don't drown first." One of Hjalmar Schacht's ancestors had twenty-four children by four wives and lived to the age of 120. At least, these are the facts as chronicled by Schacht himself, with the understanding that people from seafaring areas are prone to exaggerate and are permitted a certain artistic license.[1] To this day, many Schleswig-Holsteiners speak that peculiar Anglo-Scandinavian brand of German called Plattdeutsch, which is a

---

1. Hjalmar Schacht, *76 Jahre meines Lebens*, p. 27.

friendly singsong, neither English nor Danish, nor really German. Visitors from the rest of Germany, with their precise Hochdeutsch, like to hear Plattdeutsch. It is calming and pleases the ear. But the Frisians' gentle accents are deceiving. They are hard and determined people. Their flat landscape has always invited disaster. Wild storms at sea and widespread coastal floods have drowned many fishermen and wiped out whole farm families ashore, with all their cattle. The salty North Sea and the Baltic are shallow, like America's Great Lakes, and their storms are vicious.

Today's local Schleswig-Holsteiners have learned to shrug their shoulders and take the money when rich big-city folk from the rest of Germany to their south transform little thatched-roof cottages into millionaires' summer homes. Even the placid Holstein dairy cows have learned to bear the exhaust of Ferraris. Just like the Hamptons.

Then, as now, Frisians appear slow; but they are quaintly witty and also very, very tough traders. Hjalmar Schacht's ancestors settled in the village of Büsum. The local cattlemen and dairy farmers bargained so fiercely that even the cleverest cattle dealers, most of whom were Jewish, were aghast. The Büsum people usually outfoxed them. The Christian Frisians were not prejudiced; they just knew who did what, and who was what, and were even better traders.

The northern part of Schleswig-Holstein was Danish, then German, and after World War I, once again Danish. Though their sovereigns changed, the Frisian people remained on an even keel, at home with both Danish and German ways. They never considered kings or emperors their masters. They reserved that respect for one another. On the beautiful, wood-carved, brightly colored front doors of their small houses, they still mount signs with the names of both spouses. Not just "Johansen" but "Peter und Greta Johansen." Women called their husbands by their last name. Hjalmar's grandmother from Friedrichstadt never called her Danish doctor husband anything but "Schacht!" In Schleswig-Holstein, women had to be equals and towers of strength because all too often their men died young, leaving them to take care of the family.

Hjalmar's titled Danish mother, the Baroness Constanze von Eggers, was just such a woman. Her sense of independence was inherited. Her famous liberal father had helped abolish serfdom in Denmark. The match was well below her station, but Constanze had married for love; and even though aristocratic, the von Eggers did not prohibit her from marrying into the middle class.

Hjalmar's father, William Schacht, was a young schoolteacher in the small town of Tondern and the son of an eccentric country doctor who spoke Plattdeutsch and charged all his patients, rich or poor, the same fee of sixty pfennigs for treatment and medication. Despite his waiting room full of poor country folk and fishing people, Dr. Schacht had brought up twelve children. When Denmark ceded the province to Prussia by treaty, every citizen of Schleswig-Holstein was given the option of taking Prussian citizenship or leaving the province without any loss of personal property.[2] William Schacht decided to escape the clutches of Prussia and its military conscription. Like many people from Schleswig-Holstein, he went to America.

Constanze, his future wife, soon decided to follow him — at the time an act of extreme personal courage and independence. Because young ladies of good upbringing did not travel without a suitable escort, the young countess was accompanied by an elder brother and a servant girl. They boarded a ship to Copenhagen and from there, on Friday, October 13, 1871, went to New York. Friday the thirteenth lived up to its reputation. It was a fierce crossing. The small liner *Franklin* arrived two weeks late, but Constanze was undeterred. Despite shifting cargo, a bad list in stormy seas, and a lack of fresh water, she stayed calm and confident. There was even a rumor that the ship carried cholera, so when they docked in New York, Constanze and her companions were confined aboard, quarantined through the Christmas holidays. They were finally allowed to disembark, and on January 14, 1872, the impatient Schachts were married in St. James Episcopal

2. Norbert Mühlen, *Schacht: Hitler's Magician*, p. 2.

Church on Fifth Avenue and Madison Street. He was twenty-six and his bride twenty-one. At the end of the year, on December 11, William, who worked in a German brewery, became a naturalized American citizen.

The two newly minted young Americans were enthusiastic citizens. Their great hero was Horace Greeley, the New York journalist and politician, one of America's most influential voices. Greeley, an early abolitionist and liberal, represented everything Constanze and William Schacht held dear, and they devoured his editorials in his daily New York Tribune.

In the wake of the Civil War, hatreds still ran deep, but Greeley believed in amnesty for the defeated Southerners and in suffrage for all Americans. He angered many New Yorkers when he helped post bail for Jefferson Davis, the former Confederate president. The Schachts were ecstatic when Greeley, backed by a coalition of liberals, ran for the presidency. Although he lost, and lost badly, William and Constanze remained his fervent admirers and, even after their return to Germany, never gave up Greeley's brand of liberal Americanism.

The Schachts' first child, Eddy, was born in Brooklyn in 1872, the year Greeley died. Sadly, William had failed to take Greeley's famous advice to "Go West." He stayed in the East and held a variety of jobs, among them one in a typewriter factory in Ilion, New York, but nothing worked out.[3] He even tried to open a business in New York City but failed. The new young parents had to give in and return to Germany. In his memoirs, their loyal son Hjalmar offers more positive reasons for their return. He wrote that while things were precarious in America, Germany was in an economic upsurge (which was true) and that his parents "were homesick" (which is unlikely).

In 1876 the returned emigrants settled in Tinglev, an inland town just north of today's Danish-German border, with the Baltic seven miles to the east and the North Sea twenty miles to the west. William found a job teaching in a private school. It was

3. Ibid., p. iv.

an ill-paid position, one of many that plagued William until late middle age. The Schachts were often on the edge of bankruptcy.

On the blustery and snowy night of January 22, 1877, their second child was born. They planned to name him Horace Greeley, but grandmother Eggers insisted that the Danish name of Hjalmar should come first, "so that he would at least have one proper name." The compromise resulted in Hjalmar Horace Greeley Schacht. The family's persistent monetary perils threw a long shadow, and little Hjalmar began a lifelong revolt against empty pockets and set out to prove that the Schachts were every bit as good as the von Eggers.

Schacht's multinational first names confused generations of bankers and journalists in many countries; they even rattled the fledgling Nazi Party of the twenties. The Nazis (short for National Socialist German Labor Party) began as a thoroughly socialistic and anticapitalist sect. When Schacht's prominence as the commissioner of currency made him their target, the party newspaper printed a story that "this manipulator" was "a Moravian Jew named *Chajm Schachtel*."[4]

William Schacht remained an American, in passport and spirit, despite all the setbacks he had suffered in his beloved America. Like so many people of the German north, he loved the English-speaking world, with its sense of individuality and independence. Schleswig-Holsteiners were loyal to the string of Hanseatic ports from Hamburg to Danzig, which were much closer in attitude and temperament to the English and the Americans than to the Prussians. A standing joke in Nazi times, when the Gestapo was out of earshot, was to ask, "Which English city has Germany ever held?" The answer was, "Hamburg!" To this day, people in Hamburg say that "if it rains in London, everyone in Hamburg opens his umbrella."

In the case of William Schacht, the Hanseatic sense of personal independence was in strong evidence, but the sense of com-

---

4. Schacht, *76 Jahre meines Lebens*, p. 25.

merce was missing. His son Hjalmar would eventually more than restore the balance.

To the Hanseatics, Prussia possessed a landlocked mentality and a near horizon. The Hanseatics loved open oceans and distant places. They also loved the profit made in duty-free world trade. They admired England but deified America. Their biggest steamship line was the Hamburg-Amerika Line, which was the creation of one of Hamburg's leading citizens, the Jewish Albert Ballin.

In contrast to the Prussians, Hanseatics disdain landed ancestral titles. Hamburg's aristocrats are the great trading families, the patricians. Hanseatics live in constant optimism that something better lies ahead, just over the horizon. Hjalmar Schacht told the story about the old Frisian woman who had only a miniscule bit of butter to spread on her slice of bread. She was perfectly happy to butter only a tiny corner of the slice and to chew first the dry part, because she knew that, eventually, she would reach the best part, the butter.[5] People from Schleswig-Holstein always hope for the butter in their future.

In 1878 the Schachts and their two sons moved west from Tinglev to Heide, a cattle market town where William Schacht was hired as editor of the local newspaper, the *Heider Zeitung*. The determined Constanze opened a trimming store. While she had some success, her husband's paper floundered. William was a sarcastic commentator and was not afraid to tackle the most touchy of local political problems. The paper soon lost money, and the owner decided to replace him. The Germans have an expression for men like William Schacht — *Stehaufmännchen,* a kachina doll that can be knocked down but keeps regaining its feet. He was like a prizefighter who immediately bounces up after a knockdown, dizzy but willing to face his fate. By 1883 the Schachts were once more on the move, this time to Husum, "a gray town by the gray sea," as Hjalmar later described it.[6]

William went to work for a man named Gold, a Jewish soap

5. Ibid., p. 37.
6. Ibid., p. 39.

manufacturer. A short time afterward Gold went bankrupt, and later Hjalmar speculated that his father may have been the whipping boy for the impending bankruptcy. But in all fairness, he also thought that his father may have contributed to it. Another debacle!

In 1883 the Schachts were on the move again, this time south to the large port city of Hamburg. Constanze was expecting another baby, and the time had finally come for William to suppress his unshakable sense of self-esteem. He became a bookkeeper in the coffee-importing firm Schmidt-Pauli. The Schachts barely stayed a step ahead of the bill collectors, but they managed, somehow, to send their eldest son, Eddy, to Hamburg's finest high school, the Johanneum. Hjalmar soon followed him there. They lived in a shabby rental apartment in the cheap back building of a working-class apartment house. They still seemed jinxed. After some failed speculations in the coffee market, Schmidt-Pauli, an old and distinguished importer, went bankrupt. Once more, William Schacht was condemned to go job hunting.

Then, at long last, he found the perfect employer. He became a bookkeeper for the German branch of American Equitable Life. In some strange way, it was like a return to his America. Equitable soon promoted him and sent him to Berlin to run its central office; from then on, the flagpole in front of the Schachts' small family house was never without the Stars and Stripes. Only Constanze was left to carry on the Scandinavian tradition. In 1887, when she bore a baby boy, she saw to it that he was named Oluf. She seemed untouched by all their privation and drudgery, remaining a self-confident woman, a great beauty, and someone perfectly capable of ignoring her surroundings. Despite living in Germany, she often spoke Danish until her death in Berlin in 1937. Her self-assurance marked Hjalmar's life as much as his father's failures. Hjalmar would always jealously guard his place in society, his standing, his status. Although it was never mentioned, there was a distinct social gap between the titled von Eggers and the bourgeois Schachts, but his mother's graceful acceptance of whatever the fates provided made things easier for the most ambitious of her sons.

When the senior Schachts moved to Berlin, Hjalmar stayed in Hamburg to finish his studies at the Johanneum. Eddy had gone on to university, so Hjalmar moved in with a doctor and his family, friends of the Schachts'. His room was comfortable, and the daughter of the house was both pretty and forthcoming. It was his first serious love affair.

Strangely, Hjalmar's teachers at the Johanneum reported that he was a poor mathematician, but that did not faze him. He frequently told the story of the great mathematician who was asked to divide nine by three. The genius consulted his slide rule and, with wrinkled brow, came up with an answer. "Nine by three is 2.999999, *say three!*"

Hjalmar Schacht credited the Johanneum with his lifelong interest in the classics and the humanities. He explained his ability as a banker by suggesting that successful bankers needed psychology, common sense, and a grasp of economics. To Schacht, the nature of all credit was psychological.[7] You extended a loan, no matter how well secured it might be, only if you were convinced that the borrower was worthy of credit. To Schacht, banking was an art, not a science.

His late teens in Hamburg were probably the key to some of the forces that moved him later. He loved his parents and recognized the sacrifices they made for their sons. He had watched helplessly as they tried to cling to a style of life that they claimed by virtue of birth and education, and he pitied them, as well as himself. He knew their struggle was hopeless, and it left him angry, embarrassed, and determined never, ever to let it happen to him.

Sometimes his father's Frisian arrogance infuriated him. On the day Hjalmar graduated from the Johanneum with his precious *Abitur*, he telegraphed the good news to his family in Berlin. William Schacht later rebuked him. "A postcard would have sufficed!"[8]

7. Ibid., p. 52.
8. Ibid., p. 80.

Hamburg's jeunesse dorée lived the life of parties, sailing, and rowing at the elite clubs along the Outer Alster, a basin that reaches almost the middle of the city. Even today, spring to fall, many Hamburg lawyers, businessmen, and students still go to "the club" before lunch or after work for an hour of rowing or sailing. Hjalmar could never afford membership in any of these clubs.

For his graduation at the Johanneum, he had to borrow the traditional white tie and tails from another student. After graduation all his classmates traveled abroad, but he was penniless and stuck in Hamburg. For Hjalmar, the lack of funds was more than just a dilemma. It was a plague, and he hated the unending penalties it imposed.[9]

The year 1889 is known in German history as the *Drei Kaiser Jahr,* the year of the three kaisers. Two kaisers — one expectedly, the other unexpectedly — died within a few months of each other, and the heir to the throne was Wilhelm II, the man who eventually sent Germany into World War I. Wilhelm was an ambitious and rambunctious young man who responded to a withered left arm and neglectful parents by frequent shows of bombast. He made no bones about his wide-ranging plans for Germany, both nationally and internationally. The coalition of Germany's kingdoms, duchies, and provinces — including the ports of the Hanseatic League — was too loose and voluntary to suit his designs. Germany was technically a united empire, but each of its parts still exercised a certain independence. The kaiser, as king of Germany's kings, was still king of Prussia, which dominated two-thirds of the empire. The Catholic south leaned toward Bavaria's Wittelsbach kings. Kaiser Wilhelm seemed bound and determined to conquer his own empire and then possibly go on to the lands of others.

The north German Hanseatic ports of Bremen, Hamburg,

---

9. In 1929, on the four hundredth anniversary of the Johanneum, the wealthy and successful Schacht gave an endowment to the school so that top students could travel abroad.

Kiel, and Danzig were a special thorn in his side, especially Hamburg. The ports were Germany's only access to the open ocean, but they did not contribute one pfennig to the empire by collecting import duties. The Hanseatics had always resisted the imposition of duties on imports. They insisted on reciprocal free trade with the rest of the world. In 1889 Kaiser Wilhelm II came to Hamburg to perform a ceremonial duty. The splendidly uniformed twenty-nine-year-old monarch gave three symbolic taps with a hammer to the cornerstone of an important new bridge in the port, but the ceremony masked the real purpose of the kaiser's visit.

Eventually, Hamburg's senate surrendered to the wishes of the kaiser. It decided to introduce import duties. Eighteen years after Bismarck, the "Iron Chancellor," had tenuously assembled the new German Reich, the Hanseatics finally capitulated their independence to Prussia. They would not have collapsed under military threat or economic pressure, not the Hanseatics. In the end it was they who had sold themselves on the idea of the profitability of joining the greater German Reich, of Bismarck's vision of the empire.

Along with thousands of others, schoolboy Schacht had gone to the port to see the kaiser. He was impressed with the grave young man in the fine uniform, but in time he realized the true meaning of the visit. As he later wrote, "the three hammer blows were to remain in my memory."[10] With schoolboy idealism, he hated the end of "free" Hamburg. Throughout his life, Hjalmar Schacht remained a "free trader," and it remained one of his *Leitmotifs*. Even in the controlled time of Adolf Hitler, he still insisted on fighting all restrictions to international trade.

Most European upper-school students were more than aware of politics. It was their passion. Germany's teenage students of the day argued about politics with the fervor American schoolboys reserve for sports.

After Hamburg's remaining "free trade" liberals had failed to

10. Schacht, *76 Jahre meines Lebens*, p. 61.

block the marriage with the Prussians, Schacht developed contempt for most political liberals. The kaiser's three hammer taps convinced him that liberals were "usually right in theory and wrong in practice."[11]

In 1892 all studies at the Johanneum were interrupted by an outbreak of cholera.[12] Hjalmar's parents, who now lived in Berlin, sent him to stay with his grandfather until the epidemic had subsided. For three months, the gangling sixteen-year-old accompanied the tall, bearded curmudgeon on his medical rounds. Dr. Schacht treated his grandson to a daily demonstration of duty and decency. Money meant very little to the old man. His patients meant everything. Young Hjalmar admired his grandfather's attitude but would not accept it. He was sure that the doctor's fees could have been much higher without causing damage to the patients or to his grandfather's ethics. Later, whenever Hjalmar Schacht reminisced about his grandfather, he did so with a certain patronizing forbearance. When the epidemic ended, Hjalmar returned to Hamburg and his studies. He was never to see his grandfather again.

His Hamburg romance soon collapsed. His landlord's daughter told him their affair was over, so Hjalmar moved out. He rented a cheap room from a watchmaker, made money by giving lessons to slow students, and even splurged on his first bicycle.

In 1895 he visited his parents in Berlin, to meet another new baby brother, William, the first of the Schacht sons without a Danish name. When Hjalmar brought up the subject of what to study, his parents thought that like Eddy, he might want to consider medicine, but Hjalmar had little inclination to follow his brother's example. Perhaps his feisty grandfather's philanthropy had discouraged him. Nevertheless, at Eddy's urging, he made a halfhearted attempt at premed studies for one semester at the University of Kiel. Then he quit medicine, but the two handsome

11. Ibid., p. 60.
12. Ibid.

brothers did collaborate in another field. They were almost identical in looks, so Hjalmar often substituted for Eddy on blind dates.

Undergraduates at that time made frequent changes, both academically and geographically. The four years between 1895 and 1899 were eclectic for Hjalmar.[13]

> Summer 1895, Kiel: medicine, Germanistics, history of literature
> Winter 1895–96, Berlin: Germanistics, history of literature, journalism
> Summer 1896, Munich: economics and Germanistics
> Winter 1896–97, Leipzig: journalism and economics
> Summer 1897, Berlin: economics and public speaking
> Winter 1897–98, Paris: French and sociology
> Summer 1898, Kiel: economics
> Winter 1898–99, Kiel: economics
> Summer 1899, Kiel: doctorate in philosophy

Although Hjalmar Schacht claimed he had "tried a bit of everything," the recurring theme was economics. After his first semester he transferred from Kiel to Berlin University, where he launched himself into a field that had barely arrived on the academic scene: journalism. He also had classmates who later were among Germany's leading journalists and publishers, such as Monti Jacobs, later the editor of Berlin's *Vossische Zeitung,* and Arthur Dix, who was to edit the *Nationalzeitung.* He also befriended young Franz Ullstein, eventual head of Ullstein, Germany's leading publishing house.

For the following semester Schacht transferred to the University of Munich to launch himself deeper into the study of economics. Arthur Dix sent a letter of introduction to Lujo Brentano, one of the leading economists of the time, who was teaching in Munich. The antimilitarist Brentano, an eventual Nobel Peace Prize laureate (1927), fascinated his young students, but

13. Ibid., p. 83.

Hjalmar Schacht was ever the skeptic about antimilitarists. While his pro-trade liberal background convinced him that any military action was an admission of failure, like most political realists of his day, Schacht also believed in the value of keeping a nation well armed. In the prenuclear world, powerful nations that were virtually army-less (like today's Germany and Japan) would have been unthinkable. Then as now, nations were considered opponents or allies, and their zones of influence and trading markets were seen as accessible or inaccessible based on their political alignment and strength to enforce that alignment. Our contemporary notion of power is based on intercontinental ballistic missiles. Prior to or between the two World Wars, nations were judged by the might of their armies, the heft of their fleets, and, ultimately, the reach of their bombers. When told of the Pope's opposition to certain Nazi plans, Adolf Hitler was said to have asked, "How many divisions [of troops] does the Pope have?" Schacht's later aims were to abolish the Versailles Treaty and to establish Germany's industrial strength, with the emphasis on export. He felt he needed a mighty and powerful nation to do so.

Schacht then went on to the university at Leipzig in Saxonia, where Professor Karl Bücher lectured on journalism as a major influence. At the turn of the century, journalism was still considered suspect and not to be taken seriously. Many people accepted Bismarck's definition that "journalism was for those who had failed at their professions." Bücher, who had edited the *Frankfurter Zeitung,* one of Germany's great dailies, put the importance of journalism into modern cultural and political context. From then on, newspapers — and the men who ran them and wrote for them — continued to intrigue Hjalmar Schacht.

When he mentioned a future in journalism, he found his father sympathetic. After all, William Schacht was himself a former journalist. He introduced Hjalmar to a man named Leipziger, who ran a small paper called *Das Kleine Journal,* and the nineteen-year-old undergraduate began his journalistic internship on February 2, 1896, in Berlin.

Although Hjalmar had been hired by the managing director, the paper's city editor was skeptical.

"Schacht, have you ever written?"

Indeed. Volumes. He had even been published.

"What did you write?"

Poetry! He loved poetry.

"Poetry?" The editor was unimpressed.

He gave the cub reporter his first assignment: a twelve-line story about the construction of a new Berlin bridge. It was not earthshaking news. Berlin was and is riddled with canals and river bends and, most of all, bridges. New ones or reconstructed ones are a constant. To take away the banality of it all, Hjalmar wrote a gripping, romantic piece about the river, the gray water, and the swirling gulls and handed it to his city editor.

An hour later, he was complimented by the managing director. Good piece for a beginner. Schacht had not yet seen it in print. When he finally did, he realized that they had not used a single word of his romanticized report. The city editor had rewritten the story, and while Schacht hated to admit it, it was a good piece. The old hands at the paper had all colluded to give the cub reporter a boost.

Das Kleine Journal was a tabloid, filled with innuendo and gossip. Schacht's job was to scout Berlin for scandal, rumor, the seamy side. The editor who had saved him during the bridge episode cajoled him to "write for the masses, to forget what interests *you,* and to write what interests *them!*" The advice was delivered in Berlin's raucous and well-targeted street argot. Hjalmar haunted Berlin's back alleys and the *Kneipen* (pubs), its coffeehouses and theaters, its dance halls and society galas for bits and pieces of gossip. He reported disaster and accidents. He learned journalism in the raw.

At heart, Hjalmar Schacht always remained a journalist. Because he understood effective reportage, he always knew exactly how to present his ideas to the press. Even at the height of his busy career, Hjalmar Schacht never needed speechwriters. He also continued his early knack for poetry, begun during his short stint as a medical student, and he continued to frame many written thoughts in verse. He even admitted to having coauthored an operetta with another student, though he hints it would have impressed neither Strauss nor Lehár.[14]

Berlin at the turn of the century was one of Europe's great theater towns. Its many stages featured productions of everything from Shakespeare to musical comedy by creative new entrepreneurs like Max Reinhardt. Hjalmar, who had a talent for mimicry, impersonation, regional accents, and vernacular, became a lifelong theater fanatic.

He met his future wife in 1896 while playing tennis at a suburban Berlin tennis club at Schlachtensee. Her name was Luise Sowa, a slim, dark-haired, and vivacious girl, the daughter of a Prussian police official in the Schachts' residential district. Hjalmar was a handsome fellow, with the craggy looks of his Danish-German ancestry. Although Luise was quite certain that he would be her future husband, their romance went slowly. Both sets of parents were supportive; but for Hjalmar, anything serious was out of the question, at least for the moment. He was an undergraduate and had no intention of assuming responsibilities he could not handle. He remembered the disastrous financial consequences of his parents' early marriage, and he had vowed never to let that happen to him.[15] In the fall of 1897 he left for Paris to study French. On the westbound train he got into a shell game known in America as three-card monte, and he lost all but twenty marks of his monthly allowance. He swore never again to gamble with his own money, a rule he followed throughout his long career. He even distrusted any banker who played the stock market for his own account.[16]

While Hjalmar studied in Paris, Emile Zola published his famous article "J'accuse," in the Paris newspaper *L'Aurore*. The article dealt with the three-year-old Dreyfus Affair.

Captain Alfred Dreyfus, a Jewish French artillery officer, was

14. Ibid., p. 109.
15. Ibid., p. 100.
16. Ibid., p. 101.

accused of high treason. Despite his protests and an impeccable record, Dreyfus was found guilty, expelled from the Officers' Corps, and sent to prison on Devil's Island. The Dreyfus Affair dragged on for years, tearing at the social structure of France. Emile Zola's attack on the anti-Semitic French reactionaries who had condemned Dreyfus brought him such enmity that he had to flee to England. The real traitor, a titled Hungarian serving in the French army, was finally caught. After years of disgrace and harsh treatment, Dreyfus was eventually cleared of all guilt, reinstated as an officer, and promoted.

Hjalmar was only mildly interested in an internal French political matter. He felt sure that this sort of miscarriage of justice could not happen in Germany, and with some reason. Since Bismarck, Germany's Jewish citizens lived in an atmosphere of comparative benevolence and security, and many had risen to prominence; a few states, other than Bismarck's Prussia, allowed Jews to hold army commissions. Nobody knew the kaiser's true feelings toward his Jewish subjects, but he depended on their good advice in matters of trade, finance, and shipping.

In 1898 Hjalmar's immediate problems were not political, but those of the heart. On his return to Berlin and Luise, he explained once more that any wedding plans would have to be postponed. He was preparing for his doctoral work and would never marry without an income. She seemed to understand, and they decided to separate temporarily. But Luise was a determined girl.

The uncompromising code of Britain's tiny, imperious Queen Victoria ruled the households of middle-class Europe. Parents with a marriageable daughter were frequently quite tyrannical, and it was unlikely that Luise's father, the proper Prussian police official, was particularly willing to show patience. Proper young ladies married, and married early. They did not sit on the shelf waiting for a reluctant suitor. No matter. His strong-willed daughter insisted on making her own romantic decisions and was a match for him.

While Luise fought her battle, Hjalmar returned north to his "home" university of Kiel to work on his doctoral thesis. His first meeting with the dean was tense. The professor began by accusing him of returning to Kiel because it "was an easier university" for a doctorate. Besides, Hjalmar had chosen journalism as his subject, a field that the dean refused to accept as fit for a thesis. Hjalmar compromised. He asked the dean for suggestions, and luck was on his side. The academic was in the middle of a stormy dispute about certain economic theories with a rival expert, so he hinted that Schacht might write a thesis supporting his, the dean's, views. Since the dispute involved the British economy, research would mean a trip to England. Schacht was not averse to that idea, and he accepted the assignment. He arranged cheap passage by freighter from Kiel to Hull, and from there by train to London. He planned to live inexpensively. He then persuaded Kiel's leading newspaper, the *Kieler Neuste Nachrichten,* for whom he had been writing pieces on theater and art, to sponsor his trip. Hjalmar had some leverage with the paper. Some of his more controversial articles on art had displeased the owner of the paper, but the powerful local art association had backed Hjalmar's views and the publisher surrendered.

His first visit to gray, foggy January London was a letdown. He rented a room in a drab boardinghouse on Tottenham Court Road and spent long hours at the British Museum library. At the end of each day of research, he took a short walk, then had dinner, took another walk, and went to bed. There was only one unexpected academic bonus. In the middle of his dull research, he discovered new meaning in the legendary children's story *Robinson Crusoe.* He became convinced that Daniel Defoe's tale of adventure was actually the depiction of a primitive economic system in an experimental micronation.[17] It was his only bright moment. Schacht would pay many visits to London, but his first trip was disappointing after he had tasted the attractions of Paris. He decided that "no one should go to London for two weeks in January," and he was happy to return to Kiel to finish his work.[18]

His dry doctoral thesis was titled "The Theoretical Content of

17. Ibid., p. 110.
18. Ibid.

British Mercantilism." It was tailored, quite diplomatically, to support his embattled dean's views, and it quoted much original text in English, partly to obfuscate but also to impress. The shrewd young man realized that most people, even academics, were susceptible to a certain amount of showmanship.

He was left with one final hurdle. His doctorate could not be granted until he passed an oral examination in his assigned category: philosophy. It was not his favorite field. He had neglected the subject and knew only the rudiments because he hated dealing with abstractions. He preferred the practical.

The examiner, a charming professor of philosophy, greeted him courteously, and Hjalmar managed to bluff his way through a superficial discussion about some of the great philosophers and their theories. In the manner of many German universities, there was much emphasis on a candidate's ability to present his point of view in spoken form. Schacht, who was gifted with the ability to parry, thrust, and riposte in open debate, would have welcomed a verbal examination, though not in the field of philosophy. German higher studies were still classical and ignored "modern" subjects. Doctorates were not granted in Schacht's specialties, economics and journalism, but they were granted in philosophy. While Schacht valued the power of psychology, he resented the abstractions of philosophy and knew he was on shaky ground. There was no way around it. Paraphrasing Schacht's version of the exchange that then followed:

> The examiner pointed at an armoire. He asked, "What is that?"
> Puzzled, I said, "An armoire, sir."
> "Good," said the philosopher, clearly relieved that I recognized the object. Then he asked, "What is this armoire?"
> I had never thought much about armoires, except that I used one to hang up my suits. Impatiently, the examiner repeated, "Well, what is this armoire?"
> I was getting annoyed. "Brown," I shrugged.
> "What else? Don't you know anything else about it?"
> I was getting desperate now. "It's square. Like a cube."
> "And?"

I had no idea what he was driving at. Finally I said, "It's wooden."

He snorted disdainfully. "Good God, candidate, it's roomy. That's what it is, *roomy!*"

I stared at him, still baffled. He began to laugh, until the tears came and he needed his kerchief. "You economists," he complained to the world at large, "what do you know about philosophy?"

I rebutted by citing a little Locke and Hobbes and some passages from my thesis.

"Well, thank you, candidate." I was dismissed.[19]

Schacht went home, quite unsure about the outcome. Two days later he received a hand-delivered envelope from the university. He had been awarded his doctorate of philosophy.

This time, he sent no self-congratulatory telegram to his parents. Instead, he carried the message to Berlin. The newly minted Dr. Schacht moved in with his parents for the winter of 1899–1900. He attended some academic lectures, but it was time to loaf, and he made the rounds of all the new plays and operettas. He loved Berlin. It was "cozy, witty, malicious and human, showing the tolerance of the Prussian kings, not really German, but a colony of foreigners, French Huguenots, Dutch reformers, eastern Jews, Polish conspirators and Italian *carbonari*. Everyone who lives there is part of Berlin. One need not be a native."[20]

Indeed, since the days of Frederick the Great, Prussia's kings had been men of tolerance. Frederick, who brought the revolutionary thinkers Voltaire and Rousseau to his Potsdam court and who preferred speaking French to German, believed that "everyone should be happy in his own fashion." (*Jeder soll nach seiner eigenen Façon seelig werden!*) Who could fault a king who invited Voltaire by writing:

P

Venez   (*Venez souper!* or Venez sous P)

19. Ibid., p. 111.
20. Ibid., p. 113.

and received the affirmative answer

J- a   (*J'ai grand appétit!* or J, grand, a, petit)

The twenty-two-year-old Hjalmar Schacht and the city of Berlin were a perfect match. He was already cynical, skeptical, bored with the traditional view, hardheaded, and ambitious. Like most Berliners, he was an outsider who was, in the words of today, "on the make." He was more realistic than most men his age. Marriage would have to wait until he could afford it. There was a Berlin beer hall song that went, "Berlin girl, I ain't gonna marry you just because we're dancing!" (*Du Baliner Pflanze, denkst De denn ick heirat Dir weil ick mit Dir tanze!*) He "knew the angles," such as citing footnotes in English for effect and playing sides to his own advantage by slanting his thesis to manipulate his professor.

Typical for the senior Schachts was the family's 1899 New Year's Eve, which would usher in the twentieth century. At twenty minutes before midnight, they were all assembled in Villa Equitable, as the Schachts called their Berlin house, drinking William Schacht's powerful and traditional New Year's Eve hot punch. Constanze Schacht turned to her husband. "My God, William, Nineteen hundred! It's twenty-seven years since we got married! All the things we've seen in our time."[21]

William Schacht looked at Constanze, took the cigar out of his mouth, cleared his throat, replaced the cigar, and poured drinks for everyone. Then he took the cigar out of his mouth once more, walked over to his wife, and kissed her and patted her hand. Obviously, William Schacht, the old rebel and wanderer, was touched. "Yes, *Mudding*" — he used the Plattdeutsch word for *Mommie* — "twenty-seven years. And now we have grown sons, one a doctor and one a philosopher. Who would have thought it." The two elder sons were amused. They knew that their father's show of emotion was unusual, un-Frisian and rare. One did not mark major events with shows of sentimentality.

21. Ibid., p. 113ff.

One sent postcards, not telegrams. The two younger boys were goggle-eyed. Papa had actually kissed Mama!

They drank a silent toast while, outside, churchbells, cannon fire, and shouting announced the twentieth century.

Hjalmar Horace Greeley Schacht's boyhood days and student days were over. One of his professors at the Johanneum had written, probably with a tinge of maliciousness, "Schacht seems to feel he is destined for great things."[22]

The time had come to enter the arena.

22. Edward N. Peterson, *Hjalmar Schacht: For and Against Hitler*, p. 19.

3

THE NEW CENTURY

TO MOST TURN-OF-THE-CENTURY GERMANS, Prussia had come to mean much ambition, much dominance, some arrogance, and, above all, power. Prussia was an overwhelming reality, which pleased most of its own citizens, infuriated many non-Prussian Germans, caused edginess and derision in London, and fostered widespread paranoia in Paris. The French were still crushed by their 1871 defeat at the hands of Bismarck's Prussianized Germans, and the bumptious and aggressive style of Kaiser Wilhelm II did not reassure them.

Much time had passed since Prussia's nineteenth-century patriarch king, Wilhelm I, had set an example for all ruling monarchs. The first Prussian Wilhelm, a model of modesty and duty, despised all show, display, and bluster. His was a "revolution from the top." As he wrote to Prince Leopold of Anhalt-Dessau, "In this world, nothing but effort and work." Historian Christian von Krockow called it the "perfect preparation for the industrial age."[23] In 1871 Bismarck finally realized his dream of forging Germany into an empire, with Prussia's king as emperor, or kaiser. Wilhelm I, the most Prussian of kings, was in tears. "Tomorrow we are carrying the kingdom of Prussia to its grave!" He had no wish to be

23. Christian von Krockow, *Die Deutschen*, p. 41.

Germany's kaiser.[24] By the time the twentieth century came, the original Prussia of modesty, duty, and tact was no more. Like other generations of leaders that follow great founders, Wilhelm II was neither modest nor tactful.

Still, some of Frederick the Great's original eighteenth-century inheritance had survived. There was a certain tolerance for different ideas and other religions. As Schacht had noted, fin de siècle Berlin was a haven for a wide diversity of ideas and people. There were even early glimmers of a social conscience. In the 1880s "Iron Chancellor" Count Bismarck had introduced social security. It showed that in some respects he was a man of the future. His successor, Count von Bülow, expanded it after the turn of the century. To be sure, he also enlarged Germany's navy, to suit the wishes of the new, ambitious Kaiser Wilhelm II, the well-tailored young monarch whom the schoolboy Hjalmar had gone to admire that day in the port of Hamburg. Those three symbolic hammer blows still threw their echo. The kaiser had brought Germany's assortment of kingdoms and duchies into line. The newly expanded German navy would show England that there was more than one naval power, and Germany's multiprovincial and multiuniformed armies would soon be unified into one field-gray phalanx. Whenever he compared his realm with the vast empire of his Saxe-Coburg cousin at Buckingham Palace, Wilhelm II seemed ridden with inferiority. He was also plagued by his withered left arm, carefully camouflaged by the parapher-nalia of his uniforms. All his subjects knew of his affliction, but none dared mention it. In London there were no such restric-tions, and the kaiser — "Kaiser Bill," as the British had dubbed him — was on constant and paranoid guard against insults from across the Channel.

In 1900 the only international excitement was in faraway South Africa, where Boer settlers and the British army battled over the fate of the colony. Germans openly sided against Great Britain and with the outnumbered Afrikaners and their leader,

24. Ibid., p. 60.

"Ohm" Paul Kruger. The German newspapers exploited widespread German envy of British imperial power and influence. They enthusiastically backed the Boers and told tales of British atrocities. German schoolboys devoured books of adventurous tales praising the heroic, outnumbered Boers and condemning the ruthless English. Most Germans were highly indignant when the German merchant ship *Bundesrat* was stopped on the high seas and boarded by the British navy, which claimed that she was carrying contraband for the Boers. The British withdrew their allegations, but it created a mighty tempest in a journalistic teacup. There was much pouting in Germany when the Boers finally had to surrender. To this day, revisionist German historians like to point out that concentration camps for civilians were invented by the British during the Boer War.

Wilhelm II's envious dislike for his royal British cousins was imitated by many of his loyal subjects, who adopted a love-hatred of "perfidious Albion," about whom the kaiser often vented his spleen. Finally, he went too far. In 1908 he told a senior reporter from the London *Daily Telegraph* that the "German people are against you. I am for you." It raised eyebrows in Buckingham Palace and Whitehall but, quite unexpectedly, also caused an uproar in the Reichstag, Germany's parliament. After all, this was the twentieth century. The question of constitutionality suddenly arose. How much power should a modern kaiser be free to wield? It came nowhere near a true crisis, but for Wilhelm II, it was the first inkling that he was not an absolute monarch. His chancellor, von Bülow, became the sacrificial lamb and eventually had to resign.

Despite these occasional flurries, peace prevailed. In 1900 educated young men like Hjalmar did their military year and then concentrated on commerce rather than on soldiering. Hjalmar was disqualified from military service because he was found to suffer from "extreme myopia." The German economy was booming; everyone was optimistic; and for the cream of the university graduates, getting jobs was comparatively easy. In one of the business journals, Hjalmar read an ad inviting job applicants to participate in an evening of economic discussion, sponsored by an organization called the Center for the Preparation of Commercial Treaties. The center was supported by a powerful group of exporters and bankers and was headed by a man named Vosberg-Rekow. He impressed Schacht as a man of intelligence who was very good with people but, he noted, slipshod and superficial.[25] As if to second this impression, Vosberg-Rekow soon informed him that he was the only candidate who was offered a job, because "you were the only one dressed in a dinner suit. I like my gentlemen to make a good appearance."[26]

According to Hjalmar Schacht, this was the only time he ever had to apply for a position. All other employers sought him out. He detested having to "audition" and promised himself that any future job negotiations would be conducted from a position of strength, not need. He would never compromise himself because he needed the money or because he had to repay a loan. Hjalmar Schacht insisted that he never borrowed money personally, a strange guideline for someone whose business life was devoted to loaning money, pursuing credit, earning interest, and satisfying debts. From the beginning, Hjalmar Schacht always seemed to separate his personal self from the profession of banking, the way a surgeon makes his incisions without empathy for the patient. It is unlikely that Schacht ever wished to amass a fortune, but he was determined to protect himself against the kind of financial buffeting he had witnessed during his boyhood. At heart, he would always remain a publicizer and a journalist whose most valued asset was a free hand, without the need to kowtow.

The center represented some of Germany's most formidable banks, exporters, merchants, and shipping firms, whose managing executives were on the board of directors. Among them were Emil Rathenau, the founder of AEG, Germany's leading electrical combine; Dr. Achelis, the chairman of North German Lloyd, the big shipping line; and Georg von Siemens, the head of the

25. Schacht, *76 Jahre meines Lebens*, p. 119.
26. Ibid.

Deutsche Bank. All were free traders and strongly opposed import duties and tariffs.

Young Dr. Schacht was eminently suited for his new position.* He had spent his boyhood listening to his father's Hanseatic free-trade views, and his stint of tabloid journalism in Berlin had taught him the value of raw publicity. It now became his job to launch a propaganda campaign against those German industrialists and landowners who wanted to raise protective barriers against foreign industrial and agricultural products.

Considering his youth, Hjalmar Schacht showed astonishing business insight. The senior executives who were on the center's board reinforced his conviction that Germany's future would best be served by inventiveness and productivity instead of hiding behind protectionism. German brains and skill could be counted on to produce superior goods. Germany's real profits lay in the sale of manufactured goods, not in the export of its coal, chemicals, and ore.

He also wrote essays against the formation of cartels. He believed instead in the creation of industrial trusts. As he saw it, the purpose of a cartel was to keep prices artificially high, while trusts lowered prices and raised productivity by creating vertical source-to-manufacturing organizations.[27] In one of his reports to the members of the center, he described cartels as "morphium" and trusts as "elixir."[28] In another, he argued against small, local utility companies "who sell overpriced energy." These think pieces gave him a wonderful chance to impress his influential audience.

The board members were very pleased. His antitariff statements found their way into many public speeches on the economy and were often quoted by would-be politicians. As a result, friends encouraged him to run for a seat in the Reichstag parliamentary elections of 1901. Schacht refused, but a colleague whom

---

* He became the director of this public relations cum lobbying organization.

27. Ibid., p. 122ff.

28. Ibid., p 122.

he proposed won a seat. Schacht was more interested in econom-ics than in politics.[29] He was sure that once he had mastered the former, the latter was sure to follow.

By 1903 the twenty-six-year-old economist-publicist had gained a fine reputation. He received several flattering offers. The most premature but pleasing came from the kaiser's brother-in-law, Prince Ernst Günther of Schleswig-Holstein. An aide invited Schacht to visit the prince at his private Berlin residence. Schacht was shown into the prince's study, where his royal host stood wreathed in cigar smoke. Without being seated, the young econ-omist was asked to take charge of the prince's personal finances. Schacht declined as gracefully as he could, explaining that he lacked the qualifications. Although the prince may have been dis-appointed, it must have elated the poor boy from Schleswig-Holstein to hear this offer from its prince.

Next, he was approached by southern Germany's leading chambers of commerce. Again, Schacht declined. Even when the patriarchal Emil Rathenau tried to convince him to come work for his electrical empire, Schacht managed, most politely, to stall the great man.

These flattering and seductive offers were heady stuff, but his eyes were on banking. The offer he finally accepted came from one of Germany's most prosperous and successful institutions, the Dresdner Bank. Waldemar Müller, one of its chiefs, inter-viewed the young publicist. When they discussed salary, Schacht told Müller that he was earning over eight thousand marks a year while working at the center. Müller was shocked. It was much more than the bank paid its junior executives. The self-confident Schacht told Müller, "Pay me what you think I am worth, and I promise that you will pay me what I have just asked for within a year." He was quite right. By the end of his first year at the bank, he was earning a comfortable salary.[30]

29. Ibid., p. 125.
30. Ibid.

Schacht became head of Dresdner Bank's press department. He created prospectuses for new loans and ventures, a task that went hand in glove with his earlier work at the center and his knowledge of publicity.[31] It called for a delicate mixture of optimism and fact. Schacht was in his element when creating perceptions. Besides, he loved the cut and thrust of big-time banking, which had its buccaneers and its pirates.

At the center, he had met several of the major players at Germany's four great banks, the so-called D banks: Deutsche Bank, Diskonto Company, Dresdner Bank, and Darmstädter Bank. His new chief at Dresdner Bank, Eugen Gutmann, famous for his business agility and courage, had a flamboyant and generous way of doing things. When some of Schacht's early work helped launch a difficult issue of stock for a foreign client, Gutmann handed him a thousand-mark bill. Schacht never forgot it.[32]

Now that his days of borrowed tailcoats were over, and he was earning more than his father did, he returned to Luise, the girl who wanted to wait for him. Were they passionately in love? With typical Frisian restraint, Schacht confined himself to *"gefiel mir so gut wie am ersten Tag,"* or "I liked her as much as I did on the day we met." In 1902, five years after they had met, Hjalmar Schacht and Luise Sowa got engaged. They were married on January 10, 1903, seven years after they first saw each other at the tennis club in Berlin. At twenty-eight, Luise was two years older than her bridegroom.

On the way to the registry office the wedding party formed a small convoy of horse-drawn cabs. Schacht suddenly realized that he had forgotten to give the rings to his best man. So, "top hat jammed firmly on my head and tailcoat flying," he jumped from their rolling carriage, rushed to the one containing the best man, handed him the rings, and then returned to his own cab, much to the amusement of Berlin's pedestrians. Schacht, often

31. Mühlen, *Schacht*, p. 7.
32. Schacht, *76 Jahre meines Lebens*, p. 129.

known as the most calculating of men, called this little incident "typical of my impulsive nature."

Luise's father had just died. Schacht described Police Commissioner Sowa as a man who spent much time in the immediate surroundings of the imperial household and who had developed "a pathological distrust of everyone."[33] The Sowa daughters had always been under the tightest of surveillance, and had Police Commissioner Sowa lived, he would have been an extremely burdensome father-in-law.

In November of that year, Luise bore their first child, a girl they named Inge.

Schacht admits that he was not the ideal young husband. From early morning, when he commuted to the bank by bus and trolley, to late in the day, when he returned home to continue work at his desk, he was consumed by his job. He wrote that a "comfortable bourgeois existence" was "not for him." His career and his work became the Schachts' *Leitmotif,* and their marriage took a strangely avant-garde form. At a time when most wives were subservient or slyly manipulative, Luise became his teammate, his partner. He called her an "imposing woman" with strong opinions of her own, which she never hesitated to express. They traveled and entertained together, and they became "the Schachts." It was a "marriage of comradeship." In 1910 their son, Jens, was born and they built a small villa in the upper-middle-class Berlin suburb of Zehlendorf.

Banking was his passion, but there were still many lessons ahead. As chief of his bank's press department, Schacht issued a challenge to the *Morgenpost,* one of Germany's most important newspapers. For some time, the *Morgenpost* financial correspondent had been making derogatory comments about each new venture or announcement by Dresdner Bank. When a major newspaper attacks a great financial institution, it makes for spicy reading; or perhaps it was just an attack of self-importance on the part of the writer. At the same time, salesmen from the paper kept

33. Ibid., p. 151.

soliciting Schacht for the bank's advertising. During his days at the center, Schacht had learned all about what he called the "cancerous" relationship between advertising revenues and a free press, but he was not above using pressure whenever it suited his purpose.[34] To teach the *Morgenpost* a lesson, Schacht flatly refused to give them any further advertising. It flew in the face of traditional dealings between distinguished banks and great newspapers.

He soon found himself in the eye of a storm. *Morgenpost* belonged to Ullstein, one of Germany's most powerful publishing houses. Schacht's draconian stratagem had come to the personal attention of chairman Louis Ullstein, who launched a complaint with Schacht's chief, Eugen Gutmann. Louis Ullstein was outraged by the brash young bank executive who was running roughshod over accepted business practice. Schacht was ordered to report to Gutmann's inner sanctum. He asked his chief for permission to handle the matter, and shortly thereafter he sat in press lord Ullstein's private office, being lectured about freedom of the press. Schacht rebutted by asking what Herr Ullstein would do if the newspaper's outdoor advertising on billboards was invariably followed by posters that said, "Do not read the *Morgenpost*. It is the worst newspaper in Berlin!" Would Ullstein keep buying space on those same billboards? Reluctantly, the press lord conceded his point, and after some Schacht apologies, peace was restored. The attacks eased, and the bank continued to advertise.

Next, Schacht got his first taste of Berlin's stock exchange, and he liked the rough and tumble, the close contact among traders, and their overwhelming cynicism. His greatest disdain was reserved for the speculators, who bought stock on margin for quick turnover. Schacht himself never played the stock market and could never convince himself to trust anyone who did. His favorite stock exchange quip was about the man who was described

34. Ibid., p. 134.

as the most straightforward man on the exchange. "He looks like a crook and he *is* a crook."[35]

In 1905, in part because of Schacht's admittedly tenuous knowledge of English, he accompanied board member Hans Schuster to the United States to work on the details of a contract between Dresdner Bank and New York's J. P. Morgan. Schuster, who was Eugen Gutmann's son-in-law, had a fine reputation of his own, and Schacht was flattered to be chosen. It was Schacht's first visit to his father's beloved America, to brother Eddy's birthplace, and to the city of Horace Greeley, his namesake. He accompanied Schuster to the White House, where they were received by Teddy Roosevelt. He even saw Niagara Falls; he could not wait to report everything to William and Constanze Schacht back at Villa Equitable.

His deepest impression was the open banking floor of the House of Morgan, which looked and functioned like the city room of a great metropolitan newspaper. He spent seven days at the House of Morgan, fascinated by its informal style. Morgan executives were constantly accessible to their staff and to outside visitors. For Schacht, it was the first of many future contacts with John Morgan, J. P.'s son, and Thomas Lamont, later Morgan's chairman. His greatest admiration was reserved for the "man with the Cyrano nose and the kindly eyes," the senior John Pierpont Morgan.[36]

In 1911, only eight years after joining the Dresdner Bank, the thirty-one-year-old Schacht was promoted to assistant director, the equivalent of an American vice president. He remained the bank's press chief and house economist but was also put in charge of its branch operations.

He soon got involved in his first battle with a rival bank. The Prussian state government had given Dresdner Bank the highly confidential assignment of buying up the stock of Hibernia, a German coal-mining concern. The state wanted to guarantee

---

35. Ibid., p. 138.
36. Ibid., p. 141.

that the coal-driven Prussian state railway system could count on a regular and inexpensive supply of fuel. Utmost discretion was needed, and purchases were made in small blocks. Any hint that the state was buying Hibernia shares would have caused a feeding frenzy. Berliner Handelsgesellschaft, a smaller bank that had handled some business for the state railway, smelled a rat. Its chief, Karl Fürstenberg, convinced several other small banks to help him purchase large blocks of the remaining Hibernia shares. Financing the Hibernia stock purchases was easy for Dresdner Bank. They were using Prussian state money. Their smaller rivals had to use their own hard cash, so Fürstenberg and his group formed their purchases into a dummy corporation and sold its bonds, offering 4 percent interest. The bonds quickly sold out once word was let out that Hibernia was the target. While Dresdner Bank earned only a fee for acting as purchasing agent, Fürstenberg and his partners earned a real trading profit on the transaction. Not that Fürstenberg was unpatriotic. Since he was left out of the deal, both the state of Prussia and his friend (but rival) Gutmann at Dresdner Bank had become fair game. Schacht, who knew and admired the quirky Fürstenberg from his days at the center, was impressed.

The Jewish Fürstenberg's wit was legendary throughout the German financial world. When someone addressed him as "Herr Director," he riposted, "I'm no director. I employ directors." When someone asked him if he was part of the very aristocratic Fürstenberg-Januschau family, he said, "No. That's the other bunch." When offered a court honor, he was asked by the imperial chamberlain to choose between a decoration and a title. He asked for a title. "Which one?" said the court chamberlain. So Fürstenberg shrugged. "You can offer me only one title, but you can't give it to me. It's for Christians." Fürstenberg was one of the few men in his position who never converted to Christianity.

Another venture taught Schacht the art of flexibility. A group of London investors formed a company to exploit the hydroelectric potential of South Africa's Victoria Falls on the Zambezi River. The London group commissioned Dresdner Bank to explore both the technical feasibility and the financing of the project, and the bank retained Germany's AEG electrical combine to investigate the technical problems. AEG reported that the cost of harnessing the falls was prohibitive. Instead, it suggested using the large untapped coal deposits at Witwatersrand in South Africa. Coal-fueled steam-turbine power could produce electrical energy at a fraction of the cost. Dresdner Bank then floated a successful issue of stocks to finance the venture, which AEG then carried out. The Zambezi River and its massive Victoria Falls remained undisturbed, and Witwatersrand Utility came into being. Schacht's role was to boost the sale of stocks by touting a romantic pioneering project in faraway South Africa to German investors.

During his trip to New York, young Schacht once asked J. P. Morgan for his formula for success. The great banker told him, "I have always believed in the financial future of my country."[37] Germany was peaceful and booming, and Hjalmar Schacht must have found it easy to take J. P. Morgan's advice. Like many German bankers, he believed in the financial future of Germany.

Schacht's great hobby, hiking, was one of the most popular German pastimes. They even coined the word *Wandervögel,* "wandering birds," for the millions of German hikers. Schacht would hike anywhere, anytime, not just in Germany but into far-flung corners of Europe, like Bosnia, Serbia, and Herzegovina. When Schacht passed through Sarajevo, a Bosnian tailor promised to produce a local folk costume within two days, but Schacht had to stand for hours while Bosnian passersby hovered at the door of the tailor shop, giving unsolicited advice to the tailor and staring at the tall German, who was stripped to his skivvies. His sangfroid and patience were rewarded. A few months later, at Berlin's annual Colonial Ball, Schacht cut a dashing figure dressed up in his Sarajevo finery and wearing a fez.

In 1908, like his Americanized father and his Danish great-grandfather, Schacht became a Mason. He joined a lodge in Berlin. He stayed a member even after Adolf Hitler had declared

37. Ibid.

Masonry a mortal enemy of Germany and as dangerous as Judaism. Masonry brought Schacht interesting contacts abroad. Following his Balkan adventures, he took a hiking tour across Turkey, this time carrying introductions to some Turkish Masons. They, in turn, introduced the young German banker-hiker Mason to some revolutionaries, the so-called Young Turks, all Masons, who eventually overthrew Turkey's decaying sultanate. Schacht returned from the trip with a powerful attack of malaria, for which he was treated in Germany. It never returned and proved a minor annoyance compared with the rewards his Turkish adventure provided.

With some of his fellow hikers, he formed a fraternal trade group, which they named the German-Turkish Society. In 1911 the society was asked to host a group of forty Turks who were visiting Germany. Among other events, there was a flight on one of Count Ferdinand von Zeppelin's great new airships. It was Schacht's first flight and an act that called for a certain amount of courage, considering the history of crashes by dirigibles. It was also the first time he was proposed for a decoration by his government. The official in charge of the Turkish desk at the Foreign Ministry was delighted by the success of the Turkish junket. He proposed Schacht for a mid-level Prussian decoration but found himself in a battle with the minister of trade, who thought that at thirty-four, Schacht was too young for the honor. During the ensuing bureaucratic squabble the Foreign Ministry proposed various decorations of lower rank, until the disgusted Schacht told them that he would decline any decoration.[38]

After a boyhood of setbacks and obstacles, he had learned to deal with trouble. But no matter how grim things looked, he often seemed able to call on his storm-defying Frisian steadiness and agility to see him through. While his career advanced, Hjalmar's personal life lagged behind. Once more he had to cope. His "comradly" marriage soon showed signs of trouble. In his memoirs, Hjalmar explained, with some generosity, that Luise had "in-

38. Ibid., p. 161.

herited certain Prussian traits from her late father." These could on occasion "lead her into pedantic ways," while he preferred to see things "more diplomatically" and "to make allowances for human frailties."[39]

Schacht's elliptical description of Luise may well point out her intolerance of his own personal frailties. According to some contemporaries, Schacht had a roving eye. He was also more adventurous than Luise about his business associates and friends. After all, the world of finance was not a social club. Luise held to a strict bourgeois Prussian code of manners and was, in the style of the Teutonic Queen Victoria of Britain, often "not amused." Schacht's stiff appearance hid a surprisingly romantic man. Her appearance hid nothing.

Despite the compromises his marriage began to force upon him, Hjalmar's own life still seemed on course. Two of his brothers were not as lucky. Eddy, the doctor, married a Swedish girl, had children, and then divorced her. With brotherly forbearance, Hjalmar said that Eddy was "careless" about the education of his children, so Hjalmar took over. He was particularly fond of Eddy's eldest son, Sven, who became a talented writer.

Oluf, one of Hjalmar's two younger brothers, lived the adventurous colonial life as an engineer in the Cameroons and South Africa until he contracted several tropical diseases and was forced to return to Germany. He deteriorated rapidly. One day he stopped his car at the side of a rural road, stepped out, and sat down in a ditch. Minutes later, he was dead of a heart attack. His three children then became Hjalmar's responsibility. He was a man who took the word *responsibility* very seriously. His parents had shown him the way. Despite their chronic financial distress, they had sent him to expensive schools and had always cared for his well-being.

Hjalmar Schacht made responsibility into a fanatical religion, an arrogant preoccupation that was probably the key to the man. Many of his actions were guided by the wide range and lofty

39. Ibid., p. 154.

heights of his self-assigned responsibilities, and he often took immense risks to make his point. Even as a young man, he saw himself as a bastion of strength, a master patriot, an arbiter of political right or wrong. Whether this was a matter of hubris or of morality stays open for discussion, but throughout his long life he was usually absolutely sure that his way, Schacht's way, was the right way.

He was often accused of being ambitious, but he refused to accept ambition as a harmful trait. "As if ambition were a fault. I have always wanted to achieve things, not only for myself but for the common good. I have never tried to hide this ambition."[40]

40. Ibid., p. 157.

4

WORLD WAR

―――――――――――

ON JUNE 28, 1914, Crown Prince Franz Ferdinand of Austria and his princess were assassinated while riding in an open black automobile. They were paying a show-the-flag visit to Sarajevo, the capital of the Austrian province of Bosnia. The assassin was Gavrilo Princip, a Bosnian Serb who hated the Austrian Empire. The assassination was regrettable and shameful, but in Berlin it was considered a regional matter, brought on by the hatred the local Serbs felt for the Austrians. As the Serbs in Bosnia saw it, Vienna had annexed their native land. They counted on the loyal support of their cousins, the citizens of the neighboring kingdom of Serbia. The Serbians might have been sympathetic to the Bosnian Serbs, but had they actually supported the Black Hand, the Serb resistance movement in Bosnia? More to the point, did the royal Serbian government know about the plan to murder the Austrian heir to the throne and his princess, and had they endorsed or even supported it? The Austrians strongly suspected that the Serbian government was behind the murders. Yet, the man who was sent out by Vienna to investigate the facts, Baron Friedrich von Wiesner, found no evidence at all to support these suspicions.

This sad event began the convoluted political twists and turns that led to a World War.

At first, "Sarajevo," as the assassination came to be known, brought little concern or worry to Kaiser Wilhelm's loyal subjects.

After all, their newly rich German Empire was strong and secure and quite removed from all those "obscure" Austrian problems in the Balkans. In Berlin most people shrugged their shoulders and said that these things happened all the time in the Balkans. Certainly the kaiser would remain above the squabble between a midget Balkan state and what he considered the pitiable and crumbling Austrian Empire. As a safety precaution, a French delegation traveled to Saint Petersburg, the czar's capital, to convince the Russians to keep Austria from attacking Serbia, a Russian "client."

At first, everything seemed in control, but then suddenly events got out of hand. Below the surface, the European political arena was filled with harsh feelings. Some countries lusted to go to war, others were forced to go to war, and the decisions for war and peace were in the hands of a few royal people, often capricious and unqualified but unopposed by their subject citizens.

Czar Nicholas was trying to govern a vast rebellious anachronistic nation that had been left behind during the Industrial Revolution. Emperor Franz Joseph of Austria clutched at the reins of a collapsing multiethnic empire hungry to free itself from its masters in Vienna. The world's most powerful nation, Great Britain, found itself under challenge from an aggressive Germany and a voraciously ambitious kaiser. France was still writhing after her defeat by Prussia in 1870–71.

No one would wait. Everyone wished to act or thought they had the duty to act immediately. Within a few days the Austrians sent an ultimatum to Serbia, the Russians objected because the Serbs were under their patronage, and the French promised to back the Russians against Austria. Britain tried to organize a last-second peace conference, which the Austrians turned down. The British then asked the Russians to stand down.

The German government still refused to discuss the entire matter. The kaiser wished to stay above it all. Then, on July 28, afraid to lose Bosnia, Austria declared war on Serbia.

The Russians had mobilized along their German border, thereby angering the Germans.

Finally the kaiser raised a clenched fist. Germany declared a state of national emergency and told the Russians to withdraw their troops from the border. The French would not guarantee their neutrality if the Germans came to blows with the Russians. They would side with the Russians.

The British then wanted Germany to guarantee that if it fought the French, Belgium would not be invaded by the kaiser's troops; but Germany would give no such promise.

On August 1, at 3:55 P.M., the French mobilized.

At 4:00 P.M. the Germans mobilized.

At 7:00 P.M. Germany declared war on Russia because the Russians had not withdrawn their troops from the German border.

The Germans then invaded Luxembourg and Belgium in case they wished to launch a preemptive strike against the French flank.

On August 3 Germany declared war on France.

On August 4 Britain declared war on Germany.

Soon everybody got involved. Cobwebbed treaties and allegiances were brought into play. The Japanese against Germany; the Turks and their decaying Ottoman Empire on Germany's side; the Italians against Austria; the Bulgarians against France and Britain. Next, Romania, Portugal, China, and in 1917 the United States got involved. By 1918 even Peru, Guatemala, Nicaragua, Costa Rica, Haiti, and Honduras had declared war on Germany.

Nobody could have guessed that the events in Sarajevo would produce a major war. Nobody had even worried about it; but when war broke out, all sides joined the fray with great enthusiasm. The French were hungry for revenge after their 1871 humiliation in the Franco-Prussian War. The British saw their chance to teach the Germans a lesson about global power. The czar saw an opportunity to unite his country and avert serious interior social upheaval. He also wanted to prove that Russia had changed since its disastrous loss against Japan in 1904 at Port Arthur. The Turkish emirs thought they could cement their sprawling, fissured Middle Eastern empire.

Kaiser Wilhelm II and his Germans were absolutely sure that they had nothing to fear. After all, their army's belt buckles said *"Gott mit uns"* ("God is on our side").

God was on everybody's side; to the singing of Te Deums, young men of many nations set out from great cathedrals with as-

surances that their specific national deity would steady their hands
and shield their hearts. An oft-played old German cavalry song
said, "Mount up, mount up / A man still is worth something on the
field of battle!" (*"Im Felde, da ist doch der Mann noch was wert!"*)

No one understood the true horror of modern World War.
There had been some grim battles in the American Civil War and
in the Franco-Prussian War, but no one could have envisioned the
hellish years of static trench warfare, poison gas, tanks, warplanes,
and the killing of millions of men.

In 1913 Schacht had prepared a brochure for Dresdner Bank's
fortieth anniversary. He wrote about the speed with which Germany had grown from an agrarian society into a leading industrial
nation that had doubled its population, with worldwide shipping
lines, low national debt, and highly paid industrial workers. To
counter any accusations that Germany was overly aggressive, he
quoted some interesting figures. These set out to prove that Germany spent proportionately less money on its military establishment than did France and Britain (twenty-one marks per citizen,
compared with twenty-seven for France and thirty-two for Britain).
As the son of a man who had once emigrated from Germany,
he now found it a cause for great optimism that the flood of Germans emigrating abroad had shrunk to a trickle. He was proud
of Germany's "benign" colonial policies. According to Schacht,
German colonies were never used as springboards for imperialist
adventures. There were only six thousand soldiers in the German
colonies, and Germany never used native colonial troops to fight
abroad, whereas Britain and France forced native soldiers to fight
in their foreign wars. It was a fairly convenient point of view,
because Germany had small colonies and could raise only small
armies of native colonial troops.

He claimed that Germany's success had produced a degree of
envious isolation. Great Britain "was spinning a worldwide network" of trade alliances to defend herself against German competition, while France was financing Russia's military expansionism.
But, he concluded, despite certain tensions, a major war would not
break out. Some of his logic seemed to emerge from the same
primer that won him his doctorate by pleasing his professor; still,

this was the opinion held by most Germans of influence. Obviously, they were all wrong.

Germany's soldiers, in their multicolored Prussian and Württemberg and Bavarian and Hessian regional uniforms, were soon homogenized into a field-gray soldiery. They marched to war from Berlin's Unter den Linden and Munich's Maximilianstrasse, their heads held high and flowers stuck into the muzzles of their rifles. Pretty girls strewed petals in their way. *Im Felde, da ist doch der Mann noch was wert!*

5

BRUSSELS, 1914-15

GERMAN TROOPS quickly swept into Luxembourg and Belgium. In October 1914 Schacht, whom the army had deferred from military service, was given a leave of absence by Dresdner Bank. He was then ordered to Brussels to join the military occupation authorities. A former Reichsbank executive named von Lumm was named senior financial advisor to the German military governor in Belgium, and Schacht became one of his assistants. Von Lumm carried the nominal rank of major; Schacht stayed a civilian.

The German military governor was Field Marshal Colmar von der Goltz, an old soldier who was also known as Goltz-Pasha. His Turkish title was awarded after the Turkish government asked him to reorganize the slovenly army of their far-flung sultanate. Schacht had met the field marshal through his German-Turkish organization and had invited Goltz-Pasha to address several admiring groups of Turkish junketeers.

When Schacht arrived in Brussels, he was immediately confronted with a challenge to his sense of decorum and personal status. He reacted with typical self-protectiveness. As a member of von Lumm's advisory staff, he expected to take his meals in the German officers' mess. When Schacht requested credentials, von Lumm, who was rigged out in his major's uniform, informed him that no mere civilian could become a member of a German officers' mess. A furious Schacht quietly asked to speak with the military governor directly.

Von Lumm was outraged by this request. How could a minor

civilian member of the occupation authorities bother a field marshal? It was a laughable idea, but he gave Schacht leave to try. Perhaps the myopic young banker would learn his lesson. After
sending his personal card to the military governor, Schacht was
immediately invited to Goltz-Pasha's headquarters, where he was
given the warmest of receptions. Schacht appeared that night as
Goltz-Pasha's guest at the officers' mess, in the seat of honor to the
field marshal's right. It obviously did not endear him to von Lumm.

Those who conquer take what they want. In Belgium the German army did things the old-fashioned way, by simply requisi-
tioning what it wanted. The immediate task of the financial
advisors to the military government was to clean up the manner
in which the Belgians repaid their occupiers for the expense of
occupying them. Until World War II, this was the strange, cruel,
but historical system of all military occupations. Those who get
conquered pay tribute to their conquerors.

Von Lumm decided to organize and sanitize this military
gouging of the conquered Belgians by introducing a special occupation currency. This new occupation money would serve to
pay debts incurred by either side and to avoid the army's arbitrary requisitions. It was almost impossible for von Lumm to
conduct properly accounted financial transactions in the occupied country when every German general, colonel, or major
could arbitrarily hand out a chit that read, "This is in full payment" for ten horses or an estate or a ton of coal.

There were more ruffled feathers between von Lumm and his
new subordinate when Schacht pointed out that the Belgian government, with its gold reserves and even its money-printing
plates, had fled into exile in England.[41] Belgian money would
have to be raised to back von Lumm's special new Belgian occupation currency. Schacht proposed that the individual Belgian
provinces combine to raise a bond issue that would secure this
new currency. It was an inventive way of financing, and typical of
Schacht's talent for improvisation. Von Lumm was extremely

41. Peterson, *Hjalmar Schacht*, p. 24.

doubtful about Schacht's idea (and probably also jealous of him) until a 480-million-franc bond issue was launched and successfully sold. Now German troops could be paid in the new occupation currency instead of grabbing what they wanted.

This began a murky chapter in Schacht's career, which would continue to haunt him. Schacht later claimed that the Deutsche Bank had requested a considerable block of occupation currency to be discounted at a profit against German marks through its Brussels branch. Schacht did as asked. Shortly thereafter, his former civilian employer, Dresdner Bank, asked him for a similar block of currency for the bank's use with its Belgian clients. Schacht knew that the use of highly discounted occupation currency was very profitable for German banks, but he protested that there was nothing wrong about fulfilling the request from Dresdner Bank. After all, Deutsche Bank had already been accommodated.

Schacht had made an implacable enemy of his chief, the snubbed von Lumm, who now accused him of unethical conduct. As a government employee, Schacht should not have used the power of his position to create massive profits for his former employer. Von Lumm informed Schacht that he was sacked.

Other versions of these events are available. In 1923, during Reichsbank proceedings to confirm Schacht's appointment to an important government post, the "Brussels matter" came up. Apparently, there was a July 6, 1915, inquiry (prior to Schacht's dismissal), in which Schacht was accused of giving "far-fetched" explanations[42] for his actions, explanations that showed "disingenuousness" and a "lack of openness."[43] Others felt that von Lumm had "made a mountain out of a molehill."[44]

Schacht's influential friend von der Goltz could play no role in the matter. He was back in Turkey, commanding a Turkish army, which did some damage to the British general Townsend's Near Eastern units. He was one of the few military men who had

42. Ibid., p. 25.
43. Mühlen, *Schacht*, p. 9.
44. *International Military Tribunal*, vol. XIII, p. 67.

Schacht's unstinting admiration. Von der Goltz died of typhus in Turkey in 1916. Dr. Eddy Schacht, who served in Goltz-Pasha's army as a medical officer, was charged with bringing the field marshal's body back to Germany.

In 1916, after the unpleasant end to his time in Brussels, Schacht returned to Berlin, which, like capitals all across Europe, was beginning to feel the pinch of food shortages. The Schachts added a goat for milking and a vegetable garden.

Schacht's antagonists (and there are many among historians) claim that shortly after his return to Dresdner Bank headquarters, he was fired. This seems unlikely, since he had produced substantial profits for the firm during his supposed transgressions in Brussels. His own explanation for his departure from Dresdner Bank in 1916 is more in character. As soon as he returned to Berlin to resume his duties, his chief, Eugen Gutmann, gave him to understand that he was in line for election to the board of directors. By the end of the year, he saw no sign that this was about to happen. He asked Gutmann if he could still count on the promotion, and the embarrassed chairman confessed that a member of the board, his own son Herbert was against the idea. Schacht then met with Herbert Gutmann, who confessed, "Dr. Schacht, if you were to join the board, I'd be afraid that you'd take over all my consortium business." He meant consortiums of banks for joint ventures.

According to Schacht, he told Herbert Gutmann, "If you have these fears, then I'm leaving." Before the end of the day, he had handed in his resignation. Supposedly, Eugen Gutmann later called his fellow board members fools for letting him go.

Luise Schacht, never the complaisant wife, was furious about what she considered her husband's precipitous decision. "What now?" she asked. "You like to burn your bridges before you know what comes next!"

He shrugged off her complaints. "My dear," he preached, "material gain or loss isn't so important. Staying true to oneself is."[45]

45. Schacht, *76 Jahre meines Lebens*, p. 179.

He made it clear to her that he had absolutely no worries about their future but that the first thing he would do was report for military duty. He did, indeed, register his name at military head-quarters. Did he count on the fact that it was probably an empty gesture? There was no way he could be sure he would be rejected again. He was as myopic as ever, but by 1916 the German army was beginning to enroll men with lesser physical qualifications because the war in the western trenches was grinding up the sup-ply of soldiers. Schacht's antipathy to war was not cowardice but simply a matter of rational belief. For Schacht, war meant waste and failure, and he probably considered himself — or any other young man of intelligence and achievement — too valuable to squander. The obituary he offered for his son, Jens (who died in World War II), typified his disdain for war. He called Jens a good man and an intelligent man, whose death was a great waste. "He could have been a fine leader of commerce."[46]

Schacht could never permit himself be openly antiwar. Dur-ing both World Wars it was considered treasonable for a German to speak of anything but a "hero's death," and the loss of a man's life was a "valuable gift to the Fatherland." Though Schacht's thinking was frequently ahead of his time, his actions often re-mained shackled to German convention.

He did not have to wait long to find out whether he would be wearing a uniform. Before the military doctors had a chance to give their learned opinions, he was called back to bank-ing. High positions in German industry, banking, and govern-ment invariably guaranteed deferment from military duty. His departure from Dresdner Bank had not gone unnoticed, and he was contacted by a smaller bank, rather grandly named the Na-tionalbank, that specialized in joint ventures. Strong personali-ties were usually the catalysts for these joint ventures or consortiums. Nationalbank's chairman, Julius Stern, was such a man, and when he died unexpectedly, the bank began to floun-der. It offered the job to Hjalmar Schacht because of his persua-

46. Ibid., p. 156.

sive presence and great inventiveness, and he accepted. It was a good opportunity.

A few days later, Karl Friedrich von Siemens offered him the position of financial vice president of the great Siemens industrial complex. Had Schacht known earlier about the Siemens position, he would have preferred it, but he had given his word to the Nationalbank.

Luise Schacht had complained needlessly. Her thirty-nine-year-old husband was obviously in demand and had every right to feel self-confident. Many people in the German financial community considered him a man of the future. Schacht was never openly a self-promoter. Yet, somehow, time after time throughout the years, each one of his achievements was much discussed and extremely well recognized.

His ability to attract the cooperation of other banks was soon on display. Among those who sought him out at the Nationalbank was a small consortium of princely investors, a suitable epithet for the partnership of Princes Hohenlohe-Öhringen and Fürstenberg. Sick of watching the rise of the newly rich industrialists, the princes had invested heavily in industrial holdings through Deutsche Bank but had soon lost 90 million marks. Now they were anxious to move their portfolio into the hands of Schacht's Nationalbank. Schacht, whose bank was still a minor player in a big game, was anxious to guard his relationships with the powerful "D" banks. He arranged to meet with President Havenstein of Deutsche Bank, who handled the princely account. Schacht explained that he had been approached and that the two princes wished to leave Deutsche Bank. However, he thought that Deutsche Bank would prefer to have their former clients handled by a banker who would stay in close touch with their former advisors. The Deutsche Bank was pleased. Schacht and the Nationalbank restored the princes' portfolio to a semblance of health through the sale of certain holdings and, it is assumed, with some profitable reinvestments. Throughout the transaction, he stayed in constant touch with Deutsche Bank.

Schacht's daily pursuit of banking, his beloved affliction and obsession, took place against the backdrop of an increasingly brutal war. The only clear-cut German victories had been against the ill-equipped and badly led Russians early in 1914 and 1915. German troops were commanded by the elderly semiretired Field Marshal Paul von Hindenburg and his clever and younger associate, General Erich Ludendorff. Their victories at Tannenberg in East Prussia and in the area of the Masurian Lakes made a national hero out of the dull von Hindenburg and boosted the ambitious gambler Ludendorff into a position of great power. Ludendorff, an earlier-day Patton, suited the average German's picture of a true soldier, and he quickly displaced the kaiser and his chancellor as leader in the mind of the average German. People listened to Ludendorff. They felt they could *trust* Ludendorff. The kaiser retreated into imperial seclusion, from which he occasionally and ineffectively implied that behind the scenes he was still the true commander. Until the disastrous end of the war, the fate of the German people was largely in the hands of General Erich Ludendorff, backed by Field Marshal Paul von Hindenburg, the "hero of Tannenberg." The kaiser, his chancellor, and the cabinet were in the shadows.

In September 1915 the czar had fired his incompetent imperial relative, the Grand Duke Nicholas Nicholaievich, from command of Russia's forces. The czar then took personal command, another bad decision. Like most of Russia's lower class, the huge, neglected Russian army was chafing under the czarist regime. Except among the aristocrats and the very wealthy *haute bourgeoisie,* rebellion was brewing at all levels of Russian society, from intellectuals and professionals to the poorest peasant. Ludendorff and the German High Command were quite willing to take advantage of this unrest. With German permission and encouragement, Russia's most potent revolutionary, Vladimir Ulyanov (Lenin), left his Swiss exile and got passage through Germany to Russia and the revolution. Because of the obvious participation of the Germans, some Russians considered him a German agent provocateur. Others saw him as their savior. Russia's revolution gathered strength. At first, it was bourgeois, middle-class, and quite civilized, styled more after the American model of 1776 than the French one of 1789, but soon it deteriorated into bloody insurrection.

The czar, who was still tenuously in command, tried to relieve the pressure on the Allies fighting in France by launching a final risky attack into Polish Galicia. His army was badly beaten, and the result was a peace treaty signed at Brest Litovsk. Russia's war was over. Its revolutionaries of all shades were delighted that the fighting had ended, and mangled Russian soldiers and idle sailors were about to join them.

With Russia no longer a military threat, Ludendorff turned his attention back to the French and the English, who had refused to collapse as he had planned. He plunged German troops ever deeper into the meat grinder on the western front. The "west," with its maximal attrition and minimal victories, became part of every German's daily vocabulary, as typified by Erich Maria Remarque's antiwar novel *Im Westen Nichts Neues* (*All Quiet on the Western Front*). Most German leaders, with the exception of Ludendorff, lost all their conceits and delusions about the war, but Ludendorff still held the reins. He now launched Germany into unlimited submarine warfare, hoping to starve the British out of their islands. This brought the certainty of war with the United States, but American military effectiveness was dismissed by the German High Command. One of the heads of Germany's navy, Admiral Capelle, saw the Americans as "the equivalent of Zero."[47]

For more than two years, Ludendorff's powerful personality had dominated all decisions. In his view, Germany would win or perish. Several opportunities for peace negotiations, using the freedom of occupied Belgium and the suspension of the U-boat war as pawns, were cavalierly ignored by Ludendorff, while Germany's civilian government remained in name only. On the Allied side the scenario was reversed. David Lloyd George of Britain and Georges Clemenceau of France were in full control of their military commanders and of the conduct of the war.

Ludendorff had miscalculated monumentally. In 1917 the United States sent its troops into battle at Ypres. German U-boats failed to starve the British Isles into surrender, and Paris re-

47. Golo Mann, *Deutsche Geschichte des 19 und 20 Jahrhunderts*, p. 626.

mained French. The Russo-German peace treaty brought little
relief to Germany's struggle in the west. On March 21, 1918, Ludendorff launched his final, desperate attack. It involved 750,000
men and six thousand pieces of artillery in a sector of only forty
miles, near the Marne River. It stalled. Then one last German attempt failed in early July, and it was all over. There was nothing
left. No ammunition, no supplies, and no will.

On August 8, 1918, Ludendorff, anxious to shift responsibility,
informed his oft-ignored kaiser that "there was no way left to
break the enemy's will to fight." It was the end of Ludendorff's influence, the end of the kaiser's rule, and the end of Germany's
war. It led to the revengeful peace treaty signed in 1921 at Versailles, which the Germans usually called the Versailles Dictate. It
would haunt the world into the next great war.

Unable to ignore what was happening on the war front but
unwilling to let it distract him, Hjalmar Schacht continued his
daily work. With a journalist's ability to read between the lines, he
was probably more aware of the true shape of events than were
most of his colleagues. There was some excuse for their mis-
guided optimism. Military bulletins were still inexcusably positive. Germans felt falsely secure because there was still not a
single foreign soldier on German soil. Although there were shortages of many daily necessities, long casualty lists, and vast lines of
wounded and disabled soldiers being carried from Berlin's railway stations to hospitals, people told themselves that this was the
ugly price of any war. Until late 1917 most Germans were still
lulled by the reassuring words of its supposed military experts,
like Ludendorff and old von Hindenburg. Nobody really cared
what the kaiser or his civilian ministers had to say.

Schacht's personal outrage about what was really happening
often took a curiously bankerlike direction. Privately, he praised
Germany's Franco-British enemies for imposing heavy taxes on
war industrialists, who had most to gain during a war, and condemned Germany's war profiteers, who remained untaxed. One
of Schacht's heroes, the shipping magnate Albert Ballin of the
Hamburg-Amerika Line, told him the following story. While visiting in Copenhagen, Ballin spotted a group of German hustlers

arranging illegal shipments of high-priced luxury foodstuffs into Germany. When Schacht asked how much Ballin thought their total transactions were worth, Ballin said, "Probably thirty years at hard labor."

The Jewish Albert Ballin was a great patriot. Schacht visited him in 1916 at his Hamburg headquarters. They both detested the enormous wastefulness of war, but Ballin was more optimistic than Schacht. He said, "It will all blow over and reason will rule. Eventually the merchant, with his logical mind, will always win out over the politician." Ballin was also sure that all the hatreds born of war "can be eliminated by commerce, and that Germany can best benefit humanity through worldwide trade." This was virtually the creed of Schacht's Hanseatic youth. Sadly, as Schacht later pointed out, Ballin was wrong. Everything he held dear, including the Germany he loved, seemed lost. At war's disastrous end, Ballin committed suicide.

Schacht called him "a Jewish German patriot, whose only wish was for Germany to excel."

The patriot Ballin was one of two people who had great influence on Schacht during the 1914–18 war. The other was August Thyssen, with his genius for dealing in Schacht's favorite commodity: credit.

August Thyssen, the credit master of German industry, was tiny, bearded, and modest. He amassed Germany's greatest fortune by trying to teach others the great power of building the trust that breeds credit. As a young man working for the Center for the Preparation of Commercial Treaties, Schacht had touted the benefits of verticalization. Thyssen was the master of vertically integrated industrial production, from iron ore to finished machinery.

Thyssen was a genius in the creative use of credit: many of his biggest deals were guaranteed by the vaguest of promissory notes rather than by hard currency. Occasionally, Thyssen's methods worried his creditors. Once, during a car ride, a banker pointed out that he held a large block of Thyssen's "currency." He was quite concerned and asked, "What's to become of it, Herr Thyssen?"

Thyssen sat back and seemed to be in deep, silent thought. When they reached their destination, he turned to the banker and said, "You're right. What's to become of it?"[48]

Schacht's original interest in politics had been demoted to second place once he began banking, but it still existed. About 1905, when he was still a junior executive at Dresdner Bank, he had some tenuous contact with a politician named Friedrich Naumann, who headed a political movement called the National Social Union. Naumann's theories involved a socialized contract with the working class, a somewhat utopian upper-class way to combat the Marxists by preempting their promises. Though Naumann's ideas sounded seductive to Schacht, he eventually found them unrealistic.

Schacht's next political flirtation went deeper. During the war, he joined the Berlin political club *Klub von 1914*. Its members were young democratically minded professionals and businessmen, all increasingly worried about the rise of the radical Left. As Germany rushed forward into disaster on the battlefield, members of the club decided it was time to take an active part in politics.

They may have been too late. The abyss was near. On November 3, 1918, German sailors mutinied in their home port of Kiel. At the same time, a large group of leftist soldiers declared a rebellion, the Spartacus movement (named after the Greek slave who rebelled against the Romans). The German government was then led by its last imperial chancellor, Prince Max von Baden, who, despite his noble title, believed in democracy. On November 9 he announced the abdication of the bitter and angry kaiser, who then exiled himself to Holland. Even old von Hindenburg had urged the kaiser to leave the throne. Strangely, Wilhelm II shed the title and position of kaiser but never abdicated his throne as king of Prussia, probably hoping for some future miracle. He blamed Germany's defeat on everyone from the Jews to the Communists, and he was judged paranoid by several medical observers.

On November 11 the German High Command was forced to

48. Schacht, *76 Jahre meines Lebens*, p. 186.

sign an undignified armistice in the dining car of a French train that stood in a clearing near Compiègne.

It was the end of Germany's war, and it had cost the Schacht family dearly. Brother Oluf died of an illness contracted during the war, and William, the baby of the family, was killed during the frightful Battle of the Somme.

Many German monarchists and reactionaries refused to accept defeat as a fait accompli. They insisted that the German army was never beaten in the field but had been stabbed in the back by a group of left-wingers, Marxist agents, and war profiteers in Berlin. While Germany's far Left threatened revolution in the manner of Saint Petersburg, frustrated former army and navy officers raised the Freikorps, armed vigilante militia units ready to occupy Berlin to eliminate the leftist "backstabbers." Early in 1920 one of these Freikorps, led by an ex-bureaucrat named Wolfgang Kapp, did indeed move into the center of Berlin.

The so-called Kapp Putsch was stalled and then stopped by Berlin's working-class people, who mounted a general strike and forced Kapp to flee by airplane. Finally, in 1919 the first German republic was in place and began to function, though very tenuously. It is usually called the Weimar Republic because its constitution was written in the "poets' city" of Weimar, although its seat was in Berlin.

On the day of the Armistice, Schacht and several other members of the *Klub von 1914* assembled in a Berlin apartment and formed the Deutsche Demokratische Partei (DDP), the German Democratic Party. It was their political answer to the excesses of both the Left and the Right. They believed in parliamentary government rather than in the revival of the discredited Hohenzollern monarchy or the brutality of a Marxist system. They were sure their new DDP would offer sound, conservative, but enlightened solutions.

One of its founding members, a prominent newspaper editor named Theodor Wolff, had drafted the party's platform, which he read to the assembled lawyers, editors, businessmen, and other future members of the party. He began with "We are republicans . . ."

Strangely, Schacht objected. "I can't sign that. I am a monar-chist!"

The others were shocked, until Schacht pointed out that he did not mean the return of the Hohenzollern kaisers. After all, Britain and other countries had constitutional democratic monarchies, with full parliamentary representation. This was his idea of good government. To compromise with Schacht, they set-tled on "We rely on a republican structure . . ."

Schacht viewed democracy as a system rather than as an ide-ology. He stated in his memoirs that as he saw it, democracy de-pended on the voice of the majority, *no matter what the majority favored.*[49]

Since his memoirs were written long after World War II, this explanation may have been his way of rationalizing how he could accept the Nazis. There is a frequently offered argument that the 1932 vote which finally forced the German president to appoint Hitler as chancellor was indeed "the voice of the majority." In ac-tual fact, under the Weimar multiparty system, a party could be dominant without gaining an absolute majority. As little as 35 percent could suffice, if other parties had won fewer votes. Usu-ally the party with the most votes sought a coalition to gain extra strength. It was the democratic way, and Hitler predicted in *Mein Kampf* that he would come to power by "using democracy to de-feat democracy."

Though he had taken part in founding a political party, Schacht did not become a politician. He made a few speeches to explain the DDP and its program. One was before an association of reactionary former officers. Sensing the deep antagonism of the audience, he began, "Ladies and gentlemen, I represent the DDP, the party of the liberal press, the Jewish bankers and the 'gilded Marxists.'" Each of these self-directed insults was greeted with applause and shouts of approval.

Then Schacht continued, "You see, ladies and gentlemen, I used all these foolish descriptions so that I could find out quickly

49. Ibid., p. 194.

what sort of people I was speaking to." According to Schacht, his audience seemed taken aback and then began to pay attention.

Schacht's direct involvement with politics would remain a side issue, though he often used his connections and talent as a banker to further his favorite patriotic and political goals. For Schacht, banking would always remain intertwined with his very personal view of patriotism.

Every breath of the newborn Weimar Republic was inhaled in the poisoned atmosphere of the Treaty of Versailles. The German historian Golo Mann, an anti-Hitler exile who is not known for his reactionary views, describes the Versailles terms as "careless of justice, a monstrous instrument for suppression, looting and permanent insult. Germany lost a tenth of its population, half of whom were Germans by descent, an eighth of its territory, most of its iron ore and much of its coal, and all of its colonies with the insulting explanation that 'Germans were too barbaric to be a colonial power.'"

Its locomotives, ships, and cable stocks were requisitioned. Its army and navy were reduced to the size of police forces, the historic Rhineland was occupied for fifteen years as a "buffer" for France, the mineral-rich Saar territory was separated from Germany, and crushing financial "reparations" were to be paid annually to the victors. Among the hardest terms to digest was the infamous (to Germans) Article 231, which stated that Germany admitted to *Alleinschuld,* the sole responsibility for causing the war. Although this clause was purely rhetorical, it did unending damage, since few Germans, no matter if liberal or conservative, believed it to be true.

President Wilson, the only voice of reason among the Allies, was scuttled by his own isolationist Congress, so America never joined the League of Nations, an anemic predecessor of today's United Nations. With American participation, the league might have been a much more potent instrument. Many rational Germans felt betrayed because they had believed in Wilson's constructive Fourteen Points for a peace treaty. Instead, they had to accept the brutal Allied terms. Those German leaders who signed the Versailles Treaty, no matter how reluctantly and with how much revulsion, were never forgiven by most of their fellow countrymen. By accepting Versailles, the Weimar Republic ordained its eventual doom.

Friedrich Ebert, the Weimar Republic's first president, was buffeted by one disaster after another. In October 1919 a group of Rhinelanders backed by the French began to plan a separatist Rhineland republic. Ebert's chancellor and his cabinet resigned rather than have to ratify the terms of the Versailles Treaty, and Ebert had to patch together a new cabinet, which then dealt with the unpalatable Allied terms. Matthias Erzberger, who headed this new cabinet, was soon assassinated by right-wingers. Three chancellors and their cabinets resigned or were eased out within a year.

Schacht was asked to travel to Holland as part of a very downhearted German delegation to meet at The Hague with the victorious Allied Commission on Reparations. He was charged with finding the way in which various chemicals and raw materials would be delivered to the victors. Schacht was stunned by what he considered the overbearing ways of the Allied officials. It was typical of Allied arrogance that when there were not enough chairs, the German participants were left standing during long meetings. Despite fear-filled warnings from his fellow German delegates, he complained to the general who headed the Allied group.

"General," he said, "we are quartered in The Hague's worst hotels. During meetings, when there are not enough chairs, we are just left standing on our feet. We are even limited as to where we can go in The Hague and when!"

The answer should have prepared him for things to come. The general shrugged and said, "You seem to have forgotten that you lost the war."[50]

Schacht was aghast that after being defeated and escaping the danger of a Communist revolution, Germany was now haunted by a new specter: the Allied demands for harsh and excessive reparations. This, as he saw it, quickly brought on the disease of inflation.

---

50. Ibid., p. 205.

6

THE MOMENT

IN 1920, HJALMAR SCHACHT was a well-known young German banker. By the end of 1923 he was world-famous in banking circles and often garlanded with the term *genius.*

His sudden rise to prominence was brought on by Germany's economic inflation, which was described as "creeping" in 1921, then "galloping," and finally "runaway" in 1923. To this day great nations quake at the very word *inflation,* and each modern country has installed economic emergency mechanisms to avoid it. The crustiest of today's government economists still get nightmares when seeing old newspaper photos and newsreels of Germans bringing wheelbarrows filled with devalued paper money to buy a loaf of bread, or of reichsmark banknotes, overprinted with a succession of ever increasing zeros, from 10 to 1,000 to 10,000 to 1,000,000 and even 1,000,000,000,000. Every time the chairman of America's Federal Reserve Board raises the nation's interest rate by a small fraction, he risks being called an "initiative killer." But he cannot help himself. Subconsciously he is being manipulated by the atavistic echo of a financial disaster that happened three-quarters of a century earlier in another country. The word *inflation* has become the unfailing tool, the bogeyman threat, used by modern politicians during almost every election campaign. The avoidance of inflation has become a lofty achievement, like a balanced national budget and a positive balance of trade.

Runaway inflation, the apocalyptic spasm that struck Germany's economy in 1923, provided the stairway for Hjalmar Schacht's climb into the pantheon of international banking.

Inflation occurs when a government prints paper money without being able to ensure that this currency is backed by solid value. In the nineteenth century and at the beginning of the twentieth, the internationally accepted standard of value was gold. A banknote promised that every mark or pound or franc was worth its value in gold; the only changes came with the fluctuation of the value of gold on the international market. International finance depended on this gold standard. (In the 1930s several leading nations decided for reasons of flexibility to disassociate themselves from the gold standard and to back their currencies with their own future productivity or other internationally acceptable assets.)

Any nation printing paper money without solid backing for the promissory amount on the face of its banknotes is causing the currency to lose value and to be "inflated" like a hot air balloon. Hjalmar Schacht was a conservative man who always believed in gold as the standard for international finance.

After the ruinous consequences of the lost war, the mark had lost half its value against Western currencies. When this weakened mark was confronted by the need to pay large reparations and also to rebuild a decimated industrial structure, the German government's panicked response was to print more paper money so that employers could pay their workers and factories could pay their suppliers. As these inflated marks weakened even further against foreign currency, *Raffkes* (as the Berliners called profiteers) with borrowed foreign money and marauding foreigners with dollars, pounds, and francs bought whatever land, houses, factories, and businesses they could grab. These German properties multiplied in value by the day — and even by the hour — while the value of the mark slipped. Many German *Raffkes* with access to borrowed foreign funds made fortunes during the inflationary years.

The German *Raffkes* and foreigner marauders were getting rich while the sound and solid burghers of Germany became instant paupers. Their savings accounts became valueless within weeks. What did it matter that one had diligently saved a respectable 100,000 marks over a lifetime? That amount could no longer even pay the rent for a single month. Respectable, reliable people — the backbone of German society — were bankrupted. It also caught up with the working class. Factory workers, whose pay rose astronomically, found that it was not enough for even the barest necessities of life. A meal could double in price as you were eating it.

Why did the German government keep printing money? One view is that they were inexperienced, without a democratic tradition or precedent, and too weak to say, "Not another mark will be printed." The president of the Reichsbank, Rudolf Havenstein, the man who was supposed to control the flow of currency, seemed to have lost his head.

An opposing view holds that several powerful men in the German government were purposely letting Germany slip into financial disaster in order to shed the burden of Versailles. They hoped that it would become clear to the Allies that a bankrupt Germany could no longer pay war reparations, but their stratagem had gotten out of control.[51] The average German could not survive the harsh cure.

Against this background of doom, many German businessmen considered it a ray of hope and an excellent opportunity when Russia's new Communist leaders offered to open trade relations. In April 1922 Foreign Minister Walter Rathenau met with the Soviets in the Italian resort of Rapallo to sign a mutual trade agreement. Two months later he was assassinated by a group of right-wing ex-officers who thought that the "Jew-sow" Rathenau had betrayed his country by dealing with the Reds. Rathenau was one of Germany's outstanding leaders, a man who had given up a comfortable place in his father's vast AEG electrical empire to serve his nation.

In January 1923 Premier Poincaré of France, the most irasci-

---

51. Wolf von Eckardt and Sander Gilman, *Bertolt Brecht's Berlin*, p. 17.

ble of the former victors, accused Germany of purposely defaulting on reparations and unilaterally occupied the German Ruhr district, the heartland of its coal and steel industry. Backed by Germany's chancellor, Wilhelm Cuno, the Ruhr Germans mounted a campaign of civil disobedience. While this hampered some Ruhr industrialists, others in German industry prospered. They manufactured and exported goods, for which they were paid in solid foreign currency while they paid their workers in inflated German marks. The manufacturers' profits were immense, but their workers faced daily troubles when their ballooning paychecks shriveled in actual purchasing power. The social fabric of the country was beginning to tear, and many feared a Communist insurrection.

On November 8, 1923, General Ludendorff, the man who was most responsible for Germany's fate during the war, teamed up with Adolf Hitler, the head of the small and vocal National Socialist (Nazi) Party, in an attempt to take over the Bavarian government as a prelude to a right-wing march on Berlin. The Munich police put down the putsch with a few volleys of musketry. After being tried for insurrection, Hitler and his aide Rudolf Hess were sent into genteel imprisonment at Fortress Landsberg in Bavaria, while Ludendorff was released with barely a rap on the knuckles. Normally, high treason was punishable by long prison sentences, but the right-of-center Bavarian government was hedging its bets.

At the end of the war, when Schacht was at the head of the prosperous, conservative Nationalbank, Jakob Goldschmidt joined the executive board. Schacht explained that one of Nationalbank's top executives had to leave, and the business was then run by himself and an old colleague named Wittenberg. To ease the workload, Schacht was eager to add a senior executive. A member of his board then persuaded him to make room for Goldschmidt, a member of the firm of Schwarz, Goldschmidt & Co., stockbrokers and investment bankers. Goldschmidt, a stock-market expert, had begun as a young Jewish bank clerk from a small town near Hanover. He became a highly successful market operator with a reputation as a speculator and a gambler. The volatile time of inflation suited his talents, and he was in his element. Some called Goldschmidt courageous and visionary, but others dismissed him as a hustler, interested only in quick profit. No matter how his contemporaries judged Jakob Goldschmidt, he became a new and powerful voice at Nationalbank and, of necessity, in the career of Hjalmar Schacht. It is most unlikely that the ever alert Schacht knew nothing about Goldschmidt, whose stock-market speculations were everything he detested, but to Schacht's horror, Goldschmidt immediately began to buy stock in companies to make them into clients. Schacht thought this added to the risk of the bank and of its clients, whose money was used for the purchases. For once, he was outvoted. The board of Nationalbank saw no harm in backing what they considered the verve and imagination of this new associate, whose manipulations were on a grand scale. Goldschmidt was even compared to Nathan Rothschild.[52]

Schacht's previously quiet and reliable Nationalbank was now boosted into the world of giant deals. It was always in Schacht's nature to sell short and to minimize his risks, and he now found himself challenged within his own kingdom. In Schacht's words, "it soon became clear that Goldschmidt's temperament and, sadly, his view of banking were diametrically opposed to mine."[53] Even the colorful personal style of Goldschmidt offended the standoffish Schacht, and there must have been many moments when he faced his long-submerged distaste for this "cattle dealer," for the prototypical Jew of his Frisian boyhood.

As if to explain himself, Schacht mentions in his memoirs the heavy flow of Eastern Jews who came to Berlin during the years immediately following the war. Rather than express his own aversion for these newly arrived Jews, he diplomatically hid behind a lengthy report by Berlin's police commissioner. This official, though not necessarily an anti-Semite, was certainly displeased by the thousands of impoverished refugees from Russia's and Poland's ghettos. They spoke only Yiddish, that tauntingly com-

52. Mühlen, *Schacht,* p. 10.
53. Schacht, *76 Jahre meines Lebens,* p. 216.

prehensible but deeply annoying (to Germans) brand of medieval German spiced with particles of Hebrew and delivered in
an Oriental sing-song. Even their posture, gestures, side curls,
and long, black caftans branded them as strange outsiders.
Schacht hints that the police official reported that these strange
interlopers "did not only cause annoyance in Germany, but else-
where in Western Europe."[54]

It is likely that Schacht saw Goldschmidt as a Semitic inter-
loper. He tells of a failed deal that drove Goldschmidt into such a
frenzy that Schacht said, "For God's sake, Goldschmidt, calm
down. This situation must not be handled *with Jewish hyper-
activity, but with Aryan calm* [italics added]."[55] (It should be
mentioned that this style of open reference to religious prototypes was not unusual in the Europe of the twenties. Even Jews
were inclined to chastise one another for doing things with "Jewish haste." In turn, German Jews were inclined to dismiss certain
daredevil activities as *goyim naches,* or "Christian stupidities.")

Undeterred by Schacht's opposition, Goldschmidt played
from strength. He soon persuaded the board to unite Nationalbank with Deutsche Nationalbank of Bremen and then to merge
with the large Darmstädter Bank, one of the old "D" banks. The
new consolidated unit was named the Danatbank, and it was a
powerful institution. The Nationalbank's old board was delighted; Schacht was aghast. He felt it would only encourage more
speculation.[56] Goldschmidt assured the board that the time had
come to concentrate on bigger deals and that their increased capital would ease the way.

By the end of 1922 Schacht had clearly lost leadership, and his
daily disagreements with Goldschmidt grew increasingly loud.
Schacht was too conservative to go along with Goldschmidt's
gambles and too vain to allow himself to be elbowed out of the
way by someone he considered an uneducated parvenu. Their

54. Ibid., p. 215.
55. Ibid., p. 217.
56. Ibid., p. 218.

open rows became the scandal of the banking community.[57]

As if to point out the difference between them, Schacht traveled to Paris and to London on semi-institutional business, using each opportunity to take on the role of unofficial ambassador. He would explain to his foreign colleagues the folly of heavy reparations and warn about the danger of German inflation and the possibility of national bankruptcy. While bankers in France or Britain seemed sympathetic to his arguments, they were in no position to change the terms of the Treaty of Versailles. Earlier he had met in Berlin with the young American lawyer John Foster Dulles, former counsel to the American delegation at the Versailles peace conference and later American secretary of state. Dulles was impressed by Schacht but unable or unwilling to intercede for him in Washington.

By the fall of 1923 the storm of uncontrolled inflation grew into a hurricane. Like the aborted Hitler-Ludendorff coup in Munich, other riots of the Right and Left broke out all over Germany. Schacht was a patriot but no fool. He knew that any leading banker might have to face an angry populace. He called Germany a "powder keg" and a "witches brew."[58] After all, whom can the man in the streets blame for his money troubles except those who deal in money? He sent Luise and the children out of harm's way to Lausanne, in Switzerland. Daughter Inge, who was twenty, enrolled in the University of Lausanne, and Jens got a chance to improve his French at a Swiss private school. Luise's reaction is not known, but the move to Switzerland might even have been made at her suggestion. Her political views seemed to be drifting far to the Right of her husband's, and she probably feared a Communist insurrection. Now Schacht could face whatever trouble was brewing without worrying about the safety of his family or about Luise's phobia of a Red uprising. It is even possible that her increasingly rightist views could have caused him embarrassment among his largely democratic associates.

57. Peterson, *Hjalmar Schacht*, p. 27.
58. Schacht, *76 Jahre meines Lebens*, p. 223.

One of the most remarkable politicians of the Weimar era was the left-of-center moderate Gustav Stresemann. On August 12, 1923, Stresemann replaced Wilhelm Cuno as chancellor. Cuno, who had run the Hamburg-Amerika Line since Ballin's suicide, returned to the shipping business. Stresemann's two most immediate tasks were to settle the standoff with France over its occupation of the Ruhr, where the local Germans were displaying passive resistance, and, even more urgent, to put an end to inflation. He did his immediate best to persuade the German citizens of the Ruhr to end passive resistance against the French, but inflation took center stage.

Many plans were suggested. One of the most forceful was proposed by the big landowners. Among the few Germans who had benefited from inflation were Germany's farmers. Their agricultural products were inflation-proof, and according to German law, they could settle their fixed debts, like rents and mortgages, in newly inflated marks. Anxious to show his solidarity with them, a leading rightist Reichstag delegate named Karl Helfferich, formerly the Kaiser's minister of finance, proposed that a new sort of mark be introduced, the roggenmark, or ryemark, which would be inflation-proof when backed by Germany's total grain crop. This would have put the currency firmly into the hands of Germany's agricultural interests, who could have hedged the usual fluctuations in crop prices. The proposal was immediately squelched by the left-wing politicians. As a final compromise, it was agreed that a new form of mark should be introduced to replace the ruined reichsmark and the many private currencies issued by various industrial enterprises. It would be called the rentenmark, or the lease-mark, and would theoretically be backed by all of Germany's land values, which in turn were mortgaged against Germany's remaining gold supply. It was a tenuous arrangement because no one could gauge the true value of Germany's total publicly owned real estate, but it was a step in the direction of perceived stabilization. The system had once been used during the French Revolution to stabilize the currency. The idea was born of the fertile mind of Finance Minister Rudolf Hilferding, a socialist, who was better at planning than at executing. Chancellor Stresemann soon replaced him with Hans Luther, a less imaginative but more forceful man.

The chancellor then managed to get the Reichstag to grant him complete control of all questions relating to currency. The Reichsbank would distribute the new rentenmark, which would be printed by a newly created so-called Rentenbank. The idea behind both financial maneuvers, the roggenmark and rentenmark, was to build some form of backing for a rigorously limited issue of currency. It would be exchanged at a fixed rate and pegged to the U.S. dollar against the discredited old currency and against all private issues of currency. All credit would be shut down to end speculation by the *Raffkes*. At the same time, there would have to be massive dismissals of hundreds of thousands of government employees, a brutal process.

Most of the machinery and laws for defeating inflation were now in place. It then became the Stresemann government's task to find someone strong and unshakable to enforce both.

Hjalmar Schacht's moment came on the morning of November 12, 1923, when Hans Luther, the new minister of finance, asked Schacht to come to the ministry for "an urgent meeting."

When Schacht's male assistant, Herr Müssigbrodt (literal translation, Lazybread), who was nicknamed Fleisskuchen (literally, Diligentcake), asked his boss whether he needed to take his usual red leather envelope, in which he always kept important documents, Schacht said, "No. Not needed. Thank you, Müssigbrodt." Schacht was quite certain that the meeting would be about the newly created post of national currency commissioner. He had heard that two other bankers had already been approached and had turned down the job.

Luther came straight to the point and offered Schacht the post. Schacht asked the obvious question, "Herr Minister, why don't you do it yourself?" Luther claimed an overload of work.

Next, Schacht asked, "Why did the two gentlemen who were offered the post ahead of me turn it down?"

Luther was not surprised by Schacht's question. "They were both too scared. One of them was naive enough to say he would accept only after the new currency had been introduced. Ridiculous! The job *begins* with the introduction."

"Why," asked Schacht, "don't you ask the Reichsbank to handle the introduction?"

"Dr. Schacht," said Luther, "you know very well that the president of the Reichsbank is not on good terms with President Ebert." This was true. Ebert had been trying to convince Reichsbank president Rudolf Havenstein to resign, but the presidency of the Reichsbank was awarded for life. Besides, Havenstein, who was a right-wing conservative, would have wanted right-wing politician Karl Helfferich of the old imperial treasury (and of the roggenmark) to succeed him. Unmentioned was the obvious fact that Havenstein's weakness was partly responsible for inflation. After all, his signature as president of the Reichsbank could be found on each of the monstrously inflated German banknotes.[59] When they reached trillion denominations, they were printed only on one side to save time, and clerks in the banks used the backs for scrap paper, since they had little other value.

Schacht knew that eventually there could be no solution except to back the mark by gold, but he also understood the urgent need for a stopgap measure like the rentenmark. He, of all people, understood the importance of perceptions. He asked Luther for a few days to think it over, but Luther shook his head. He gave Schacht until the end of the day. Things were that critical.

Schacht then demanded absolute assurance that he would have a completely free hand and could function outside the normal channels of organization, without needing any approval from the cabinet. In effect, he asked for dictatorial powers, and he was promised that he would have them "if he accepted the post by the end of day."

On his return to Danatbank, he called a special meeting of the board. He then told the directors that he had decided to resign from the board and to take Luther's offer.

According to Schacht, there was no truth to the rumor that he

59. Mühlen, *Schacht*, p. 11.

received a huge separation payment. The parting was no jolt for either side. The Danatbank's board was tired of Schacht's conservatism, his lack of adventuresomeness, and his constant quarrels with Goldschmidt. On his side, Schacht was eager to sever connections with the dangerous and risky Jakob Goldschmidt.

He began his new position as Reich currency commissioner on November 13, 1923, four days after the aborted Hitler-Ludendorff putsch in Munich.

A more cynical view of Schacht's appointment as currency commissioner points to Jakob Goldschmidt as the puppeteer. Goldschmidt was doing all the innovative work at Danatbank, while Schacht's contribution was limited to open criticism of the bank's new and increased scope and plans. He had produced no new business and had become a costly liability. In this version, Goldschmidt set out to lobby Luther and Stresemann to appoint Schacht as currency commissioner, a job that would create a valuable contact for Danatbank while getting Schacht off the bank's payroll. If true, this cynical scenario was not out of character for Goldschmidt, but Schacht never complained of having been manipulated, and he was not a man to hide a grudge.

On November 13, the day Stresemann installed Schacht as his cure for the currency, the chancellor obtained emergency powers from President Ebert to deal with other, equally urgent problems, such as the Ruhr insurrection, without having to wait for parliamentary approval.

These emergency powers could be granted by the president, on a temporary basis, under the Weimar constitution. At first, they were given sparingly, then as the republic's problems multiplied, more and more frequently to chancellor after chancellor.

The new commissioner took charge at once. He and his long-time secretary, Clara Steffeck, moved into a small room at the Finance Ministry that had been used for storing the janitor's supplies and had a persistent smell of carbolic. It was a strange place from which to try to save Germany and her reputation as a great nation. He met with the *Regierungsrat* who was the ministry's *Staatssekretär,* or chief of staff, and announced that he would bring along Fräulein Steffeck. There was some discussion about his salary and hers, and according to Schacht, he informed the shocked official that he would take no money but that he wanted six hundred marks per month paid to his secretary. This was the total amount that had been budgeted for the new commissioner's post and was also the sum Steffeck had been paid at the bank. *Herr Regierungsrat* was appropriately taken aback.

While Schacht had not invented the anti-inflation strategy, it was the fierce and combative execution of the rentenmark plan that gained him a worldwide reputation as "the banker who saved his country." On November 15, 1923, the printing presses stopped and began to turn out the new rentenmark. One rentenmark would be exchanged for one trillion (1,000,000,000,000) inflated old marks, take it or leave it.[60] Each owner of private or commercial real estate could obtain a bond in rentenmarks at 4 percent, redeemable at 5 percent, though the length of the bond's term stayed vague. There was a violent struggle with the speculators. Cutthroat *Raffkes* had bought everything in sight (real estate, textiles, foodstuffs, jewelry) from desperate owners. ("A thousand dollars for your villa, not a penny more, take it or leave it.") They had used borrowed foreign currency, paid high interest for their capital, and made a quick killing when they sold their "plunder," but the *Raffkes* did not stand a chance against the tough new commissioner. German property owners took heart and would no longer peddle away their holdings. By November 20 most speculators had capitulated.

The fight with Germany's export manufacturers did not end quite as quickly. They had paid minimal taxes by using inflated marks. The mark was now pegged at the old rate of 4.2 rentenmarks to the U.S. dollar, and they had never expected to settle their debts in deflated currency. Now they had to pay everything and everyone in the foreign currency they had earned. Eventually, though reluctantly, they saw the sense of Schacht's draconian regulations and exchanged their *Notgeld* (emergency money), the currency they had privately printed to settle their debts and pay

60. *Review of Reviews* (November 1924), p. 541.

their workers, for rentenmarks. They had enjoyed earning foreign currency through their exports, but they also needed a domestic market — and could not have one as long as the average citizen was bankrupt. At the time, people said that *Notgeld* clearly proved that "every man could be his own Reichsbank."[61] But not while Schacht was in charge!

Now one could once again buy things that cost two or three marks. A 1924 New York article about Schacht by Isaac Marcosson of the *Saturday Evening Post* said that "there was really nothing behind the Rentenmark except the iron determination of the Currency Commissioner to make it a stable medium of exchange."[62] Schacht stated, "I have tried to make German money scarce and valuable."[63] As usual, Schacht showed that credit is often psychological and not necessarily rational.

During the battle, Schacht had great need of his inherited Frisian humor, and he valued others who took the lighter view. Karl Fürstenberg, the famous banker whose terse pronouncements were legendary, heard a quip that one of the big "D" banks had added two floors to its building, "just to accommodate all those inflationary zeros." Fürstenberg said he saw no need for the extra floors, because "all the zeros at the bank were already housed in the executive offices."

Clara Steffeck was asked by some reporters what the currency commissioner really did all day long.

She answered, "What did he do? He sat in his dark room, which smelled of old cleaning rags, and he smoked [cigars]. Did he read letters? No. And he dictated no letters. But he phoned a lot all over the world, about domestic and foreign currency. Then he smoked some more. We didn't eat much. He usually left late and took public transportation to go home. That was all."[64]

Schacht was helped in no small measure by some cruel steps

61. Schacht, *76 Jahre meines Lebens*, p. 232.
62. *Review of Reviews* (November, 1924), p. 540–01.
63. Ibid., p. 541.
64. Schacht, *76 Jahre meines Lebens*, p. 235.

that had to be undertaken by Stresemann and his successor. Between October 1, 1923, and March 31, 1924, the German government discharged 397,000 employees, mostly lower-level managers and clerks, at a savings of 421 million marks.[65] There was also a substantial increase in taxes.

Only one week after Schacht's appointment as currency commissioner, Reichsbank president Havenstein died. Chancellor Stresemann immediately proposed Schacht for the post in order to forestall the departed Havenstein's choice of Karl Helfferich, an antirepublican right-winger. Stresemann's candidate ran into immediate opposition from the board of the Reichsbank. A letter of December 17, 1923, to the chancellor, signed by two senior members of the Reichsbank's board, stated that they considered Schacht "unqualified" because of his lack of experience in the specialty of national reserve banking. They added that his Brussels "problems" of 1916 also disqualified him on ethical grounds. Although there was no proof of any wrongdoing on his part, the accusations sufficed. Not a single speck of stain must be attached to the head of the nation's official bank. Paul von Schwabach, a senior board member, had moved in a meeting on December 17 that Herr Dr. Schacht was unqualified for the post of president of the Reichsbank, and the board had so voted. Twenty-two were against Schacht, three for him.[66]

Despite this forceful opposition, Schacht was appointed Reichsbank president on December 22, 1923. He was the man the leftist delegates in the Reichstag wanted, he was supported by the trade unions, and he was the liberals' choice over the right-wing Helfferich. Most important, he was the choice of Friedrich Ebert, Germany's president.

President Ebert and Hjalmar Schacht met that day, and their conversation was comparatively short and clear. Ebert asked Schacht what he thought of becoming president of the Reichsbank. Knowing that Ebert's government was a liberal and demo-

---

65. Mühlen, *Schacht*, p. 19.
66. Ibid., p. 16.

cratic one, Schacht said that he was no socialist and that he believed in individual enterprise. Ebert waved off his *confessio* and said, "That is neither here nor there. Will you be able to carry out stabilization?"

Schacht replied, "I am clear about the things I must do. I am confident I can do them. I will use all my strength to see it done!"[67]

It was not the last time Schacht would tell a head of state that he did not agree with him but could do the job.

On December 22, 1923, Schacht added the presidency of the Reichsbank to his post as currency commissioner of the Reich. Like his predecessor, he was appointed for life. Within a few weeks he had virtually become Germany's economic dictator. He could attend all cabinet meetings but did not need the cabinet's approval for his decisions.

Stresemann was not as successful in convincing the Ruhr insurrectionists to call off their passive resistance against French occupation, so his plan for negotiating with Poincaré evaporated. On November 23, 1923, he resigned and was replaced by Wilhelm Marx, a moderate of the Catholic Center Party. Stresemann took the portfolio of foreign minister.

Schacht's life had changed substantially. He claimed that his private life was happy. After all, he had family, friends, and a comfortable, cozy home. He even insisted that "I shared my daily [banking] business responsibilities with capable associates," and he concluded that he could have "lived out his life in a quiet and agreeable way," had he not been gripped by "the burning desire to be of help to his people."

However, despite this seeming tranquillity, there were signs of estrangement in the Schachts' marriage. Luise and the children were still in Switzerland, and Schacht claimed that this was the reason he had not asked for her opinion before resigning from the bank. He wrote, "My wife was in Lausanne, and I could not consult with her. I did not inform her until shortly before my de-

---

67. Schacht, *76 Jahre meines Lebens*, p. 229.

cision [to resign from the bank], so I had to act without her counsel." Recalling her fury the last time he resigned from a job without her advice, he then added, rather enigmatically, "The way into loneliness had now begun for me."

Nevertheless, he immediately telephoned Luise to present her with the fait accompli of his resignation and his new government appointment, and he got on a train to Switzerland. They had a makeshift Christmas celebration in their rented rooms. Schacht remembered that "we tried to make things as harmonious as possible."[68] He then returned to Berlin, and Luise and the children followed him on December 27. He made no mention of any discussion that surely must have taken place with the far-from-meek Luise.

68. Ibid., p. 239.

7

THE HERO

FOR THE NEW COMMISSIONER and Reichsbank president, it was time to plunge into the next phase, establishing a gold reserve to give real backing to the mark (instead of relying on the somewhat mythical value of the rentenmark), followed by easing the reparations. Schacht had to impress the Allied governments that Germany was at the abyss. Despite temporarily stemming inflation, he now had to destroy the illusion that all was well again, and that reparations payments would flow.

Before actually moving from his janitor's closet in the Finance Ministry into the presidential suite at the Reichsbank, Schacht had a meeting with his future number two, an old-fashioned member of Prussia's minor nobility named von Glasenapp. Schacht asked whether the Reichsbank had developed any plans to stabilize the currency against gold. His guess was confirmed; there was no such plan. He told von Glasenapp that it was his intention to go to London as a first step toward pegging the mark to a gold standard.

He also chronicled his first meeting with the Reichsbank's senior executives, which was held after his return from London. With the fierce opposition of the Reichsbank's board of directors to his appointment in mind, he told the executives that he would understand if they decided they could not work with him. Within a half hour, von Glasenapp announced himself as their delegate. The executives wished to stay on at the Reichsbank under his leadership.

A form of temporary stabilization, the most urgent of Schacht's three tasks, seemed well launched. The Berlin of 1923 was wild, cynical, and hard to impress, but Schacht was a hero. In the cabarets, in the streets, they sang a ditty:

> The Rentenmark has saved the day,
> Our hero Schacht has shown the way!

Next in order of importance came the need to secure solid backing for the rentenmark by anchoring it to gold. Through the German embassy in London, he initiated an urgent request for an immediate meeting with Montagu Norman, governor of the Bank of England. He asked for a rendezvous in London around December 30, 1923. Schacht was quite aware that the meeting might interfere with Norman's New Year's celebrations, but he took the chance of offending his British opposite number. He received an instant and friendly reply. Mr. Norman would be delighted to meet with him, and the Reichsbank booked passage for him and secretary Steffeck by train and ship to London.

To Schacht's happy surprise, when his train arrived at Liverpool Street Station at 8 P.M. on New Year's Eve, Montagu Norman himself was there on the platform to greet him. Norman told Schacht he was delighted that Schacht "had accepted his invitation so quickly" and suggested a meeting at 11 A.M. on New Year's Day at the Bank of England. When Schacht expressed his surprise that Norman was willing to meet on a holiday, Norman insisted it would be a joy to get together "as quickly as possible" and that he was looking forward to it. "I hope we shall become friends!"[69]

Dufour-Feronce, commercial attaché of the German embassy, who was also there to meet Schacht, confirmed that Montagu Norman was more than eager to begin a close working relationship with the new president of the Reichsbank.

Schacht was painfully aware how critical the meeting would be. The mark was only tenuously stabilized, Germany's economy was anything but strong, and the Allies had just formed a com-

69. Ibid., pp. 243, 244.

mittee of financial and economic experts under the leadership of the American Charles Dawes to review the relationship between Germany's economy and its ability to pay reparations. The so-called Dawes Committee was scheduled to have its first meeting in London on January 14. Dawes was what the Germans called a *Tausendzassa,* a multitalented man, who had achieved success at almost everything he touched. He was a banker of renown, a general during the war, a persuasive charmer, a Nobel laureate, and, eventually, vice president of the United States. The American S. Parker Gilbert was named to represent U.S. interests on the committee. Schacht's meetings with Norman were to be held with the threat of the Dawes Committee's findings looming in the near future.

Understandably, it was a serious and concerned Schacht who checked into Mayfair's luxurious Carlton Hotel in the midst of gala New Year's Eve celebrations. Though usually not a man to dodge a party, Schacht did not feel like joining the glossy evening-gowned and white-tie-dressed crowd.

The three days of meetings with Montagu Norman were an unqualified success. Schacht told Norman that he was in no position to wait for the proposals of the upcoming Dawes Committee and the negotiations that were sure to follow, because there was too little time. Instead, he convinced Norman to cosponsor a new Gold Discount Bank, partly based on some of Germany's sparse gold reserves but mainly capitalized by British investors. He painted a persuasive picture. German export industry would be the main borrowers so that foreign capital could be earned by Germany. British capital investment in the Gold Discount Bank could then be repaid within three years. Because the original capitalization would be comparatively small (200 million pounds sterling), additional shares in the bank could be sold to British investors on the open market since all capital and loans would be in pounds sterling only. The Gold Discount Bank's business would be managed by the Reichsbank. After a day to think it over and confer with his associates, the Bank of England accepted Schacht's proposal. Montagu Norman even offered to furnish capitalization at 5 percent interest (as opposed to 10 percent in

Germany). It was one of Hjalmar Schacht's great acts of salesmanship, but it would have been impossible without Norman's
conviction that a healthier German economy was of international importance.

Over lunch with the directors of the Bank of England, Schacht
was treated with much fraternal warmth and good humor. When
he stepped into his limousine to begin the voyage home, it was
snowing hard. His new friend Montagu Norman reached into the
front of the car, pulled out a blanket, and handed it to Schacht. It
was the beginning of a long friendship, and the British banker
even became godfather to one of Schacht's grandchildren.

Montagu Norman thought it politic to inform the Dawes
group, then meeting in Paris, of their mutual plan, and Schacht
did so on January 21, 1924.[70] He testified before the committee.
Then, after meeting with Governor Robineau of the Bank of
France and President Millerand of France, a socialist, he paid a
visit to Premier Raymond Poincaré in his offices on the Quai
d'Orsay.

Actually, as Schacht relates this event, things were not so simple. The visit began with a typical Schachtian contretemps. Jean-
Louis Barthou, the French delegate at the Dawes Conference, said
to Schacht, "You cannot visit the president and ignore Premier
Poincaré." Schacht assured Barthou that he would be delighted to
visit the premier, if he was invited to do so. Barthou told Schacht
that Poincaré was very eager for a meeting, and Schacht patiently
repeated his request for an invitation. Two days later he gave in,
made an appointment, and visited the Quai d'Orsay. There, Poincaré kept him waiting in an antechamber for thirty minutes, so
Schacht reclaimed his hat and coat and left a message that, most
unfortunately, he had to leave. Just as he reached the street, two
liveried flunkies rushed after him and begged him to return.
Poincaré and Schacht then had a frosty meeting. Schacht quoted
himself as saying that reparations could be paid only through
German exports, while Poincaré insisted on cash. Schacht finally

70. *Current History Magazine* (March 1924), p. 1071.

broke off the conversation with "I am sorry, but I cannot see any purpose in continuing this conversation. I leave this room with less optimism than I had entering it."[71]

Poincaré was later quoted as saying that "a German had finally talked straight" and that "this was the first person to break off a conversation with me." For Schacht, the chance to speak his mind was a balm, both for his vanity and his sense of affronted patriotism. The *New York Times* of January 24, 1924, calmly reported: "Premier Poincaré received Dr. Schacht, head of the German Reichsbank, this afternoon, conversing with the German financier at considerable length on German financial questions and the work of the [Dawes] committees of experts."

No wonder that Robert Long, reporting in London's *Fortnightly Review* of August 1, 1924, wrote: "Today he [Schacht] is Germany's most prominent man, not only at home, but also, though he has never held a diplomatic post, in international relations. He is the only German who holds the ear of British and American finance. Germans, like the rest of the world, are won by achievements."

When the Dawes Committee began to stall about the Gold Discount Bank as one of the concrete measures to deal with the future of reparations, Schacht used a technique he often applied later; he "went public." At a speech in Königsberg in front of the financial press and other bankers, he related the Dawes Committee's delaying tactics and blamed it for any disasters that might befall. He had made the same remarks earlier, in private to the German delegation during a meeting in a Paris hotel room. The informal gathering included Germany's minister of finance and its famous foreign minister, Gustav Stresemann. One of the participants described how Schacht, "in his harsh Frisian German," insisted that "we cannot accept the terms. We can never fulfill them." Schacht was the only dissenter.[72] Led by Stresemann, the others wished to find a way to fulfill, no matter how reluctantly, the obligation of reparations.

71. Schacht, *76 Jahre meines Lebens*, p. 263.
72. Ernst Klein, *Road to Disaster*, p. 248.

Eventually, the Königsberg speech took effect. Schacht had developed a strong reputation, and the Dawes group did not want to appear obstructionist. They no longer delayed the immediate steps that had to be taken to form the Gold Discount Bank.

When Schacht was in London, he had also managed to parry a dangerous threat to the authority of the Reichsbank. With French encouragement, a group of Rhineland industrialists — led by Hugo Stinnes, a major industrialist, former wartime production czar, and member of the Weimar Reichstag — wished to found an independent Rhineland Reserve Bank. The French government had approached the Bank of England for its help and cooperation, and Montagu Norman asked for Schacht's views. The Rhineland bank was part of a French plan to separate the Rhineland provinces from Germany. The French had twice been invaded from across the Rhine, and they were anxious to create a controllable buffer nation. On October 21, 1923, a provisional Rhineland Republic was founded but not recognized by Berlin, London, or Washington.

Schacht convinced Norman of the danger of challenging the authority of the Reichsbank at this critical juncture, and just before Schacht left London, the Bank of England informed the French that it was not interested in the Rhineland proposal.

On January 31, 1924, the so-called new Rhineland Republic collapsed after its provisional president Heinz was assassinated, but plans for a Rhineland bank went ahead anyway. When the Bank of England failed to collaborate with them, the Rhinelanders, led by Stinnes, were furious. They thought they had been deceived by their Berlin contact, a senior Prussian government official named Bracht, and they were certainly aware of Schacht's opposition. They were sure he had torpedoed them in London. They got rid of Bracht, but Schacht was harder to tackle. On his return to Berlin, Schacht was asked to meet with Chancellor Marx at his office, where a group of the angry Rhinelanders, led by Hugo Stinnes, awaited him. They accused him of throwing the fate of German currency into foreign hands with his plan for the Anglo-German Gold Discount Bank. Schacht assured them that the capitalization of the bank was only in the form of a loan, which would be repaid within three years, and that the Reichsbank would keep complete control of the enterprise. Chancellor Marx then decided against the disgruntled Rhinelanders. The next skirmish was with Karl Helfferich, the anti-Schacht fiscal conservative in the Reichstag. Schacht needed the Reichstag's approval to carry out his plans. When Helfferich heard of the low (5 percent) rate of interest for the British loan, he had no further objections.

The new law was passed by the Reichstag, and on March 13, 1924, Schacht's dream, the Gold Discount Bank, came into being. This stabilized the temporary rentenmark and thereby the future of Germany's currency, since the Reichsbank now used the new Gold Discount Bank as its link to gold.

Schacht greeted the Rhinelanders' defeat with one of his laconic poems.[73]

> The Rhineland group is furious,
> Finds Schacht and Bracht injurious.
> They have already scuttled Bracht,
> But cannot faze the wily Schacht!

He also took his revenge on those Reichsbank board members, in fact the majority, who had earlier opposed his appointment. At very short notice he called a meeting in the large and pompous Kaiser Hall of the Reichsbank. Formally decked out in morning coats and striped pants, they waited for him at the long board table. He appeared in a normal business suit, nodded to a few of the gentlemen whom he knew, took his place at the head of the table, and announced, "Gentlemen, I have the honor to greet you as your new president. It is, of course, known to me that, with a few noticeable exceptions, most of you voted against my confirmation as president of the Reichsbank. This fact was of great use to me during my recent trip to London, because people abroad have taken notice that the fiscal policies of the Reichsbank

---

73. *Current History Magazine* (March 1924), p. 254, translation by the author.

will now change radically. You will learn more about these new policies in the coming weeks and months. For today, that should conclude the meeting, unless some of you have some comment [emphasis added]."[74]

The three members who had voted for Schacht's appointment sat there, grinning ear to ear, when the famous Berlin banker who was originally Schacht's main opponent asked to be heard. He assured the new president of the complete loyalty and cooperation of the entire board.

The Reichsbank, founded by Frederick the Great, was filled with tradition and staffed by flunkies in navy blue livery with red collars and many brass buttons. Its offices were filled with upholstered armchairs, wood trim, oil portraits, and vast desks. The whole atmosphere suited Schacht because he could use the stuffiness of his surroundings and its tradition to demonstrate his own informal Frisian style. He indicated that he was available to everyone, from messenger boy to cleaning woman. He was proud that his desk was usually empty of papers and bric-a-brac, with the exception of a statuette of the founder. He asked for punctuality and in return kept no one sitting in an anteroom. To save time, he introduced the telegraphic transfer of funds, a jolting jump into the future.

The Schachts moved into the roomy presidential apartment in the Reichsbank, a gloomy red building on the Jägerstrasse. Their quarters adjoined Schacht's presidential office and provided a constant connection between privacy and work. Fräulein Steffeck administered his business day. Luise was in complete control of all social plans, such as musicales with prominent artists, theater parties and boxes at the opera, dance parties for their children, and dinners for foreign diplomats and bankers (with ensuing business discussions). They became friendly with President Ebert and his wife, a warm and unpretentious couple. He was a saddlemaker by craft. When she spoke admiringly of a certain painting by Giotto in the Pitti Palace in Florence, a

---

74. Schacht, *76 Jahre meines Lebens*, p. 240.

snobby aristocratic fellow guest asked her how she could have seen it. Germany's First Lady calmly answered, "When I accompanied my master and mistress to Italy as a ladies' maid."

Luise soon learned to expect these occasional faux pas in their newly democratic surroundings. When the papal nuncio, Eugenio Pacelli (later Pope Pius XII), called on the Schachts, the elegant churchman extended his hand to one of their maids so that she could kiss his ring. The sturdy East Prussian serving girl, a Protestant, promptly grabbed it and shook it vigorously.

Meanwhile, the Dawes Committee made sure that the new Gold Discount Bank was not the idealized two-way partnership between the Bank of England and the Reichsbank that Schacht had envisioned. Half the new bank's board of directors were Germans, half were foreigners. The liquid capital of the bank would at all times be 400 million gold marks, half raised in Germany, half abroad.[75] Credit was advanced to German manufacturers only for the import of raw materials, which were then re-exported as finished products. Part of the proceeds from these exports were earmarked for the payment of reparations.[76] This was not exactly what Schacht had planned, but at least it finally gave him a chance to peg the shaky rentenmark to gold.

Schacht was fully aware that a great battle loomed ahead and that the Allies would eventually have to give up their demand for 225 billion goldmarks in reparations. He and many others considered this sum outlandish, and many financial experts on the Dawes Committee agreed. For the moment, Schacht felt that the committee presented Germany with its best opportunity, but he saw it only as a first step toward the end of what he considered financial enslavement.

The details of the so-called Dawes Plan were signed on August 16, 1924, and ratified by the Reichstag on August 29, 1924. According to its terms, for the years between 1924 and 1928, Germany would pay cash reparations of 1 billion to 1.75 billion

75. R. C. Dawes, *The Dawes Plan*, p. 65.
76. *Fortnightly Review* (August 1, 1924), p. 165.

goldmarks annually. Yearly payments would then rise to 2.5 billion goldmarks. Germany would be given a permanent open credit of 800 million goldmarks, to be secured by German import duties and taxes. As part of the plan, France would end its occupation of the Ruhr within twelve months.

There were still some speculators, now dealing in the newly backed rentenmark. Schacht felt they had to be stopped. On April 5, 1924, he had imposed a short-term stoppage of all Reichsbank credit. This caused a panic among speculators and bankrupted some of the weaker new business ventures, which he probably considered a healthy catharsis. It was the second time since his days as currency commissioner that Schacht had gained a temporary reputation as a business-killer, which is still the occasional lot of any tough reserve banker.

In an interview with financial reporter Isaac F. Marcosson in the *Saturday Evening Post* of October 4, 1924, Schacht was quoted as saying that "the German capital famine is fundamentally due to war exhaustion, reparation deliveries, and to the seizure of goods in the Ruhr which have not been paid for. It cannot entirely be remedied by national saving. The only remedy is to attract foreign capital into German industry and mortgages and other long-term investments. What I have tried to do is to clean house preparatory to the enactment of the Dawes Plan. The Rentenmark is nothing, more or less, than a stop-gap, a bridge, so to speak, between the chaos which prevailed late last year and the new deal [sic] which will come to Germany through the international loan which the Dawes Plan provides." He continued, "Every fair-minded German has favored the Dawes Plan from the start, because it separates German reparations and reconstruction from politics and will enable us to get on our feet. Here you have the American influence strongly asserting itself. Once in operation, the Dawes Plan will mean that Germany resumes her old place as a constructive force in the economic affairs of the world."

While the interviewer was impressed, others might have thought it clever to make a politic bow toward Dawes and not to object to the principle of paying reparations. Schacht was always good with the press, but this time he was reaching all the way to the White House, because Charles Dawes had just been nominated as a candidate for vice president. In an earlier interview (June 14, 1924) he had told T. Ybarra of the *New York Times* that "the nomination of General Dawes for the Vice Presidency of the United States gives a most valuable lead to people everywhere who seek a settlement of European problems."

The ancient Reichsbank was reorganized in tandem with the Gold Discount Bank's dual control. Reichsbank shares were still privately owned, but as of August 30, 1924, the bank was no longer dominated by the German government and its all-German board of directors. A fourteen-member board of advisors came into being, half of them Germans, half foreigners. Schacht was one of the seven German advisors, although as chairman of the Reichsbank, he was still in charge. He welcomed the new multinational influence. He hoped it would help him fight short-term "frivolous" borrowing from abroad.

The growing attachment between a troubled Germany and the American world of banking brought blessings as well as problems. Americans, who were in the midst of their wildly optimistic Jazz Age spree, were hungry to invest anywhere, anytime. What better place to loan out your money than in honest, hardworking Germany, which was guided by that banking genius Hjalmar Schacht? American financial publications were filled with flattering articles about "the man who saved Germany." Unfortunately, American bankers sold only short-term debentures, exactly the kind Schacht had dubbed both opportunistic and frivolous.

Schacht could keep control of things only as long as the Reichsbank was the prime conduit of credit, but now every individual German business, municipality, and state became a target for America's bankers. Once Wall Street found the range, depressed towns all over Germany were offered all the short-term foreign loans they wanted. It was difficult for Schacht to walk past the luxurious Adlon Hotel in Berlin without being accosted by some foreign banking agent trying to place investments for his clients.

On November 3, 1924, speaking to a rally of liberals in his old student town of Kiel, he received tumultuous applause when he said, "Only straightforward democratic politics will accomplish the destruction of the war-guilt lie and help us achieve our national regeneration." Having won their approval, he then took them to task by denouncing the "indiscriminate chase after foreign loans and credits. These produce intolerable confusion because of the costly intervention of superfluous middle men."[77] This began a typically Schachtian campaign, warning that it was foolish to borrow foreign capital for municipal indulgences, such as sports stadiums, theaters, opera houses, and municipal parks, when every bit of "hard" currency was needed to meet the payment schedule of the Dawes Plan. Foreign credit was there to boost industry and exports, not for entertainment and indulgences. Soccer stadiums and symphony halls would have to wait. As Schacht expected, his disciplinarian warnings upset many elected politicians, who wished to court their constituents by bringing some cheer into their depressing lives.

Early in his dealings with the Dawes group, Schacht made it his business to become closely allied with Parker Gilbert, the permanent American representative on the committee. He tried to impress Gilbert with the need to control the flow of direct American short-term loans. Even industrial companies like Daimler Benz, I. G. Farben, and United Steel took direct American loans to boost the production of domestic consumer goods rather than earmarking them for export against hard currency.[78]

In his 1968 memoir *1933,* Schacht pointed out a strange example of what he considered an abuse of easy foreign credit. Most people assume that Germany's autobahn roads, the forerunners of most superhighways, were Adolf Hitler's brainchildren. Actually, the first one, the Avus between Berlin and Wannsee, the nearby lake resort, was built in 1921 with foreign credit. It was primarily an indulgence, since it eased the commute between the wealthy resort and the city. Its traffic consisted of luxury cars such as Mercedes, Horches, and Packards. Fortunately, it was also

77. *New York Times* (November 3, 1924), p. 35:3.
78. Ron Chernow, *The Warburgs,* p. 275.

used for some international Grand Prix automobile races and brought much prestige and business to Berlin. Schacht pointed out that in 1925 even Konrad Adenauer, then mayor of Cologne and later Germany's federal leader, was seduced by short-term foreign loans to plan an autobahn.[79]

Despite all these warnings, the Weimar politicians could not muster the courage to prohibit the use of short-term foreign loans for "comfortable" public projects. In the self-indulgent postwar twenties, it was hard to convince people anywhere in the world to forgo their comfort. It was a question of living well now or paying off their debts to the future, and the attitude was "Have a good time. Who knows what will happen tomorrow?" Living in Berlin, Schacht was surrounded by those who lived in this world of instant gratification.

With its quick money, hustlers, jazz, Dada, cabarets, gangsters, drugs, drag queens, new films, theater, art, experimental architecture, and flood of foreign tourists, Berlin had become the center of the world's avant-garde. But behind the gloss, there remained abandoned and crippled war veterans, a ruined middle class, and the mocking of all patriotism and conventional social values. Much of the rest of Germany considered Berlin a strange and evil Sodom.

Worse, German industry soon learned the bitter lessons of protectionism by becoming its victims. After a promising beginning, many German exporters soon ran into trade barriers, imposed when foreign industry began to protect itself against German competition. Schacht's reputation as the hero of German banking was still intact, but the German economy was closely tied to American prosperity — and this would soon bring grave problems.

79. Schacht, 1933, p. 15.

8

CHANGES

THE TALL FIGURE of Hjalmar Schacht had become familiar to millions through thousands of newspaper and magazine photographs taken at the many international conferences. Everyone could easily identify the thin man with the high, arched nose, pince-nez eyewear, and stiff gray hair worn in the high-parted, military fashion. His slim head always seemed perched on his extra-high starched shirt collars, like a general of the old kaiser era in mufti. These tall collars became his distinctive symbol, along with his ever present cigars. At any international meeting of financiers, "the man in the tall collar with the cigar" had to be Schacht. There was no other. In winter Schacht favored fur-collared chesterfield coats and gray roll-brim homburg hats. Under his left arm, he invariably clutched a red leather envelope, which held the very few papers he needed during interminable days of international discussions. It was the same envelope he had once refused to take to his meeting with Finance Minister Luther on the day he was offered the post of currency commissioner. Among senior business and political leaders of the twenties, many wore pince-nez, and most important men were cigar smokers; but the high starched collar, Schacht's trademark, had disappeared after the war and was now a rarity.

It is difficult to believe that Schacht was unaware of the impression he created. "There he is, it's Schacht!" and "Here he

comes, Schacht!" were reactions he obviously courted. He produced the perfect image of the financial genius, the economic
warlord, a patriarch who held his shaky country firmly by the
hand and guided it through the storm. Schacht's appearance never
deviated from the style he had set for himself in the early twenties.

On February 28, 1925, the much-admired President Ebert
died. Schacht had lost one of his original patrons, but by then his
international and national place was secure.

Later that spring the Schachts decided that it was finally time
for a vacation. They booked passage for all four members of the
family on a liner owned by one of his old adversary Stinnes's
many companies, joining the ship in Genoa. From there, they
cruised to Sicily, Greece, and Egypt. In a return to his *Wandervögel* youth, Hjalmar Schacht had lively discussions about Si-
cilian, Greek, and Egyptian history with his daughter Inge,
twenty-one, and his son Jens, fifteen. Their relationship seemed
awkwardly warm, reluctantly affectionate. His Frisian self-
containment showed whenever he mentioned Inge and Jens.
Hjalmar Schacht could view everyone but his own family with
humor and detachment. He did not seem to subject them to his
usual, somewhat acidic, scrutiny.

On returning to Berlin, Schacht presented himself to former
Field Marshal Paul von Hindenburg, the new occupant of Germany's Presidential Palace. The crusty old "hero of Tannenberg"
had won the presidency by a slim margin.

Schacht's fame and prestige were such that an opportunistic
music publisher who had somehow found his aborted old student-
day operetta had printed some of its songs with "text by Hjalmar
Schacht."[80] This was not quite what the president of the Reichsbank had in mind. Such frivolities had no place in the lives of
nation-savers, so he prevented further publication; but his memoirs show a certain wry, sentimental amusement. A *New York
Times* headline on March 6, 1926, said DR. SCHACHT REGRETS POEM.

---

80. Schacht, *76 Jahre meines Lebens*, p. 276.

Early in 1926 Schacht bought a landed estate called Gühlen, which was located about forty miles north of Berlin, near the village of Neuruppin. It fulfilled a boyhood dream to own a large home in the country. Gühlen, an area of meadows, woods, and lakes, became his refuge. He wrote that Gühlen could "soothe all sorrows, heal all wounds, blunt all attacks and increase all happiness."[81] His radical methods had brought him many enemies. He was a contentious man, there were many skirmishes yet to be fought, and he needed a retreat.

For instance, a man named Roll was fined 750 marks for calling Hjalmar Schacht "a swindler." He claimed he was repeating the words of a journalist who had called Schacht "the hangman of German economic life." Roll headed a large group of people who held 1,000-mark prewar national bonds, which had become worthless. There was a very turbulent and noisy court session, and Roll's supporters flooded the courtroom. Schacht had to be escorted to safety through the back door.[82]

Later, Schacht sued several people for libel and insults. He was accused of alerting several of his favorite bankers whenever he would shut off credit, giving them an insider's chance for quick profits, but nothing could be proved.

It seemed Schacht could not live without controversy. Though he had expressed admiration for the aims of the Dawes Plan, he frequently told journalists that "Germany's obligations could not be met without the return of its lost colonies." The colonies would "furnish raw materials and be an important outlet for surplus population."[83] These statements caused some shock, although he had used the lost colonies as a ploy before. It became one of the standby weapons in his fight against reparations.

In September 1926, eight months after applying for membership, Germany was admitted to the League of Nations. The league

81. Ibid., p. 291.
82. *New York Times* (August 31, 1926), p. 4:3.
83. *New York Times* (March 26, 1926), p. 4:3.

was weak and armed with a dubious arsenal of economic sanctions, but the men who led the Weimar Republic felt that Germany had to become involved.

Despite all Schacht's warnings, the temptation to incur short-term American loans for various public and private German indulgences continued unchecked, and part of the borrowed foreign money went straight into the stock exchange for speculation. Schacht feared that he might soon lose control of the mark, and Parker Gilbert, the American representative of the Dawes Committee, seemed in full agreement. Germany was paying reparations with borrowed money while speculators were investing borrowed funds in massive purchases of stocks on margin. Naturally, the Berlin stock exchange was booming. Schacht was forced to repeat his 1923 antispeculation stratagem. On May 11, 1927, the Reichsbank informed the commercial banks that it considered their reserves too low. Two days later, on May 13 — "Black Friday" — Schacht suspended all Reichsbank credit. It precipitated another business crisis, which caused stocks to dive. The business community attacked him ferociously, as did certain politicians. That Friday night the Schachts attended a dinner party. His neighbor at table was a wealthy woman who complained that he had cost her a fortune. She had been forced to sell all her stocks. It turned out that she owned only the gilt-edged kind, so Schacht asked her why she had to dump them. It turned out that she had bought them on margin and that the bank was calling for more money, which she did not have. Schacht shrugged and told her that he knew an old New York Stock Exchange ditty, "If you sell what you don't own, you go to jail or pay the loan."

Schacht made sure to share much of the blame with the American Parker Gilbert, but Gilbert was less than cowed. After he was accused of transferring excessive amounts of foreign currency out of Germany for reparation payments and causing a credit crisis, Gilbert said, "Germans are not going to get their payments under the Dawes Plan reduced because they have been buying securities on margin at much more than their correct value and now have to sell them at a sacrifice when the banks call their loans. It's exactly what has happened in other countries. It could even happen in the United States."[84] Gilbert seemed more than prophetic.

As Schacht had hoped, some borrowed foreign currency stopped wandering into the stock market and crowd-pleasing public works. But this abstinence did not last. Germany's business was good, Germans wanted to live in comfort, and foreign loans soon resumed. In November 1927, speaking at Bochum, Schacht made yet another harsh attack on "loans for luxury."[85] He incurred the fury of many politicians, who pointed at the morale-building benefits of these "frivolous" investments and tried to prove that they were actually profitable. After all, opera houses and skating rinks charged admission.

With foreign money so readily available, reparation payments were still being made with ease and on schedule, which did not comfort Schacht. Germany was living well, but its economy was mortgaged. Between paying reparations and repaying individual foreign loans, German prosperity hinged entirely on foreign credit. As a close observer of the American scene, Schacht was leery of America's gambling spree. A crisis on Wall Street would mean disaster in Germany.

Besides the financial considerations, there were other reasons for ending reparations. With the passage of time, a broader segment of Germans had come to detest the Versailles Treaty. Stresemann's "fulfillment policy" was forgotten. Schacht had cooperated with the Dawes Committee, but he never considered reparations just. In his view, the accusation that Germany alone was responsible for the war was untrue and invalid. He had powerful company. On September 18, 1927, the new president Paul von Hindenburg dedicated a monument at Tannenberg in East Prussia to celebrate his victory over the Russians. In the speech he delivered during that ceremony, he denied Germany's war guilt and repudiated Article 231 of the Versailles Treaty. This might have come as a shock in Paris, London, and Washington, but it

84. *Literary Digest* (May 28, 1927), p. 8.
85. Peterson, *Hjalmar Schacht*, p. 71.

was greeted with warm applause by many responsible Germans.

Led by Berlin, many Germans had adopted the carefree American style. The 1925 ticker-tape celebrations of Lindbergh's transatlantic flight had set off the Jazz Age, even in Germany. America of the speakeasy days exported a the-hell-with-tomorrow attitude, which appealed to Germany's recently disenfranchised and unfocused middle class. Berlin's rambunctious new cabaret life was tied to American joie de vivre, and the American dollar.

Despite his forbidding appearance, Schacht was no prude. He knew the seamy side of life from his Berlin reporting days. The stiff collar was topped by a witty and incisive mind, but as a fiscal conservative, he realized Germany's enormous risk. How could anyone tie his future to America when even New York taxi drivers bought and sold stocks on the widest of margins? He was sure the American boom would soon bust, and his fights with the loan-hungry politicians became angrier. Each time they borrowed money from the willing and eager New York bankers, he accused them of pandering to the voters instead of protecting them.

While America was still riding high, Western Europe had begun to stumble. Britain had barely survived a disastrous general strike in May 1926, and its leftist Labour Party was knocking at the door of 10 Downing Street. The British strike had been a temporary boon to Germany's coal exports, but now no more German coal was needed.

France was equally insecure. The franc had slipped to two American cents, and the French budget could not be balanced. Cabinet followed cabinet. Devaluation of the French franc seemed in the wind, an undignified stratagem that allowed nations to pay old debts in newly devalued currency.

Meanwhile, the Soviet federation grew stronger, absorbing new, smaller republics. In 1926 Joseph Stalin had seized power, and with him came an aggressive plan to expand Russian influence, both industrially and militarily. The Russian bear loomed ominously. For the Western democracies, Communism changed from an internal to an external threat.

What if the American house of cards collapsed, if Britain turned to the political Left, and France plunged into deep economic and political troubles? More and more frequently Schacht stated in private that he would do everything in his power to stop future payments of reparations.[86] He complained that the end of the monarchy had fragmented Germany into its many original smaller states, municipalities, and districts, each represented by regional politicians out to prove their parochial worth by doing things "for the people."[87] He was losing friends in high places.

In 1923 he had alienated his fellow board members at Danatbank by opposing Jakob Goldschmidt's dangerous expansionism. Five years later the object of his alarm was a nation, not a bank. Once again, and true to form, he was willing to incur the wrath of associates by insisting on the conservative point of view. He liked to hedge his bets and view the future as a narrow, poorly charted channel. He was willing to take risks, but only if the odds were heavily in his favor and after he had prepared his fallback positions. Once he was sure that he could win, he was hard to divert; but whenever he found himself on the wrong side of a decision, he quickly withdrew.

On occasion, even Hjalmar Schacht could stumble. The Berlin bureau of the Associated Press reported on February 20, 1926, that Schacht had "put his foot in it" by telling women to cut back to one new hat per year. The article reported that "women are writing to newspapers, denouncing him for picking on members of their sex." They questioned his own salary and his travel expenses, asking, "How many hats a year does Mrs. Schacht buy?"

He did not mention this brouhaha in his memoirs.

In June he quit the DDP, the democratic party he had cofounded on Armistice Day.[88] The disagreement that led to his resignation seemed trumped up, since it involved the party's supposed unwillingness to see certain property restored to some aristocratic families. Obviously, he felt the time had come to cast himself adrift from Germany's liberal and internationalist estab-

86. Schacht, 76 Jahre meines Lebens, p. 296.
87. Ibid., p. 294.
88. New York Times (June 12, 1926), p. 5:6.

lishment and to seek political alternatives. His trust in the effectiveness of republican leadership was fading.

But first, there was one final chance to make his views felt. In the summer of 1927, he joined other leading international bankers at a New York conference on the financial situation in Europe. They focused on conditions in booming Germany, on the flow of American cash into German debentures, and on Germany's ability to pay reparations. These payments were being made with apparent ease, but Schacht warned that this was a bubble that could burst very quickly. If the flow of American investments were to dry up, reparation payments would have to cease. Among others, Parker Gilbert once more shared his doubts about the true state of German prosperity.

As a result, much of 1928 was spent preparing for yet another international conference of financial experts to deal with reparations. The meeting, scheduled for spring 1929 in Paris, became known as the Young Conference, after its chairman, Owen D. Young, a distinguished American lawyer and chairman of General Electric. Young was familiar with reparation problems, as he had been part of the original Dawes Committee.

Schacht headed the German delegation to the first conference, which was held in February 1929 at the luxurious new Hotel Georges V in Paris. John Pierpont Morgan, Schacht's idol of earlier days, joined Young at the long conference table, along with representatives from Britain, France, Belgium, Italy, and Japan. Schacht's partners were the industrialist Albert Vögler of United Steel Industries and bankers Carl Melchior of the House of Warburg and Blessing of the Reichsbank. The Germans installed themselves at the Hotel Royal Monceau and brought four limousines, loaned by Mercedes-Benz. Paul Schmidt, chief interpreter for Germany's Foreign Ministry, who accompanied the party as an observer, drew the following profiles of some of the conferees.

John Pierpont Morgan was a quiet man who made a deceivingly clumsy impression because he said little at the table. His best results were achieved later, man to man, during breaks in the proceedings or in lively chats at the bar of the hotel. Governor Moreau of the Bank of France parroted his chief Poincaré's (anti-

German) line. The Belgian banker Francqui was still irreconcilably anti-German. The Italians were represented by Alberto Pirelli of the Pirelli tire family, and the two Japanese delegates attended the entire conference smiling wordlessly. The experienced and sophisticated Schmidt found that "the most impressive personality at the table was the president of the Reichsbank, Dr. Schacht. Completely sure of himself, he relaxed in his armchair, observing the other participants through his pince-nez. He spoke excellent English and I learned to value him as Germany's finest representative [during international conferences]. He had wide experience in dealing with foreigners, particularly the Anglo Saxons [sic] and was probably a better negotiator than [Foreign Minister] Stresemann."[89]

Sisley Huddleston, who attended the conference, gives a remarkable picture of Schacht: "A vehement, intolerant man; excitable and dogmatic; impatient with the poor calculations of financial jugglers. The most tactless, the most aggressive and the most irascible person I have seen in public life. But he was fundamentally right. He knew that Owen Young meant to have a 'success'; and he legitimately harried him."[90]

A photo of the participants in the *Saturday Evening Post* shows that the hat of the moment was the derby and that even Schacht wore what the Germans call *die Melone*. J. P. Morgan sported his own special shape, a kind of half top hat, half derby.

Although the conference was sometimes harsh and often tedious, Schacht would not neglect his sybaritic side. He complained bitterly of the "ghastly food" (*Fürchterlicher Frass*) at the Royal Monceau, and he moved out to Versailles for a week of gastronomic recuperation. There were also excursions to Chez Marianne and the Casanova Bar, both cabarets in Montmartre, mostly in the company of one Mme. Eliat, the attractive thirty-five-year-old wife of the Reichsbank's Paris representative. They also took long walks in the Bois de Boulogne and in the parks of

89. Paul Schmidt, *Statist auf der Diplomatische Bühne*, pp. 165–67.
90. Sisley Huddleston, *In My Time: An Observer's Record of War and Peace*.

Versailles and Compiègne. Schacht also mentioned the company of a charming Greek playboy named Nicolaides. Mme. Eliat's husband was apparently never present.

The guest book of Chez Marianne on April 26, 1929, contains a typical Schacht verse, this time in French.

> *Voilà ce que je pense*
> *à cette conférence*
> *on a perdu balance*
> *j'ai cassé ma lance*
> *et je n'ai plus de confiance*
> *mais je garde l'espérence.*

> Here's what I think
> of this conference.
> We lost our equilibrium,
> I broke my spear,
> and lost my confidence,
> But I am keeping my hopes alive.

German foreign minister Gustav Stresemann's guiding spirit was felt throughout the conference. As Germany's most famous postwar statesman, Stresemann, a stocky, shaved-headed man with the look of a German high school teacher, considered the fulfillment of Germany's financial obligations under the Versailles Treaty a matter of national honor. He had committed himself completely to this "policy of fulfillment," no matter how painful. It would reassure the rest of the world and demonstrate that Germany was once more a valuable partner in the community of nations, and he had managed to convince many foreign skeptics.

In 1925 at Locarno, he negotiated a nonaggression pact for Germany with Prime Minister Aristide Briand of France, and it was Stresemann's reputation that had convinced the League of Nations to accept Germany as a member. He shared the Nobel Peace Prize with Briand in 1926. By 1929, the year of the Young Conference, Stresemann was suffering from a terminal kidney disease, but he insisted on guiding Germany on its last steps to-

ward normal international relations. The success of the Young
Conference was dear to his heart.

The relationship between Schacht and Stresemann was one of
mutual respect and mutual disagreement. In essence, Stresemann
was more benevolent toward expenditures that improved the
quality of life for the average German, but he was no wastrel. When
the Prussian state spent 14 million borrowed marks to redecorate
Berlin's State Opera House, Stresemann privately bemoaned this
extravagance, whereas Schacht condemned it publicly.[91]

While Stresemann believed firmly in his "policy of fulfillment," the cynical Schacht, once a fairly cooperative Dawes Plan
supporter, joined the opening of the Young Conference with
severely diminished enthusiasm. The meetings began with
a bad omen. On April 19 Lord Revelstoke, one of the chief British delegates and a man known for tact and diplomacy, died
suddenly.

A small article from the *New York Times* of December 2, 1928,
seemed to indicate Schacht's new direction:

DENY REICH PAYMENT SPLIT

The reports that Dr. Stresemann, the Foreign Minister, and Dr.
Schacht, president of the Reichsbank, have disagreed over Germany's capacity to pay reparations are without the slightest foundation, it was declared officially today.

Rumors of a disagreement were published in the Nationalistic
press on Friday.

The democratic papers hint that the story was obviously meant
to suggest that Dr. Stresemann was more conciliatory than Dr.
Schacht.[92]

The events of the Young Conference would become a key to
Schacht's political future and to his view of democracy. Another
report in the *New York Times* on the progress of the negotiations
was headed by a convoluted headline:

91. Amos E. Simpson, *Schacht in Perspective*, p. 31.
92. *New York Times* (December 2, 1928), p. 5:2.

DEBT EXPERTS DENY RUPTURE IMPENDS

Dr. Hjalmar Schacht, the chief German delegate, who still sits back waiting their proposal as if he were a creditor in position to dictate terms to his debtors . . .[93]

The Allied delegates of the Young Conference were sure that the right thing was being done, but Schacht had nothing but doubts. He was aware that many Germans of all political shadings were disgusted with what they saw as a totally undeserved form of economic slavery, and their highly respected president had already rejected Article 231 of the Versailles Dictate.

For Schacht, a more personal political consideration was the opposition of industrialist and politician Alfred Hugenberg, the ideological leader of the growing right wing in the Reichstag. Schacht was deeply troubled by Hugenberg's hints that Schacht was betraying Germany.

The next phase of the Young Conference was held in April. Probably to forestall any impression that he was a compromiser and a weakling, Schacht acted quite uncharacteristically. On April 17, 1929, he launched himself onto a perilous path without his usual fallback positions and hedges. He suddenly confronted the conference with an explosive memorandum containing demands that were bound to be unacceptable to the Allied delegates. The memorandum claimed that Germany could not meet the payments outlined earlier in Paris unless its colonies were restored, because German industry needed colonial raw materials to produce goods for export. An even more startling demand involved the important East Prussian area that had been taken from Germany by the Versailles Treaty and made into landlocked Poland's passage to the Baltic Sea. This so-called Polish Corridor separated Germany from its East Prussian area. According to Schacht, it would have to be restored to Germany so that needed agricultural products could once more flow directly from East Prussia into the country.

93. *New York Times* (April 9, 1929), p. 6:1.

On the unlikely chance that these make-or-break proposals would have been accepted, Schacht could have emerged as Germany's greatest postwar hero.

He had gambled wildly and lost. The memorandum nearly brought about the collapse of the conference. His own government was apoplectic. He had presumed to make foreign policy without consulting Stresemann.

To save the day and repudiate his memorandum, the German cabinet quickly and unanimously accepted the Young proposals on May 3 and instructed Schacht to do the same. Schacht's fellow delegate, the industrialist Vögler, resigned on May 21 and returned to Germany, protesting what he considered insufficient safeguards for Germany.[94] Schacht was furious because Vögler had agreed on every point of the negotiations until Schacht's tough and unexpected memorandum. Schacht saw it as a cowardly exit.[95]

Because of Schacht's gamble, Germany could have lost years of the goodwill Stresemann had so laboriously rebuilt. Only the efforts of the benevolent Owen Young saved the conference. To save face, Schacht had to capitulate, and in a hurry. On June 7 he accepted the terms offered by the committee, "taking full responsibility."[96] The conference had begun with a death. It was another strange omen that the huge curtains of the meeting hall caught fire at the final signing.

Now Schacht was under attack from all quarters. The government was furious that he had played fast and loose with the fate of the country. Hugenberg, his conservatives, and nationalists condemned him for having committed Germany to what they considered long-term economic slavery. On June 28 Schacht had to defend himself in front of a group of business and industrial leaders, including Krupp and Thyssen.[97] They berated him for not walking out like Vögler.

94. Schacht, *76 Jahre meines Lebens,* p. 309.
95. Ibid.
96. Peterson, *Hjalmar Schacht,* p. 92.
97. Ibid., p. 92.

A lengthy profile published by the important New York magazine *Review of Reviews* in the summer of 1929 shows a chastened Schacht. On the evening after the meetings, he was asked if he was happy with the results.

"You ask me if I am glad?" answered Schacht. "Can any man be pleased with himself when the result of months of discussion is to ask his government to pay $500,000,000 a year for thirty-seven years?"[98]

The actual terms of the Young Plan began with the founding of a new institution, the Bank for International Settlements, which was opened in Basel in Switzerland. The bank's board would be the heads of all the Allied national banks and the Reichsbank. Germany was to pay substantially decreased annual installments into this Bank for International Settlements until 1988. Payments were to increase annually during the first thirty-six years. Annual installments were never to exceed 660 million marks, and sums above this amount could be deferred for two years. Schacht claimed that the idea was his and that Young congratulated him for "giving him a wonderful idea." Schacht described it as "my" Bank for International Settlements.

This plan compared very favorably with the 1.7 billion marks per year that Germany had been paying with ease under the old Dawes Plan. Obviously, the conferees had taken at least some of Schacht's 1927 warnings to heart.

In August 1929 all the foreign ministers of the participating nations met to ratify the Young Plan, and Stresemann won yet another victory, because the French finally agreed to withdraw their troops from the Rhineland. The heroic Stresemann had attended this conference in spite of dire warnings from his doctors. He died shortly thereafter.

The residue of the Young Plan has lasted until the end of this century. On January 6, 1995, the business section of the *New York Times* reported that the final interest payments on the German debts incurred under the Young Plan were to be completed by to-

---

98. *Review of Reviews* (July 1929), p. 90.

day's Federal Republic of Germany early in the twenty-first century.

For Schacht, it was time to regroup. He was unusually unfocused. A final blow to his ego came when he joined his wife in Marienbad, the Czechoslovakian spa. She greeted him on the railway platform, shouting, "You should have never signed!"[99]

In October 1929 the board of "his" new Bank for International Settlements had its first meeting in the ancient German spa Baden-Baden. The American representative was Jackson Reynolds, and his deputy was Melvin Taylor of the First National Bank of Chicago. On October 29, a few days after the beginning of the meetings, the New York stock market crashed.

The next morning Schacht asked Jackson at breakfast in the hotel's dining room, "Why the long face?"

Jackson said, "Haven't you read the news from New York?"

"Of course. But surely that cannot concern you?"

"It does. I have large amounts invested on the New York Stock Exchange."

Then Taylor, the other American banker, appeared. He was beaming. When Schacht asked him how he had fared, Taylor said, "Fine. I knew I'd be in Europe for a while, so before I left, I sold all my stocks."[100] Taylor and Schacht became good friends and frequent partygoers. At Taylor's birthday party, Schacht bemoaned America's prohibition laws in slightly Teutonic English verse.

> Yankee Doodle, guard your wit,
> Yankee Doodle Dandy,
> Don't think it fair to prohibit
> Black Forest Cherry *Brandy*.[101]

He returned from the jollity of Baden-Baden to an infuriating discovery. There had been some negotiations between the

99. Schacht, *76 Jahre meines Lebens*, p. 310.
100. Ibid., p. 317.
101. Ibid., p. 318.

German and Polish governments over certain sums to be paid to Germany as part of the Young agreement. These payments were due for land ceded to Poland under the Versailles Treaty. Schacht felt that "his" German delegation to the Young Conference had fought hard for each clause and that this unilateral settlement with Poland was outrageous. No one had consulted with him, the former head of the German delegation. It was his chance to regain some high ground. On December 6, 1929, he expressed his anger at this "betrayal" in a memorandum he addressed to the chancellor and also released to the press. It was another Schacht bombshell that brought more enmity from the government. Schacht was not cowed. When Finance Minister Hilferding wanted to arrange a loan from an American bank, Schacht refused to clear it through the Reichsbank. Instead, he offered to provide credit in German marks. Hilferding resigned in disgust, objecting to the "interference of the Reichsbank's president in matters of national policy." The new ironical term for Schacht's high-handed style was *Lex Schacht*. Hilferding, a Jew, was to commit suicide years later in a Paris prison, after Pétain's Vichy French had handed him over to the Gestapo.[102]

The vendetta was interrupted by a family event. The Schachts' daughter, Inge, announced her engagement to the Dutch-descended young German Foreign Service officer Hilger van Scherpenberg. On January 12, 1930, the Schachts hosted a large and lively engagement party in the luxurious presidential apartment of the Reichsbank.

Early the next morning Hjalmar Schacht was on his way to The Hague to attend the meeting of all concerned foreign ministers for the final signing of the Young Plan they had ratified the previous August. No less than three German cabinet members were present. Julius Curtius, the man who succeeded Stresemann as foreign minister, headed the delegation, accompanied by Interior Minister Joseph Wirth and the new finance minister, Paul Moldenauer. Schacht immediately complained to them that the

102. Bernt Engelmann, *Germany Without Jews*, p. 258.

original Young Plan was being compromised. He referred to, among other changes, a convoluted and deeply apologetic additional clause reserving the right for the Allied side, "in the most unlikely case that Germany should fail to keep its side of the contract," to apply sanctions against Germany, "though most reluctantly." It was an obvious compromise between the more Germanophilic and Germanophobic delegations. Schacht repeated a threat he had made in a private letter to J. P. Morgan on December 31, 1929, that he would not join the board of the new Bank for International Settlements in Basel. The letter was published by an English newspaper on January 4, 1930, and had raised outrage in Berlin.[103] Schacht had added to the crisis by cabling Owen Young in New York on February 20, 1930, that he was ready to resign from the Reichsbank. Young had then informed the American ambassador in Washington of Schacht's threat, and Washington had cabled Berlin.[104] In a laggard AP report of March 8, Schacht is quoted issuing a "hot denial." "Only President von Hindenburg knew of my intention to resign."[105]

Moldenauer protested, "My dear Schacht, you know what problems your attitude is causing this government. Don't you think you ought to withdraw from the presidency of the Reichsbank?"

Schacht was combative. "I'll retire from the Reichsbank whenever President von Hindenburg asks for my resignation, not to please a temporary government." Moldenauer immediately tried to contact von Hindenburg through the presidential chief of staff, Otto Meissner, but without result.

Schacht was so discouraged by the results of the Young Conference that on March 3 he wrote von Hindenburg to tender his resignation. He then had a meeting with the Reich's president on March 6, when he repeated his reasons and request. Later that same day von Hindenburg wrote that he deeply regretted

103. Peterson, *Hjalmar Schacht,* p. 96.
104. Mühlen, *Schacht,* p. 27.
105. *New York Times* (March 9, 1930), p. 9:1.

Schacht's decision, urging him to keep the reasons for his resignation secret, "since warnings from someone of your prominence would endanger our economy and cause a flight of foreign capital."[106]

Schacht's resignation took effect on March 7. To accommodate von Hindenburg, Schacht observed the discretion that the *Reichspräsident* had requested, but he complained later that doing so hid his disgust with the crippled Young Plan, the real reason he had quit.

Resigning from the Reichsbank could not have been easy. In his memoirs, Schacht quotes from the uncharacteristically warm letter written in 1923 by his father to congratulate his son on his appointment as president. That day, the stiff and crusty senior Schacht wrote: "We are so happy to be alive to see this day. We are proud of you and hope that you will enjoy the fruits of your efforts for a long time to come."[107] Schacht treasured this letter.

One school of thought holds that Schacht was so certain after the crash of the New York stock market of the German disaster to follow that his resignation was a maneuver to distance himself from events. If Schacht did not hesitate to leave the scene of troubles, it was probably because he felt he had not caused them. No matter what was the true reason, he did not leave his post without adequate financial protection. According to historian Norbert Mühlen, Schacht negotiated a severance package of three years at a salary of 360,000 marks per annum. [108] His place at the Reichsbank was taken on April 3, 1930, by Hans Luther, the former minister of finance, the man who had once recruited Schacht. Luther also took his place on the Bank for International Settlements.

An interesting peek at Hjalmar and Luise Schacht is provided by the diary of Bella Fromm, the society columnist of the distinguished newspaper *Vossische Zeitung:*

---

106. Schacht, *76 Jahre meines Lebens,* p. 328.
107. Ibid., p. 329.
108. Mühlen, *Schacht,* p. 28.

FEBRUARY 2, 1930

Silver wedding at house of important banker. Snobbish and elaborate affair. Many celebrities who had been induced to come by the promise that other celebrities would be there. Reichsbank president Hjalmar Schacht and his wife present. I understand she adorns, or rather amplifies, her bosom with an expensive swastika in rubies and diamonds, whenever the occasion appears suitable, politically or socially. Although Schacht was helped to his present eminent position by sponsors like Professor George Bernhard, editor of the *Vossische Zeitung,* Jakob Goldschmidt and other non-Aryans, he is not above using the swastika as his insignia whenever he thinks it will suit his purpose. Tonight he said to me, "Why not give the National Socialists a break? They seem pretty smart to me."

She continued: "Schacht belonged to the Liberal party. He was a devoted Republican who turned conservative. Is National Socialism to be his next step?"[109]

Like most society columnists, Fromm often dipped her pen in acid. She was a great German patriot, decorated by the government. Jewish and quite openly anti-Nazi, she managed to stay at her post for five years after the Nazis came to power, protected from press czar Goebbels's wrath by her warm friendships in the foreign diplomatic community.

In August 1938 she finally realized that her position had become untenable and that it was time to leave her beloved Berlin. Her passage to America was booked, and her belongings were packed. Then she ran into a disastrous last-second bureaucratic snag about the transfer of her smallish personal funds to a foreign country. She remembered a promise Schacht had once made to her and "sent him an S.O.S." Schacht immediately saw to it that her case was rushed through the Foreign Exchange Office. Without his quick intervention, it would have been impossible for her to leave Germany, since the U.S. government demanded proof of an immigrant's financial responsibility.[110]

---

109. Bella Fromm, *Blood and Banquets,* pp. 24, 25.
110. Ibid., pp. 277, 278.

Meanwhile, Schacht withdrew to his estate at Gühlen, to recoup and then to regroup. A New York editorial of March 11, 1930, reported the resignation, spoke admiringly of his past achievements, and ended by regretting that "Dr. Schacht seems to have chosen the wrong moment to do the wrong thing in the wrong way."[111] But Schacht was not quite ready to go into total retreat.

111. *New York Times* (March 11, 1930).

9

DINING WITH THE DEVIL

SCHACHT'S ESTATE at Gühlen sat in a semiforested area of meadows and lakes typical of the Brandenburg district north of Berlin. Although the estate was farmed, it was not particularly profitable. Schacht was strictly a gentleman farmer, raising dairy cattle and hogs. His cream was the finest, as were his hogs, but uncharacteristically he admitted that the farm's costs far exceeded its income. Although he claimed that the estate (and his hikes through its vast surrounding woods and meadows) restored his strength and gave him peace and contentment, his daughter, Inge, described him as a lion roaming in his cage, furious with his confinement. The outside world was equally sure it had not seen the last of Schacht. His supposed retirement would last three frequently interrupted years.

In his memoirs, Philip, Viscount Snowden (who was a participant in Schacht's final Young Conference) wrote that Schacht had "terrorized the German Delegation" and described him as a "man of unbounded ambition."[112] His impression was shared by many. It was not the stuff of retirement.

The March 26, 1930, issue of *Outlook,* an influential American political magazine, commented: "It is rumored in Germany that

112. Philip Snowden, *Autobiography.*

Dr. Schacht hopes to succeed General von Hindenburg as President of the Reich" and "[that summer and fall] he continued to curry favor with the nationalists in Germany by criticism of the Young plan."

Political reporter C. H. Lambert wrote in the March 22, 1930, edition of New York's *The Nation & Athenaeum* that "Dr. Schacht declares that he is retiring into [sic] his country estate, but it is by no means certain that his retirement will be a long one. He is the hero of the moderate Conservative parties." Lambert continued: "He is generally credited with political ambitions. . . ."

Schacht put it this way: "Of course I did not wish to bury myself in Gühlen. I kept thinking over and over what I, a private citizen, could do to help solve Germany's problems. So I accepted a series of invitations from abroad to lecture."[113] He began in Bucharest and then to Berne, Copenhagen, Stockholm, and finally, America. The subject matter was always Germany, its problems through the Versailles Treaty and the danger to world stability posed by reparations.

The domino effect of Wall Street's disaster soon damaged the very fabric of the German economy. Masses of opportunistic American investments had tethered Germany to Wall Street, and when the crash came, the Americans wanted out as quickly as possible. Other American investors were bankrupt, and their investments were in the hands of receivers. Schacht had warned Germany's democratic politicians often enough. They had borrowed from abroad to curry favor with their constituents, and now it was time to pay the bill.

Voters felt deceived by their democratic and liberal representatives. The grim economic situation brought a countrywide political swing to Germany's conservative political Right. For the first time, Adolf Hitler's Nazi movement became a meaningful factor. In the elections of September 14, 1930, the Nazis won 107 Reichstag seats. They had previously held 12 seats.[114] The Nation-

---

113. Schacht, *76 Jahre meines Lebens,* p. 337.
114. Simpson, *Schacht in Perspective,* p. 63.

alist Party, conservative middle- and upper-class right-wingers, won 41 seats, and the so-called Agrarians, mainly wealthy titled landowners, monarchists, and reactionaries, won 19. This put 167 delegates into the camp of the Right out of a total of 577. Under the multiparty Weimar system, an absolute majority was not needed to take control, only the largest voting bloc. A powerful coalition of right-wingers could have forced President von Hindenburg to bring Hitler into the government. The combined democratic opposition might now have to court the Communists, who had increased their delegates from 54 to 77.

Schacht had voted on the fourteenth and had then left for London on his way to the United States. He awoke the next day to learn the startling results of the election. It is most unlikely that the Nazis, a proletarian crowd of street toughs, held much appeal for him. However, their fervent nationalism brought them into symbiotic contact and potential alliances with the conventional right-wing parties he had begun to favor. Besides, the Nazis' sudden election surge provided him with a magnificent scare tactic for his international speaking tour. He could also alarm his capitalist audiences with the strong increase of the Reichstag's Communist delegates.

Eager to learn more about this new political phenomenon, Schacht read Adolf Hitler's *Mein Kampf* during his ocean passage to the United States. He was not impressed by the style, which he considered "an assault on the German language," but was taken by some of the content. He admitted that the author displayed "a keen brain."[115]

American newspaper headlines and magazine articles of the day tell the story of Schacht and the year 1930. He had become one of the most prominent names in international politics, and his unexpected and willful political doings had riveted the attention of political reporters everywhere.

---

115. Peterson, *Hjalmar Schacht*, p. 102.

DR. SCHACHT'S DAUGHTER MARRIED

BERLIN, April 23 (AP) — ... married here today to Hilger von [sic] Scherpenberg of the German Embassy in London. Foreign Minister Julius Curtius and other prominent officials attended. [Actually, Hilger was of Dutch descent and named van Scherpenberg.]

SCHACHT TO COME HERE [NEW YORK] IN AUGUST

BERLIN, June 19 (AP) — ... at the invitation of American interests ... the journey concerns German export developments.

REICH BANKER COMING HERE

[*New York Times*] August 4 — ... on a lecture tour this Fall, it was announced yesterday by the Institute of International Education.

SCHACHT NOT TO LECTURE

[*New York Times*] BERLIN, August 11 — "My trip is purely a personal undertaking and has no professional or business purpose. . . ." Dr. Schacht denied he had been invited to deliver a series of lectures. "I know nothing of the game of politics and do not intend to get into it."

LUTHER IS HOPEFUL ON CAPITAL MARKET
SCHACHT HITS POLITICIANS

[*New York Times*] BERLIN, August 13 — ... "The most important of all the problems, however, is to find work for men."

SCHACHT TO VISIT UNITED STATES

[*New York Times*] August 17 — ... The distinguished and fiery Dr. Schacht is going to pay us another visit. He denies he is coming to lecture. ...

SCHACHT DEMANDS WAR DEBT RESPITE

[*New York Times*] October 3 — ... luncheon at Hotel Astor. ". . . This dissatisfaction Hitler tried to turn into a virulent anti-Semitic movement. In this he failed. The huge victory at the polls was a protest vote against the Versailles Treaty and not against the Jews."

SCHACHT HERE, SEES WARNING IN FASCISM
RIDICULES FEAR OF HITLER

[*New York Times*] October 3 — . . . the surprisingly large vote pulled by the Fascists is to be taken as a sign of revolt of the German people against the treatment they have received from the Allies. . . ."

"Conditions in Germany are not at all alarming. . . ."

"If the German people are going to starve, there are going to be many more Hitlers. . . ."

"You seem to take Hitler seriously. Why should not the Germans do so?"

. . . accompanied by Mrs. Schacht and their son Jens, who is to study banking in the United States . . . guest of Council of Foreign Relations and to speak at Columbia University . . .

SCHACHT SAYS REICH WILL PAY ALL LOANS

[*New York Times*] October 10 — . . . luncheon at the New York Bond Club . . . "Investors who have lent money to Germany since the war need have no fear. . . ."

SCHACHT TALKS AT YALE

[*New York Times*] NEW HAVEN, Conn., October 14 — ". . . cooperative aid in Europe . . ."

SCHACHT SEES STIMSON BUT DENIES DEBT AIM

[*New York Times*] WASHINGTON, October 18 — . . . spent a half hour with the Secretary of State. Dr. Stimson will give a luncheon for him tomorrow . . . will be presented to President Hoover and probably will call upon Secretary [of the Treasury] Mellon . . .

SCHACHT PREDICTS GERMANY WILL STOP PAYING
REPARATIONS
SEES DEFIANCE ON ARMS

[*The New York Times*] October 21 — . . . Stoppage of all reparations payments by Germany unless other countries help her extend her foreign trade . . . defiance of the disarmament provision of the Treaty of Versailles by "some German Government" in the future unless the Allied countries carry out their part of the treaty bargains and divest themselves of their armaments . . . reassured the audience by saying that Germany as a nation would do nothing violent. "Hitlerism is a perfectly constitutional movement. Nothing has occurred in Germany that might be termed as outside the limits of the Constitution." . . . took issue with John Foster Dulles, member of the now defunct reparations commission . . .

DEBT MORATORIUM TALK IN 3 CAPITALS
SCHACHT IN CONFERENCES

By Carlisle MacDonald, Special Cable to *The New York Times.* PARIS, October 21 — . . . Reports from Washington reaching here today . . . unusual importance was attached to these reports in view of the presence in Washington of Dr. Hjalmar Schacht . . .

GERMANS ARE AVERSE TO DEBT RESPITE NOW
SCHACHT VIEWS OPPOSED

By Edwin L. James, Special to *The New York Times.* BERLIN, November 5 — . . . one finds large measure of disagreement with the wisdom of the pronouncements of Dr. Hjalmar Schacht.

He began some press conferences by handing out gratuitous advice to the United States about its economic crisis, which did not endear him to American journalists. Professor Steven Duggan, who had arranged speaking dates at several universities, suggested to him at a luncheon in New York that he familiarize himself with regional American attitudes before giving advice. Schacht "reddened at once and blurted, 'Dr. Duggan, if you want to dictate what I shall say in my lectures, I shall take the next boat home!' " Duggan reassured him and told him that he wanted to brief speakers about the varying conditions in various parts of the country. Duggan failed to tell Schacht that he had been urged by Paul Warburg, who attended the luncheon, to advise Schacht to be more discreet, because, as Warburg said, "Schacht was in America to borrow money for Germany, and would get nowhere unless he spoke more softly."[116]

---

116. Steven Duggan, *A Professor at Large,* p. 63.

Schacht lectured in New York, Philadelphia, Baltimore, Boston, Cincinnati, Los Angeles, San Francisco, and New Haven, at Yale University, always insisting that Germany could not pay her reparations (under the Young Plan) unless they were suspended, and pointing at the "menace to world peace and stability."

According to his count, he slept in forty-two different beds in fifty days, half of them Pullman berths in sleeping cars. He also had to suffer the chicken-and-ice-cream routine of the American speaking tour, and he complained about it.[117] Then, finally, on November 26, 1930, from the New York Times, page 21: DR. SCHACHT OFF FOR HOME.

A routine daily report on the passenger manifest of an outbound ship, the German liner Columbus, listed Schacht among such prominences as an American Nobel laureate on his way to receive the prize, a famous Irish writer, and "Princess Erik of Denmark, née Miss Lois Booth," the heiress to a Canadian lumber fortune; but it was Schacht's name that was in the headline.

He had not finished his campaign. On the day the Columbus docked in Bremen, at a dinner in his honor at the Bremen chamber of commerce, he said that America was the only hope for the revision of the Young Plan.[118] His views are also projected in a lengthy article he wrote for the Yale Review, published in the December 30, 1930 edition.

Jens stayed behind in America to serve a one-year internship arranged by his father's friend Melvin Taylor of the First National Bank of Chicago.

An American publisher offered Schacht a contract to publish the views he had expressed during his tour, and he jumped at the chance. The book was called The End of Reparations and it appeared in New York in March 1931. It then appeared in London, after the American version had been "translated into proper English." It received an excellent review in the July 12 New York Times Book Review. The reviewer called it "the most forcible and

117. Schacht, 76 Jahre meines Lebens, p. 346.
118. Ibid., p. 349.

convincing indictment of the reparations system that has yet been framed." He promised the new German chancellor, Heinrich Brüning, the first German copy. Brüning, a moderate Catholic and former World War I officer, was appointed chancellor by von Hindenburg to stabilize the embattled republic, which was in the midst of a deep economic crisis. Von Hindenburg seemed to understand the danger in the rise of both left- and right-wing radicalism and hoped Brüning could control both.

The year 1931 marked the beginning of the final chaotic chapter in the life of the doomed Weimar Republic. There would be constant changes in leadership, as chancellor after chancellor was appointed. Schacht, who admired Brüning, got into an immediate controversy. While in Stockholm, Schacht was asked by a reporter, "What would you do if you were appointed as Chancellor tomorrow?" and Schacht replied, " I would on that very day order the end of all payments of reparations." He was immediately attacked by the Berlin government; but in fact, payments did cease soon thereafter because a moratorium was installed later in 1931.

In December 1930 an old friend of Schacht's, Reichsbank board member Emil Georg von Stauss, had invited Schacht to join him for a stag dinner at Hermann Göring's apartment.

The thirty-seven-year-old Göring was the number two Nazi and one of the few who were socially acceptable to people like Schacht. Göring was intelligent, well educated, and had been raised in comfortable circumstances; he had spent a lot of his boyhood at the castle of his titled Jewish godfather. As a former fighter pilot, he had won Germany's highest military decoration, the *Pour le Mérite,* also known as the Blue Max, which was an open sesame in German society. Göring was married to a beautiful but terminally ill Swedish aristocrat. What brought Göring to National Socialism was hard to explain, except that he carried the disappointment, hurt, and anger of many former wartime officers. After the war he had moved to Denmark and Sweden, where he did some commercial piloting, was badly hurt in a crash, and became addicted to drugs while recuperating. He met Hitler in the early twenties, admired him extravagantly, and was wounded when he took part in the Nazis' abortive 1923 Munich putsch.

Schacht had readily agreed to the dinner invitation because he felt it was time to meet one of the leading Nazis. He found the evening quite civilized and urbane. The conversation at table was lively and revolved around the perilous state of Germany's economy, although the host obviously knew little about the subject. Schacht claimed that there was nothing unacceptable or radical said during the evening.[119] Göring's lifestyle was still modest and simple, compared with his eventual legendary excesses.

Another dinner invitation to the Göring residence soon followed. This time both Hjalmar and Luise Schacht were invited, and Karin Göring acted as hostess. The purpose of the evening was to meet Adolf Hitler. The date of this first meeting with the future German Führer was January 5, 1931.

The Görings lived in a comfortable flat in a middle-class suburb called Wilmersdorf. Industrialist Fritz Thyssen and Dr. Joseph Goebbels had also been asked. Dinner was simple. The very attractive Frau Göring was obviously in frail health and had to lie down on a couch.

Hitler arrived after dinner, dressed in a Nazi Party uniform. He seemed quite unaffected and modest, considering, as Schacht pointed out, that he was the leader of Germany's second-largest political party. Schacht discovered what many others were to learn. A conversation with Hitler meant that Hitler did most of the talking. Göring and Goebbels said nothing, and Schacht was content to listen because "I was not there to sell my political and economic theories to Hitler. I was struck by his absolute conviction that he was right and his determination to put his ideas into action. He was a true fanatic and a born agitator." Though Schacht reported little of the actual conversation, he soon introduced Hitler to Dr. Walther Funk, a financial journalist, who taught him some basic principles of economics.[120]

Schacht spent the following weeks lobbying Chancellor

119. Ibid., p. 351.
120. Mühlen, *Schacht,* p. 30.

Brüning and other politicians, urging them to consider including the Nazis in a future government. He insisted this was "the only way to avoid right wing radicalization,"[121] and tried to convince them that "it was a chance to steer the National Socialists onto the right path."

The economy slid into ever deepening depression, and Schacht's criticism became a growing irritant to the Brüning government. Even a leading New York editorial headlined a piece on Schacht with GERMANY'S TROUBLEMAKER.[122] Chancellor Brüning did everything he could to stimulate the economy, but without great success. He was soon forced to rule through one of the unfortunate and unhealthy presidential emergency decrees that allowed him to function for a limited time without the consent of the Reichstag.

Rumors of Schacht's meeting with Hitler circulated. In the spring of 1931 American journalist Dorothy Thompson asked Schacht if he would be able to handle Germany's economy under the Nazis, and he answered simply, "I shall."[123] He was quoted as also saying to her, "No, the Nazis cannot rule, but I can rule through them."[124] Whatever Schacht's political ambitions, George Messersmith, former U.S. consul in Berlin (1930–34) testified at the Nuremberg war-crimes trials, "There is no doubt that he [Schacht] nourished the ambition of becoming President of Germany."[125]

On May 11 Austria's vital bank, the Rothschilds' Kreditanstalt declared bankruptcy. It was the first piece in the row of dominoes. Important German banks would soon find themselves near insolvency.

A wild rumor was circulating in Paris in 1931 during France's great annual national holiday on July 14. The story had it that

121. Ibid., p. 352.
122. *New York Times* (March 5, 1931), p. 24.
123. Mühlen, *Schacht,* p. 30.
124. Ibid., p. viii.
125. *International Military Tribunal,* document 451.

Schacht was about to become Germany's dictator. He was said to be grabbing all the country's financial controls in order to push Brüning out of office. The rumor seemed credible because coincidentally Arthur Henderson, the British foreign secretary, appeared in Paris to meet with French foreign minister Aristide Briand and with Premier Pierre Laval. It so happened that American secretary of state Stimson and his wife were also on their way to Paris. Henderson was then scheduled to leave for Berlin and meetings with his prime minister and the German leaders.[126] It seemed a time of crisis.

The explanation for the movements of these prominent statesmen was actually quite routine, but it took some time for the rumors about Schacht to die down. The probable cause for the brouhaha began on the evening of July 11, 1931, when Schacht received an urgent call at Gühlen from Chancellor Brüning's office, urging him to "come to Berlin at once." Somehow, that call was leaked.

Schacht had refused to rush to the capital as Brüning requested, but he agreed to be there the next evening. At the Chancellery, he found two groups, both arguing. The bankers were in one room, the ministers in the other. Everything Schacht had predicted had come to pass. Suddenly, the banks were nearly out of foreign currency and gold, among them Jakob Goldschmidt's high-flying Danatbank. Not only were the banks broke, but municipalities and industrial companies with foreign debts were unable to repay their loans. At an earlier conference of German bankers in Dresden, Schacht had warned that this might happen and had recommended that the Reichsbank impose an immediate moratorium on the payment of all foreign debts. The Reichsbank had refused. It argued that keeping up payments would calm foreign creditors, but Schacht had assured them it would only cause a feeding frenzy.

In the emergency meeting at the Chancellery on July 12, he had expressed his credo, The greedy man who loans money to a

126. *New York Times* (July 15, 1931), p. 16:3.

poor risk in order to get higher than normal interest is every bit as responsible as the debtor. He blamed foreign creditors. Therefore, from his point of view, a moratorium on foreign debts was justified and honorable. About the dilemma of Jakob Goldschmidt and the Danatbank, Schacht suggested guaranteeing immediate payments to small creditors, and then negotiating long-term repayment plans with the big creditors.

Once more Schacht was overruled. It was the consensus of the Finance Ministry and the Reichsbank that a suspension of payments would injure the Reich's credit. Schacht returned to Gühlen.

Brüning phoned him there the next day and asked him to become commissioner of banking. Schacht protested that this was the job of the Reichsbank president, not of some separate commissioner. Brüning then asked him, "What is the first thing you would do?"

Schacht told him to get all the banks together to bail out the Danatbank and then decide if it should be liquidated. But he still refused the post of commissioner.

Next, Presidential Chief of Staff Meissner was sent to Gühlen to convince Schacht to take the position, but Schacht remembered that von Hindenburg had hinted that Schacht was a deserter after the Young Plan disagreement. He politely refused von Hindenburg's offer and stayed in Gühlen.

It was said that the banking panic precipitating all this activity was caused by one of Jakob Goldschmidt's gambles. Danatbank was committed to the hilt, financing various major enterprises, when he took two brothers named Lahusen to lunch at Hiller's restaurant in Berlin. The Lahusens owned large weaving concerns. Goldschmidt convinced them to expand and "almost forced them" to accept a loan of 50 million marks from Danatbank.[127]

The Lahusens, who were contributors to the Nazis, were crooks and were indicted and jailed. Danatbank was stuck with a debt of 23 million marks, a loss the bank could have swallowed

127. Annemarie Lange, *Berlin in der Weimarer Republik,* p. 910.

had it not been overcommitted in every direction. Goldschmidt tried desperately to get help from the other "D" banks, but he was turned down because most of them were also Lahusen creditors.

Danatbank declared bankruptcy and was soon absorbed by the old Dresdner Bank. The Reichsbank was forced to help, and its new president, Luther, rushed to London, Paris, and Brussels to scrounge up the needed credit. The Bank for International Settlements in Basel then loaned the Reichsbank 400 million marks at 4 percent interest, and Germany lost a lot of money.

On September 20, 1931, to the international financial world's shock, the British suddenly devalued the pound and on the next day abandoned the gold standard. Schacht privately advised Luther to go to London at once to persuade the Bank of England to convert all of Germany's debts into the newly devalued pound.

In October 1931 Hjalmar Schacht finally made the decision to follow the advice he had offered to society columnist Bella Fromm early in 1930. He gave the Nazis a chance. Like many of Hjalmar Schacht's moves, it had wide repercussions, even though he hedged his risks and did not truly commit himself.

As an act of ambition and a grab for power, Alfred Hugenberg, the right-wing industrialist, instigated a rally of the so-called national opposition. It included Hugenberg's "Steel Helmet" German National Party and the Agrarian Party of the aristocratic, monarchist landowners as well as the National Socialist (Nazi) Party. He arranged this mass event in the beautiful little mountain spa Bad Harzburg in the Harz mountains. It became known as the *Harzburger Front,* the Harzburg Front. In his arrogance, Hugenberg thought he would dominate the event with great ease.

Many prominent individuals, all opponents of the democratic Weimar regime, also attended. Among them were dozens of industrialists, including Fritz Thyssen; many titled landowners; four royal princes (two of them sons of the former kaiser); and a gaggle of dukes, counts, and barons. There were sixteen former generals.

And then there was Hjalmar Horace Greeley Schacht! He had accepted an invitation extended by the head of one of the conservative middle-class right-wing parties to attend a "conference on economics."

The opening paragraph of the *New York Times* front-page report of the event tells the story.

> BAD HARZBURG, October 11 — In a setting dominated by the old imperial colors, goose-stepping Steel Helmets, parading fascists and a liberal flow of Nationalistic speeches, Adolf Hitler and Dr. Alfred Hugenberg, the fascist and nationalist leaders in Germany, today swore political comradeship and declared war on the Brüning government.

One result of the rally, its martial parades, and speeches was that Hugenberg quickly learned his place. It was Adolf Hitler who dominated the event and riveted the crowd. His brown-shirted SA storm troopers were everywhere, and the Nazi movement gained new prestige and supporters through participating in the *Harzburger Front*. The town of Harzburg was friendly to the Nazis and allowed them to wear their uniforms, which were banned in many other parts of Germany.

Another result was that Schacht, claiming he was nonpolitical and unaffiliated with any parties, made a speech that reverberated throughout the political world. In effect, he warned that the Brüning government was hiding the fact that Germany was bankrupt, that the Reichsbank was minimizing the nation's true debts and inflating the size and strength of its holdings. He implied that financial apocalypse could be avoided only if they took his, Schacht's, advice. The speech was seen as an irresponsible act of betrayal by many thoughtful and loyal Germans. American correspondent Guido Enderis, cabling from Berlin, seems to sum up the reaction of many: "It is uniformly deplored that a financier of such international reputation should have allowed himself to be carried away by what is believed to be a political ambition."[128]

The Communist Party delegates in the Reichstag were much more harsh. They introduced a motion demanding "the immedi-

---

128. *New York Times* (October 13, 1931), p. 1:3.

ate indictment for high treason of Herr Hitler, Dr. Hugenberg, Dr. Schacht," and several others. Schacht and the others were accused of planning a new inflation (to destabilize the country), with Schacht's speech as the prelude.

Hermann Dietrich, the minister of finance, while unwilling to accuse Schacht of treason, argued that his speech was bound to raise nervousness all over the world and that any man who had held Schacht's high position until so recently should not have made these statements. He agreed that some of Schacht's figures were correct but were particularly damaging because they were quoted out of context.

Although Germany's politics were in chaos, the capital, Berlin, was a haven of imagination and creativity. The front pages of the daily newspapers bannered ominous headlines, but the inside pages reported Max Reinhardt's extraordinary stage productions, Kurt Weill and Bert Brecht's strange *Three Penny Opera,* the doings of Dietrich and Garbo, the performance of Conrad Veidt in *The Cabinet of Dr. Caligari.* They reported on Gropius, Mendelsohn, and the other Bauhaus architects; books by Mann and Zweig; paintings by Grosz, Tucholsky, and Dix; and concerts by Bruno Walter and Furtwängler. Berlin was overflowing with talent and wit and creativity. All over Germany, businessmen, industrialists, and professionals who should have economized enjoyed their Mercedes, their country houses, their tennis clubs, their vacations abroad and in Germany's many splendid resorts. Fourteen democratic years had lulled them into thinking that unemployment, street riots, uniformed political thugs, and an occasional juicy financial scandal were all part of modern life.

By then, unemployment stood at 6 million, and more and more Germans went hungry.

Schacht knew the world of Germany's comfortable upper classes. Though ex officio, he lived an active social life and was much lionized. His aura and reputation as a financial genius were unshakably secure, in part because of his well-remembered heroics in the twenties and in part because he had managed to stay out of blame's way in this new depression. True, many liberals had begun to distrust his politics, but that made him no less desirable as a dinner guest. After all, Schacht was a money man, and *pecuniam non olet* (money has no smell). Besides, it was smart to stay on the good side of someone "civilized" who seemed fairly well connected with the political Right. The republic was obviously floundering, and who knew what sort of government would soon emerge? Not the Nazis, of course. They were too *proletarian*. In Berlin they called them "beefsteaks" because they were Brown on the outside and Red on the inside. What was it von Hindenburg was rumored to have said when he first saw the Nazi flag with its swastika? "Too much red in that flag!"

Meanwhile, at party after party, Schacht made amusing and unflattering remarks about the Brownshirts. They obviously seemed to need him more than he needed them. Of course, he did not speak quite as loudly when his wife was present. Luise Schacht worshiped the man with the strange forelock and the Chaplin mustache. Everyone shrugged. After all, what could you expect from the daughter of a Prussian police official?

After his controversial Harzburg appearance, Schacht planned a short vacation with his wife in Merano, Italy, but he feared a false impression with headlines trumpeting SCHACHT FLEES ABROAD!, so they returned to Berlin by express train. When it made a stop at Nuremberg, some of the news reports of the angry government reaction to his speech were brought aboard by local reporters. Schacht shrugged, disclaimed any Nazi affiliation, and said he sympathized with Finance Minister Dietrich, whom he liked immensely. But he stuck by his speech.

For Schacht, the year 1931 ended most unpleasantly. He was seriously injured in a car crash when Jens and he were on a trip from the Baltic Sea to Berlin. Near a small village in the province of Mecklenburg, Schacht's chauffeur-driven sedan skidded on ice and flipped over. Schacht was the only one injured. He was carried into a blacksmith shop, where a local country doctor bandaged his wounds before he was taken to a nearby small hospital. He had lapsed into a short coma due to concussion, had some broken ribs, and lost the full use of his legs for nearly three weeks. He stayed on crutches through Christmas 1931, resting at Gühlen.

Nineteen thirty-two was the year Germany would make its

most crucial choices for centuries to come. The Brüning government was ruling by emergency decree. The Nazi Brownshirts (they were actually tan) were prohibited from wearing their uniforms. A presidential election was scheduled for March 13.

Those in Berlin, London, Paris, and New York who had shrugged off Hitler as a temporary phenomenon got a rude surprise. To his own satisfaction, Schacht saw his political instincts confirmed. Hitler, the unimpressive but single-minded presence at the Göring apartment, had become the man of the hour, and possibly a man of destiny. The results of the election were startling.

Paul von Hindenburg received 18,651,497 votes.

Adolf Hitler, the presumptuous upstart, chalked up an astonishing 11,300,000 votes.

Ernst Thälmann, the Communist chief, was far behind with 4,983,341.

Under the constitution, von Hindenburg had to wait for a humiliating runoff vote held three weeks later, when he finally eked out the majority required for a narrow confirmation. Meanwhile, the Nazis climbed to 13.4 million votes.[129] Von Hindenburg was furious because his election victory had to be engineered through a coalition with the despised liberals, the Social Democrats, whom he disliked. He was also outraged by the impudent "Bohemian corporal" who had dared to compete with him for the leadership of Germany. For months to come, it prevented him from even considering Hitler's presence in the cabinet.

Brüning, who had engineered von Hindenburg's narrow victory, soon found himself out of favor because he proposed a law whereby the state would take over and divide certain bankrupt East Prussian estates among small farmers. It seemed a sensible measure in a disastrous economy. But he had not reckoned with the clannishness of the Prussian Junkers. Von Hindenburg was one of them, and he would have no part of Brüning's proposal.

And there was more to it. Von Hindenburg's large country es-

129. Simpson, *Schacht in Perspective,* p. 73 n. 97.

tate in East Prussia, Neudeck, had been donated on his eightieth birthday in 1927 to the land-poor von Hindenburg by his fellow East Prussian aristocrats and "a grateful nation." The estate was put into his son Oskar's name to avoid any inheritance taxes, a fact that was not widely known.

There was also the scandal involving *Osthilfe* (eastern help), the massive subsidies given since 1930 by German heavy industry to support East Prussian agriculture and to "build a consumer market." Much of the money went into the pockets of some of the richest landowners in Germany, who gambled in Monte Carlo and bought yachts, sports cars, and horses.

As a typical example, in 1932 twelve thousand small farmers received a subsidy of 69 million marks, while a handful (722) of major East Prussian landowners divided up 60 million marks among them.[130] Many of them had mismanaged, neglected, and bankrupted their estates, but they were not about to let their land be "bolshevized" by von Hindenburg's chancellor, Herr Brüning.

For the first time, Schacht's name appeared in actual connection with political leadership, when General Kurt von Schleicher, a close political advisor of the president, suggested him as a potential chancellor. For a short while in 1931 and 1932, von Schleicher, a highly politicized member of the military establishment, became one of von Hindenburg's trusted counselors. Von Hindenburg was comfortable with a fellow Prussian like von Schleicher, but the "political" general was also a worldly and sophisticated man. He bridged the gap between von Hindenburg's provincial Prussian ways and the thinking of Berlin's internationalists, but he preferred to stay behind the scenes.

In desperation, the president chose Franz von Papen, a member of the landed gentry and a slim, tweedy, horsey, well-spoken former officer and political factotum. Von Papen, who was married to an heiress, had served as a diplomat in Turkey and the United States and was one of von Hindenburg's original backers.

---

130. John Weitz, *Hitler's Diplomat* p. 55.

In June 1932 the new chancellor presented his new cabinet. So many of the ministers were aristocrats that it was immediately nicknamed the Barons' Cabinet. In a conciliatory gesture to Hitler, von Papen lifted the ban on wearing Nazi uniforms. He then attempted to rule by yet another presidential emergency decree. Though he was totally unsuccessful in any attempt to curb unemployment or to revive industry, he managed to carry out what Brüning had begun internationally. In Lausanne, on June 9, 1932, he signed the final agreement for the absolute end of reparations.

It was too little, too late. At the next Reichstag elections, on July 31, Hitler's Nazis more than doubled their presence. They won 230 seats. Now Hitler could no longer be kept from participating in the process of government. The dilemma was how to curb his radical influence once he had been appointed.

This, as Schacht never tired of pointing out, was the moment when German democracy was still in action, even though it produced an unpalatable result. Hitler's election victories, Schacht preached, were due to the masses of desperate Germans who voted for the Nazis and not to the result of sly machinations.

How did he react to this new political reality?

"I decided to emerge from my usual reclusiveness, because I had held occasional conversations with the economics experts of the National Socialists like Gottfried Feder and Carl Röver, and their theories foretold a disastrous future for the economy."[131]

Feder was one of Hitler's earliest financial advisors, as was Röver. Schacht did not hesitate to inform Hitler by memorandum about the pitfalls of the old-fashioned anticapitalist Feder-Röver theories, which dated back to 1923, when the party was different. After all, Hitler would need the support of industry and other capitalists. Hitler must have relished the *denunciamenti*. He encouraged controversy among his paladins and advisors. It assured him that none of his associates ever felt irreplaceable. Wilhelm Keppler, another Nazi financial expert, was easier for

---

131. Schacht, *76 Jahre meines Lebens*, p. 372.

Schacht to accept. Keppler, who owned a small chemical business, was a longtime advisor to Adolf Hitler and was his contact with heavy industry.

Keppler had achieved but minor success. Only Thyssen was an open and generous supporter. Keppler then approached Schacht and asked him to help with men like Vögler of the steel industry and Karl Helfferich, Schacht's old opponent but now a new ally. Keppler's fund-raising activities were organized into the so called *Keppler Kreis* (Keppler Circle), and Schacht was not reluctant to become part of it. He sensed the swing of the political pendulum, and he wanted to be involved. Many leading industrialists were still quite reluctant. Friedrich Flick, the coal-and-iron magnate, donated a token 50,000 marks to the Nazis and gave 1.8 million marks to help re-elect von Hindenburg. Von Papen met with steel king Gustav Krupp in Düsseldorf on January 7, 1933, but met resistance. The heads of I. G. Farben, Bosch, and Siemens were equally tepid about Hitler.[132]

On August 29, 1932, Schacht wrote to Hitler, assuring him of his total sympathy and strongly advising him to hedge, "Do *not* put forward any detailed economic program." Schacht ended the letter with "even if you occasionally find me 'within the fortress,' you can always count on me as your reliable helper." He signed the letter *"mit einem kräftigen 'Heil'"* ("with a forceful 'Heil'").[133]

Von Papen took the gamble of dissolving the Reichstag and calling another election for November 6. The Nazis lost 34 seats, and the Communists gained 11. While the Nazis' lost seats did little to reassure the democratic side, the gain in Communist votes was enough to convince von Hindenburg that Hitler had to be given a place in the government. Anything to prevent the Reds from making even further gains. Nazi propaganda chief

---

132. Heinz Höhne, *Die Machtergreifung: Deutschlands Weg in Die Hitler-Diktatur*, ex Weitz, *Hitler's Diplomat*, pp. 52–53.

133. U.S. Chief of Counsel for the Prosecution of Axis Criminality, Nazi Conspiracy and Aggression (NCA) document EC-457 (Washington, D.C.: U.S. Government Printing Office), p. 514, ex Simpson, *Schacht in Perspective*, p. 78.

Goebbels's diary of November 21 sounded woebegone at the loss
of seats, but he reassured himself with "Schacht is still with us."
Indeed, on November 24 Schacht told a reporter from the newspaper *Nordwestdeutsche Zeitung* that Hitler would become chancellor, "if not now then in four months."[134]

Von Papen, unable to control the surge of right- and left-wing
extremism, gave up. He was hooted down whenever he attempted
to address the Reichstag. Like Brüning, he was forced to resign
the chancellorship, and von Hindenburg tried one final tactic before handing over the government to "Corporal" Hitler. He asked
his friend von Schleicher, the very reluctant éminence grise of
the last days of the Weimar Republic, to take charge. Von
Schleicher was less than enthusiastic, but von Hindenburg knew
that this was "the last horse in his stable." Schacht considered von
Schleicher "bloodless, calculating, without a soul, guided only by
intelligence." He rightly assumed that it must have gone against
von Schleicher's better judgment to emerge from the political
shadows. [135]

After becoming chancellor on December 3, 1932, von
Schleicher took a desperate gamble. He attempted to split the
Nazi Party's leadership by approaching Gregor Strasser. Strasser,
a former World War I officer, was one of Hitler's closest and earliest fellow Nazis. He and his brother, Otto, had always seen National Socialism as a socialistic workers' movement, while Hitler
increasingly emphasized the nationalistic and classless direction.
Otto Strasser finally quit the party. Gregor remained a member,
but his point of view and influence had decreased year by year.

To undermine Hitler, von Schleicher planned to offer the
vice chancellorship to the battered Gregor Strasser. When von
Schleicher told Schacht of his idea, Schacht warned him that
Hitler had complete control of the Nazi Party. No one stood a
chance of splitting it. According to Schacht, von Schleicher's only

134. Peterson, *Hjalmar Schacht*, p. 124.
135. Schacht, *76 Jahre meines Lebens*, p. 374.

reaction was a "superior smile, but he would soon stop smiling."[136]

Between 1931 and 1932, President von Hindenburg had signed 102 emergency decrees under Article 48 of the constitution. Von Schleicher was the last democratic chancellor to rule using this crutch, but he had no further control over the delegates in the Reichstag. The 230 Nazi delegates now attended session after session dressed in their Nazi uniforms, marching in as a body, shouting and stomping their jackbooted feet. They were a frightening presence of bullies for most of the other delegates, but they represented nearly 13.5 million Germans. To describe the breadth of Hitler's appeal even among non-Nazis, Schacht pointed out that in 1932 there were only 810,000 actual Nazi Party members.[137] Obviously, not all Hitler backers were Nazis. Strangely, Schacht claimed that it was von Hindenburg who eventually had made Hitler acceptable, though it is hard to understand how the president could have ignored the leader of such a powerful political party. Actually, on November 24, 1932, von Hindenburg's state secretary, Meissner, had written a letter to Hitler, in the name of the president, in which he outlined the reasons why it would be difficult or near impossible to appoint him chancellor, primarily because "a cabinet under your leadership would become a party dictatorship."

In answer, a detailed, careful, and well-reasoned reply went forward from Hitler to von Hindenburg, which disproved all the president's objections. According to historian Joachim Fest, this letter, one of the cornerstones for the eventual outcome, was ghostwritten by Schacht at the Kaiserhof Hotel in Berlin. [138]

The final negotiations that launched the era of Adolf Hitler were about to begin. Von Papen, the stylish failure, now out of office, was still hungry for power, so he appointed himself a confidential intermediary between the conservative nationalists and

136. Ibid., p. 375.
137. Schacht, *1933*, p. 68.
138. Joachim Fest, *Hitler*, p. 786 n. 48.

the reluctant von Hindenburg on one side, and the newly
adamant and demanding Hitler on the other. On December 16,
1932, von Papen gave a speech in the exclusive, right-wing
Herrenklub (Gentlemen's Club) in Berlin, which resulted in a
meeting planned for January 4, 1933, in Cologne at the home of
right-wing banker Kurt von Schröder. The Nazi side would be
represented by Adolf Hitler, Rudolf Hess, Heinrich Himmler, and
Wilhelm Keppler, the Nazi financial advisor who knew von
Schröder. With von Hindenburg's tacit agreement, von Papen
was to use the Cologne meeting to arrive at a mutually acceptable
formula for involving Hitler in the government while still retain-
ing some sort of control over him. On New Year's Day, Hitler, a
deeply superstitious man, had invited the well known German
stage and nightclub clairvoyant Jan Erik Hanussen to his Berchtesgaden chalet to consult with him about the upcoming conference. Hanussen's findings reassured him.

In three days the bank will change all things.

(Von Schröder was a banker.)

The day before the month does end, your goal is reached, your
road will bend.

(The goal will be reached on January 30.)

Hitler felt reassured about the upcoming meeting.

The angry and betrayed von Schleicher heard about the
planned meeting from his gossipy dentist. He arranged to have it
secretly photographed by a friendly former officer who lived in
Cologne. When he eventually confronted von Hindenburg with
proof of his perfidy, the old field marshal sighed wearily and said,
"My dear young friend, soon I shall be up there looking down.
Then I'll see whether I was right or wrong."[139]

139. Höhne, *Die Machtergreifung*, pp. 254–55.

10

HITLER'S BANKER

WHAT WAS HITLER'S formula for political success? Schacht said it was no secret. It was "poverty and unemployment."

Who was this man Hitler, the Austrian artist manqué, the solitary and silent former infantry soldier who advanced only to the rank of corporal and was never promoted, because his commanding officer deemed him incapable of command?

After he was refused a place in Vienna's Art Academy, a deep personal disappointment, the young art student loafed in Vienna's bohemian subworld. He then quit his native Austria for his adored Germany. He was a worshipful foreigner, an enthusiast of the pan-Germanism that was the mantra of the elitist and chauvinistic Germanic Austrians in their sprawling and multiethnic empire. When war came, he joined the German army; fought in a Bavarian regiment; won the Iron Cross First Class (a rare honor for a simple corporal); was gassed, blinded, and recovered. Bitterly angry and disappointed by Germany's defeat and surrender, he settled in Munich working as a secret anti-Communist agent for the reactionary Munich staff of the tiny, remaining German army. He soon drifted into nationalistic, chauvinistic, anti-Communist, anti-Semitic politics and joined a small extremist party called the Socialist German Workers' Party. To emphasize its reactionary nature and patriotism, it soon became the National Socialist German Workers' Party, or Nazis for short.

He struck most outside observers as a single-minded fanatic. There seemed to be no women in his life, no smoking, no drinking, no desire for wealth, no true bonhomie or Bavarian *Gemütlichkeit,* only politics and the ability and willingness to speak to anyone, anywhere, about his harsh plans for Germany. From coffeehouses to beer halls, he intrigued other malcontents with his gospel about a great country that had been betrayed by the kaiser, then "stabbed in the back" by Communists and "world Jewry," unjustly accused of causing the war, mutilated by the Versailles Treaty, crippled by ruinous reparations, betrayed by the weaklings of the Weimar Republic, pauperized by inflation, and bloodsucked by international profiteers and crooks. Hitler's cure: "Enough discussion, enough nattering in the Reichstag; people are starving and unemployed. The time has come to stop protecting those who profited from the misery of their ruined countrymen and to return Germany to world power. Shedding the Versailles chains and rebuilding the country and its armed might was the way to provide work, food, and dignity."

Part of his program was "to return Germany to its Aryan roots and to prevent those of non-Aryan blood from participating in the decisions which affected the fate and culture of the nation."

As he wrote in his manifesto, *Mein Kampf,* Germany was lucky to have found him, and he was lucky to have found Germany. He alone would lead Germany back to the greatness it deserved. Germans were inherently qualified for leadership, and Germany had the right and the duty to assume its place among the world's leaders. Democracy was a false ideal, a destructive system that slowed a nation to the crawl of the majority, instead of spurting ahead at the speed of its born leaders. Democratic leaders were elected by the majority and therefore reflected the wishes and opinions of the slowest and least-educated citizens. The reins of government should always rest in the hands of its most qualified citizens, the way all enterprises, from armies to steelmakers, chose their leaders from among the best and the brightest. Industries and armies did not appoint their leaders by democratic election. Nor could vital national decisions be shared by consensus. They had to be made by a *Führer,* a leader. Everyone was responsible to him alone; and he, in turn, was responsible to the entire nation.

Germany was composed of groups with varied origins. Though not necessarily alike, they were mutually compatible. Groups that were not of "compatible" blood could still be allowed to live within the community.

In their original versions, all official Nazi manifestos and laws spoke of "not preventing Jews from earning their livelihood, but restricting them [as possessors of incompatible blood] from participating in those decisions which affect the life of the nation." The more virulent attacks on Germany's Jewish citizens came later, culminating in the Final Solution.

André François-Poncet, French ambassador in Berlin in the early Hitler days and considered one of the most astute chroniclers of the time, describes Hitler as follows:

> A pale face, globular eyes, the far away look of a medium or a somnambulist. At other times, animated, colorful, swept away with passion and violence. Impatient of control, bold, cynical, energetic. Sometimes a "storm and assault" face, the face of a lunatic! At other times, naive, rustic, dull, vulgar, easily amused, a thigh-slapper, a face like a thousand other faces.

> Sometimes, he was all three in one conversation. He ranted on for ten minutes, a half hour, three quarters of an hour. Then he was exhausted. At that time one could speak, and he would even smile. He was no normal human being, a morbid, quasi-mad Dostoyevsky figure, a man possessed. He was an Austrian with a passionate love for Germany, wildly romantic, full of half-baked theories of Houston Stewart Chamberlain, Nietzsche, Spengler. He wanted a new Germany to replace the Holy Roman Empire, a purified race, an elite. He lived Wagner!

> A dreamer but a cold-blooded realist and schemer. He was *lazy* and hated regular work. He wanted oral information, not written reports. He allowed great freedom but knew every move his collaborators made. He willed or tolerated every excess, all crimes. He used intuition for the sudden power of decision. He was tied to the masses and had contempt for them. He lulled opponents by signing treaties while planning to wiggle out of them.

It is unlikely that Schacht knew a great deal about the person of Adolf Hitler. Only a handful of "Old Fighters" did. Everyone had heard gossip and innuendo, but very few outsiders actually understood the man, and even his oldest political allies rarely penetrated his shell. He had no real intimates. There was only one man, Ernst Röhm, who called him by the familiar *Du*, which Germans reserved for intimate friends, and Röhm would soon be executed at the order of his old friend.

Schacht kept his reserve. In August 1932 he had concluded a letter to Hitler using "Heil," because he considered the Nazi leader a fledgling and wanted to reassure him. It was a patronizing gesture of support, not an expression of adulation. But once he decided to collaborate with Hitler, he did not wish to be identified as a Nazi factotum. He tried to stay at arm's length. Typically, he insisted on addressing Hitler as "Herr Hitler" and later *"Herr Reichskanzler"* ("Mr. Chancellor") instead of the obligatory *"Mein Führer."* In emergencies, while attempting to deal with the complex dictator, he occasionally resorted to Nazi protocol, but his use of the Caesarean Nazi formalities, both spoken and written, frequently rang with irony.

Disgusted with what he considered the failure of Germany's democratic years, Schacht subscribed to nationalism, had disdain for Versailles, and held a very chauvinistic view of modern Berlin culture. These sentiments were shared by most German conservatives and were not the exclusive property of the Nazis. Many called him an opportunist for deserting democracy and joining Hitler, but Schacht never wavered from his conservative credo, no matter how dangerous, even during the Nuremberg trials. Inflated ego or determined patriot? Perhaps a bit of each.

Most people who worked closely with Adolf Hitler learned to live with his disorganized, arbitrary, and bohemian ways. He arose late, rarely managed to be punctual, imposed his health fads and abstinences on his visitors, and trapped his guests as a captive audience until the early morning hours, leaving his entourage glassy-eyed with boredom and fatigue. François-Poncet's view was in retrospect and the result of many hours in Hitler's presence, while Schacht's original experience was limited to only one face-to-face meeting at the Görings' apartment and a few speeches, mostly heard on radio or read in the daily press. He also knew something about Hitler's credo through *Mein Kampf*. Ever the cynic, Schacht quite likely considered the most controversial Hitlerisms as campaign exaggerations, soon to be moderated by the battering of time and experience.

In one respect some of Hitler's views ran strangely parallel with Schacht's. As a banker, Schacht had spent most of his adult years with other bankers, journalists, politicians, and business-men of the Jewish faith. Some of them, like Eugen Gutmann, Monti Jacobs, and Franz Ullstein, were his benefactors and had become friends. Later, he managed to protect certain Jews and to help them as he had helped Bella Fromm. No one could have ac-cused Schacht of personal anti-Semitism or of avoiding the com-pany of Jews, but he had very specific private views on what he considered their proper place in German society.

In his own words, Schacht regretted, "for the Jews' own good," that they were so anxious for cultural leadership.

> Culture has its roots in religion, and the German religion is Christian. Culture which depends purely on reason and enlighten-ment would lose its soul. The difference between culture and civi-lization is that the latter has no soul. In a Christian state, its cultural direction must in no case be delivered into the hands of non-Christians, be they Jews, Mohammedans or Buddhists. [However,] Jews must be allowed the same freedoms as all other citizens. They deserve the same Christian affection, respect and support as all other human beings.[140]

Consequently, Schacht maintained — no doubt in contrast to his American father — that religion *is not a private matter, but at the foundation of the State.* [141]

Beginning with the first week of January 1933, Hitler's ap-pointment to the chancellorship was a foregone conclusion.

140. Schacht, *Abrechnung mit Hitler,* p. 59.
141. Schacht, *76 Jahre meines Lebens,* p. 451.

Hitler had the leverage. Von Papen had promised "control" over Hitler, but even von Hindenburg must have known this was wishful thinking. A final, crucial meeting took place in Berlin on the evening of January 22 in the suburban villa of Joachim von Ribbentrop, a wealthy international businessman whom Hitler occasionally used as one of his foreign policy advisors. In total secrecy, there was a meeting of Hitler, Göring, Nazi legal expert Wilhelm Frick, von Papen, Presidential Chief of Staff Meissner, and von Hindenburg's son Oskar. Von Ribbentrop's chauffeur did not wear his livery when he called to collect von Papen, and the family butler was banned to the servants' quarters.

A deal was struck, but only after Hitler and Oskar von Hindenburg had sequestered themselves in a separate room for two hours. When they emerged, the younger von Hindenburg was willing and eager to advise his father to appoint Hitler as soon as possible. It has often been assumed that the tense two-hour meeting involved blackmailing the von Hindenburgs over the tax status of their Neudeck estate and over the possibility of scandal over the discredited *Osthilfe.* Even so, the president was not entirely cowed. At his insistence, the last-minute choice of cabinet ministers submitted for approval contained several sound and reliable names. Arguments about portfolios continued until minutes before the swearing-in. To reward him for his mediative efforts, von Papen was slated as vice chancellor.

On January 30, 1933, a cold and blustery day with snow flurries, at shortly after 11:15 A.M., Adolf Hitler was sworn in as chancellor by President von Hindenburg. They were fifteen minutes late, which ruffled the old man's sense of Prussian punctuality. Von Papen's wife was watching as the future rulers of Germany trooped toward the ceremony through a wintery garden between the Chancellery and the Presidential Palace. She turned to Alexander Stahlberg, one of von Papen's young aides, and shivering from cold and tension, she said, "Oh, my God, oh, my God, I am afraid!" She had every reason to be.

Most of Hitler's entourage was waiting impatiently at the Nazi bosses' favorite Berlin gathering place, the luxurious Kaiserhof Hotel, across the street from the Chancellery. Finally they

spotted Hitler, a few hundred yards away. Obviously, the ceremonies were over. Could anything have gone wrong? He looked
somber, grim. At last he reached the hotel lobby, and they surrounded him. There were tears in his eyes. Their dream had come
true. He was chancellor!

Schacht had bet on the right horse.

His changed allegiance was not unexpected. It had been
signaled long before. On October 16, 1932, Schacht lectured,
"Our honor has been taken from us, our moral worth, our self-
determination, all our most precious values, the inner light by
which a nation lives."[142]

From Bella Fromm's diary, November 14, 1932:

> I bumped into Hjalmar Schacht this morning in the lobby of the
> Kaiserhof. The mob loitered there, greeting him with raised arms
> and *Heil Hitler*. I had caught him, wing collar, rather soiled vest and
> all, on his way to the Führer. He smiled wryly at me, a trifle embar-
> rassed. Wonder what he's up to? Nothing that bodes good to any de-
> cent people, you can be certain.

Then, a dispatch from Berlin, November 22: "In an interview
tonight he [Schacht] declared the Nazi leader was the only man
fit for the Chancellorship."[143]

Schacht claimed he had no contact with the new chancellor
except for a strange interlude when he was present in the room
from which Hitler held his first radio address to the German nation. The new chancellor asked Germans to "give him four years,"
and they would not recognize their country. Schacht described
Hitler as looking like a surprisingly shaken man, grimly aware of
the burden he had assumed. Schacht insisted that "this was not
play-acting. This was real." It strengthened his resolve "to help
this man find the right path."

Schacht's advice probably would not have included certain
measures being taken by the Nazis. On February 22 Göring or-

dered that the brown-shirted storm troopers, the SA, be enrolled
as "auxiliary police." This led to many incidents of brutality and
a reign of street terror all over Germany. Labor union headquarters were raided and burned; pedestrians were assaulted for fail-
ing to give the Nazi salute whenever a Nazi unit marched past.
Democratic politicians were intimidated and threatened. Anyone
deemed "Jewish"-looking — including consular officials and
military attachés in mufti from Portugal, Greece, Turkey, and
Brazil — were in danger of getting beaten up in broad daylight.
Senior police officials found themselves in a quandary. Many German police, though inclined toward the political Right, were nevertheless still law-abiding and law-enforcing servants of the state.

A newspaper dispatch from Berlin, datelined March 10, told
of the raid by "impassioned Nazi gangsters" on the Berlin Stock
Exchange, demanding the dismissal of its leaders. There were attacks on various Jewish-owned stores. The report also mentioned
that new tariffs had been imposed on the import of eggs and
cheese, which would probably bring retaliation from the Dutch
and the Danes, who were large dairy exporters. "The protests of
the Hamburg Exporters Association and of the German Industries' Trade Congress have been in vain."[144] It probably reminded
free-trader Schacht of his earliest battles as director of the Center
for the Preparation of Commercial Treaties in Hamburg, and the
display of Nazi trade protectionism probably infuriated him.
Hitler certainly could use his "help to find the path."

Even though he was now chancellor, Hitler decided that he
needed an overwhelming Reichstag majority so that he could
shake the old-fashioned conservatives out of his cabinet, the von
Hindenburg holdouts whom he had been forced to accept. Only
Hermann Göring and Wilhelm Frick, as minister of the interior,
were Hitler's men. The other cabinet members were right-
wingers or conservatives, but not Nazis or radicals. Hitler had
been prevented from assembling the Nazi cabinet he had hoped
for, and he now wanted to rid himself of old-line factoti like For-

144. *New York Times* (March 10, 1933), p. 24:4.

eign Minister Konstantin von Neurath and even the Nazi-friendly war minister, Werner von Blomberg. He had even had to accept Alfred Hugenberg, his right-wing conservative rival from Harzburg, as minister of economics. The only way to gain total control and to rid himself of Hugenberg and other reactionaries was to take a gamble. Hitler dissolved the Reichstag and called for a new election on March 5, 1933.

Before the ballot box came the matter of finances. As Schacht remembered the course of events, on February 25 Göring invited him and some leading industrialists to the Presidential Palace (which Göring would soon grab as a personal residence and which would be expensively redecorated). Historian Heinz Höhne recalls Schacht's participation quite differently. Göring, "energetically assisted by former Reichsbank president Schacht," greeted the twenty-five invited industrialists. Göring then explained the importance of financing this crucial election, assuring them that it was unlikely to recur, since "this would be the last election for ten to a hundred years."[145]

There was no need to convince them. They were no longer reluctant about Hitler. Their leader, Gustav Krupp, who had turned down a Thyssen invitation to discuss the Hitler movement only four weeks earlier, now rose to his feet and, in the name of the group, pledged full support for the new chancellor.

Göring, the host, left the room. Then Schacht said cheerily, "All right gentlemen. Now to the cash register!"[146] In short order, 3 million marks were pledged to Adolf Hitler for the coming election. Later, when Schacht was accused of having been the fund-raiser, he claimed that at Hitler's request, he had "acted only as the cashier." Göring had been right. The March 5 election turned out to be the last honest German election for years to come.

A key event occurred two days after the fund-raiser. On the evening of February 27, 1933, the immense Reichstag building, the German parliament, which was a focal point of Berlin's old impe-

145. Peterson, *Hjalmar Schacht*, p. 127.
146. Höhne, *Die Machtergreifung*, p. 281.

rial district, was set on fire and destroyed. Only the shell remained.

There are endless historical theories as to who set the fire. Most have accused the Nazis of doing so in order to destroy, once and for all, the Weimar Republic's national forum. Supposedly, a small squad of storm troopers carried incendiaries through an old secret tunnel connecting the Reichstag building with the Presidential Palace, Göring's new residence.

The Nazis claimed that they caught the arsonist in the burning Reichstag building. He was Marinus van der Lubbe, a babbling and demented Dutch Communist who was supposedly directed by Bulgarian Communist agents suitably named Dimitrov, Popov, and Tanov.

Many experts reject this claim because the huge fire could not have spread rapidly throughout the vast building after being set by only one man. To this day, the facts are not clear.

It is possible that Count Wolf von Helldorf, Potsdam's police president and a Göring protégé, organized the crime, but he was executed in 1944 as an anti-Hitler plotter. Walter Gempp, Berlin's fire chief, was immediately arrested and then found shot to death in his cell. Hanussen, the famous clairvoyant who had reassured Hitler before the Cologne meetings, was rumored to have "recruited" the hapless van der Lubbe for his friend Count Helldorf. Hanussen was found shot to death in the Grunewald forest near Berlin. [147]

Asking the legal question *Qui bono?* (Whom did the event benefit the most?) the answer must be Hitler. He presented the fire as the beginning of a Communist plot and immediately demanded absolute power, supposedly to "protect the state." Meanwhile, using an emergency decree, on January 30 he had ordered the arrest of five thousand people in Prussia and of two thousand in the Rhineland. They were all on Nazi blacklists.

On February 28, the day after the fire, more emergency decrees were drafted by Frick and then put temporarily in place, thereby allowing wide-ranging anti-Communist police actions.

---

147. Alexander Stahlberg, *Die Verdammte Pflicht: Erinnerungen 1932 bis 1945*, p. 29.

It marked the beginning of the Gestapo (then known as the *Gestapa*) as a national secret police force. The hunt for Communists became the hunt for anyone who was anti-Nazi, and a new form of arbitrary arrest and detention known as "protective arrest" was devised. It was the beginning of the end of personal freedom in Germany.

Schacht eventually admitted that Goebbels and Göring might have been guilty of having caused the Reichstag fire, but he maintained that Hitler was not involved and was, in fact, surprised by it.[148]

Meanwhile, the March 5, 1933, election achieved a 43.9 percent vote for the Nazis, but while this was substantial, it still did not achieve the overwhelming landslide that Hitler needed. Joseph Goebbels was now his new minister of propaganda, a cabinet post Hitler had talked von Hindenburg into creating. Goebbels devised a clever tactic to mollify the angry group of right-wing conservatives whom Hitler had just tried to oust in the election. He invented the "Day of Potsdam." The old garrison town of Potsdam, near Berlin, was the center of the former royal and imperial rule and the emotional capital of Prussia. Goebbels organized a solemn church service, which was to be held at Potsdam's old Garrison Church, where generations of Prussian military families had always worshiped. The date was March 21, the carefully chosen anniversary of Bismarck's founding of the Second Reich. It was a heavily publicized event, filled with military parades, martial music, and homage to Germany's most reactionary world. The newspapers were soon flooded with photographs of Hitler dressed in civilian morning coat, bowing his head and shaking the hand of the gigantic old president von Hindenburg, who was rigged out in his full field marshal's uniform and all his decorations. There were imperial princes and dukes in attendance. In the church a seat of honor was left conspicuously empty for the absent sovereign, the former kaiser, now in exile. Von Hindenburg made a small, respectful bow to it. The glitter-

---

148. Schacht, *76 Jahre meines Lebens*, p. 381.

ing military atmosphere, the booming martial music, and the fluttering imperial flags convinced many upper-class right-wingers that the Hitler movement was not averse to a monarchist restoration and was willing to draw aristocracy to its Brown bosom. As Goebbels's propaganda machine blared out, it was a "historic handshake between the old and the new Germany." The entire sham seemed to calm the conservative establishment.

It was basic doctrine that the old-line Nazi despised all reactionaries almost as fervently as he hated communists and Jews, but it was obvious that the "Old Fighters"* of the Munich days were no longer at the center of their Führer's attention.

Hitler also showed his pragmatic side when Hjalmar Schacht was called into his first meeting with the new chancellor. After all, Schacht was not a party member, and although he had more than demonstrated his willingness to be helpful, he was distrusted by most of the party establishment, who still saw Schacht as a collaborator of the Jewish bankers.

It was the middle of March 1933.

"Herr Schacht, I am sure we are agreed that the most urgent task for the new government is to end unemployment. That will need a lot of money. Do you think it can be obtained without the Reichsbank?"[149]

Schacht agreed with the immediate need to end unemployment but told Hitler it could not be done without the Reichsbank. When pressed for the amount of money needed, Schacht hedged.

"Herr Chancellor, all I can tell you is that the Reichsbank should be ready to lend all assistance until the last unemployed citizen is back at work."

Then came Hitler's pivotal question.

"Would you be willing to resume leadership of the Reichsbank?"

---

* *Alte Kämpfer* were a special category of party members who joined before 1933, and had party numbers below 300,000.

149. Ibid., p. 382.

Later, Schacht remembered his reaction. Could he accept the offer from a leader "whose political methods and individual acts he found difficult to accept"? Or should he overcome his scruples "for the sake of the six and a half million unemployed"? Besides, he was quite aware that Luther, who had held the Reichsbank presidency since Schacht had resigned, had already met with Hitler and had given an unsatisfactory answer to Hitler's question. Schacht told Hitler that he would not find it "fair" — he used the English term — to fire Reichsbank president Luther, but Hitler reassured him that Luther had already been slated for another position. Schacht then decided on the spot.

"If that is so, then I am ready, once again, to take the presidency of the Reichsbank"; and "on March 17, almost exactly three years after I had left it, I went back to work at the Reichsbank."

He insisted that it was not out of personal ambition or agreement with the National Socialist Party or personal greed. It was for the "welfare of the broad masses of our people."[150]

He negotiated an annual salary of sixty thousand marks, a fragment of his earlier earnings. He wanted to "demonstrate abstinence to Nazi officialdom" but admits that he failed to do so.

On March 23 the Reichstag, now meeting in Berlin's lavish Kroll Opera House, voted a set of new emergency laws called the *Ermächtigungsgesetz,* or "Enabling Law," which Hitler demanded "for the protection of the state" and which virtually removed all individual rights. The citizen's right to assemble, speak, write, worship, travel, read, and protest; the sanctity of his domicile; and the freedom from arbitrary arrest and detention were all surrendered in one sweeping parliamentary session. Schacht attended as a spectator. He claimed that this moment marked the beginning of dictatorship and the suicide of Germany's moderate political parties, which were, indeed, dissolved within a year. There was barely a protest from the intimidated and outvoted moderates. There was even the feeling that perhaps these laws were necessary to help the man at the helm perform his difficult

150. Ibid., p. 383.

task without undue interference. Otto Wels, the head of the SPD, Germany's centrist Social Democratic Party, formerly the main support of the old democratic regime, said on that brutal day, "Our people await achievements [with these] measures against the grim state of the economy!" [151]

Weimar Germany had made a valiant effort. The republic, saddled with enormous punitive burdens, had tied its financial fate to the West. When the West fell into deep economic depression, Germany's fate was sealed. The personal rights provided under democracy had not yet taken root in Germany, and their loss was not felt keenly. Schacht took a harsh view: "Democracy dug its own grave."

The Nazi terror spread. On Saturday, April 1, storm troopers in cities all over Germany blockaded the entrances to Jewish-owned shops and stores, smeared Stars of David and anti-Semitic slogans across store windows, and yelled, "Germans, do not buy from Jews!" It was more than a boycott, it was a mass riot. Still, New York's *Business Week* wrote: "Evidently the Hitler government realizes the boomerang possibilities of its move. The best informed authorities in Berlin expect a steady decline of jingoist action against the Jews."[152]

Schacht, like any other German, must have witnessed the excesses, the rowdiness, the cruelty, brutality, and vulgarity of Hitler's regime. Anyone walking on a German street was sooner or later confronted with the ugly ways of the Nazis.

On May 10, following Dr. Goebbels's insistence, students at universities all over Germany lit bonfires to destroy tens of thousands of books that the Nazis considered "un-German." The neo-pagan Berlin bonfire took place in the middle of the square in front of the opera. Forty thousand Berliners watched and listened as Goebbels ranted about what was suitable for the German mind. The works of Sigmund Freud, Ernest Hemingway, Jack London, and even Germany's great Jewish poet Heinrich Heine disappeared in the flames.

151. Schacht, *1933*, pp. 70, 71.
152. *Business Week* (April 12, 1933).

11

THE TASK

ABOUT 6.5 MILLION Germans were unemployed, out of a total population of 65 million and a work force of 30 million.* At
the time, worldwide unemployment stood at 24 million.

In April 1933 New York's *Business Week* reported that Germany's
railroads, once separated administratively by the Dawes and
Young Plans, would once again be fully controlled by the government. The piece continued: "It is generally believed in business
circles that Dr. Schacht, new head of the Reichsbank, is largely responsible for the shaping of this program and that in line with his
general understanding with Hitler, he will play a dominant role
in formulating government economic and financial policy."

Schacht knew that in actual fact, Germany was entirely on its
own. The country's new leader had made sweeping promises to
the German people, and now it was time for him to deliver. He
depended on Schacht to help him do so, and Schacht knew that
the only way to succeed was to have the complete and unwaver-
ing backing of Adolf Hitler. Some of the cure would be so sweeping and outrageous that only dictatorial backing could make it
workable. He had to be protected from party interference, from
cabinet obstacles, from objections of the banking establishment,

---

* Only minimal unemployment assistance was available.

and from criticism by the press. He would need unequivocal backing against complaints from abroad because some of the measures against foreign creditors were sure to make life difficult for Foreign Minister von Neurath and his diplomats.

He faced an army of foreign debts, both state and private, and a formidable wall of foreign tariffs that hindered German exports. Besides, the dollar, pound, and franc — the most important foreign currencies — had all been devalued, which caused German exports to be overpriced and imports to be bargains, while the coffers of the Reichsbank were empty of foreign currency.

German industry had to deal with a deeply depressed domestic market and a lack of available capital for expansion. Most of all, the popular euphoria that celebrated Hitler's coming to power had to be kept alive, not only for Nazi hubris but for the sake of the economic future of the country. In a stopgap measure, labor unions were abolished and a regulation against strikes and lockouts was issued on May 17. Within six months a new superlabor organization, the German Labor Front, would be established, although it merely rubber-stamped government decisions while lulling its membership with promises of vacation cruises and entertainments called the Strength through Joy (*Kraft Durch Freude*) program. But it would mean nothing without solid and guaranteed employment. Meanwhile, tax relief was instituted for employers. Subsidies were granted for improving rivers and utilities. Women were urged to leave the workforce and return home, so marriages brought bonuses from the government.

Schacht's first decision at the Reichsbank was not his creation, though he quickly endorsed it. The Reichsbank participated in Operation Reinhardt, a government-subsidized program for factories and urban renewal. It was meant to prime the housing-and-construction industry, one of the economy's building blocks. Schacht pledged 1 billion marks. Next came financing the first of the autobahns, the futuristic superhighways.* These were administratively assigned to the German state railroad system

---

* The autobahns were massive versions of the original small Avus in Berlin.

because Schacht wanted to coordinate the traffic flow and patterns of railways and autobahns. For the autobahn project, he pledged a Reichsbank loan of 600 million marks, to be repaid out of the government's total budget. Once the loan had been repaid, the Reichsbank got out of the superhighway business. Meanwhile, it provided jobs. When the first stretch between Frankfurt and Darmstadt was opened, Hitler invited Schacht to join him in his long black Mercedes convertible limousine for a well-publicized, much-photographed first trip. Hitler was amazed. "Fantastic. Even three abreast!"

The man who built the autobahns got his job through Schacht and by default. Hitler asked Schacht to choose between Feder, the old party factotum, whom Schacht had scuttled once before, and Fritz Todt, a Nazi engineer. Schacht picked Todt. Hitler asked, "Do you know Herr Todt?" Schacht's answer was typical. "No. But I know Feder!"[153] Todt would eventually become one of the Nazis' war production chiefs, one of Albert Speer's predecessors.

On June 7 Berlin's foreign press held its annual gala at the luxurious Adlon Hotel. The only two Germans invited were the tall mayor of Berlin, Heinrich Sahm, and Schacht. Somehow Schacht got into a contretemps with some American journalists. He angrily told them that "they should stick to facts, not opinions!" and was immediately trumped by the famous American journalist Edgar Mowrer, who said to Schacht, "Thank you for your support."[154]

With world depression persisting, a sixty-nation conference was scheduled in London for June 1933. To prepare for the conference, the representatives of various nations first went to Washington to meet with the newly elected president, Franklin D. Roosevelt, who had just devalued the dollar 40 percent. Schacht was chosen to represent Germany at these Washington preparations for the London conference.

When Schacht landed in New York, the press came aboard his ship and starting asking questions about anti-Semitic atrocities.

153. Schacht, *76 Jahre meines Lebens*, p. 385.
154. Philip Metcalfe, *1933*, p. 120.

Schacht completely lost his temper, crumpled up a *New York Times* dispatch they had handed him, threw it on the deck, and asked, "What atrocities? All lies!"

The *Times* correspondent, one Edwin L. James, reported archly:

> Dr. Schacht has a tempestuous disposition. He has often slammed doors at conferences, although he has always come back. There may have been some relationship between Dr. Schacht's outburst and the circumstance that since March 5, *The New York Times* has published fuller accounts of developments in Germany than any other newspaper. All of its dispatches from Germany have passed the Nazi censors.[155]

Schacht stayed in Washington for a week. He was thoroughly charmed and impressed by the ebullient and crippled Roosevelt, "an example of manly good looks," with his "formality, interrupted by his many jokes."[156]

Schacht compared Roosevelt's task with Hitler's. They both had to rebuild the economy of their nation, but Roosevelt took over a wealthy country that was in trouble. Hitler took over a bankrupt one. Roosevelt soon instituted measures he called the New Deal. Schacht's future plans would be named the *Neuer Plan* (New Plan). His closest American collaborator in Washington was Hans Luther, whom he had replaced at the Reichsbank. Luther had become the German ambassador to the United States, obviously the "new assignment" Hitler had mentioned. J. Pierrepont Moffat, a State Department official, wrote that President Roosevelt, helped and escorted by an aide, ushered Schacht and Luther into the Blue Room on Saturday, May 6, while a U.S. Marine band played "Deutschland, Deutschland, über Alles."[157] There was a luncheon for twenty, and then a working session.

Luther must have been taken aback when, in the presence of

155. *New York Times* (May 7, 1933), p. 1:7.
156. Schacht, *76 Jahre meines Lebens*, p. 389.
157. J. P. Moffat, *The Moffat Papers*, pp. 94–95.

the dour secretary of state, Cordell Hull, Schacht told Roosevelt that Germany might have to stop paying the interest on American bank loans that had been given to Germany. As Schacht describes the scene, "Cordell Hull was visibly nervous. Luther slid around uncomfortably in his chair," and Schacht expected an unfriendly reaction from the president. "Nothing of the sort happened. Roosevelt gave his thigh a resounding slap, laughed and shouted, 'Serves the Wall Street bankers right!' "[158]

The room relaxed. Schacht was amused by Roosevelt's unexpected reaction. It was clearly a victory of American partisan politics over the national interest. Wall Street had been opposed to Roosevelt, and now he relished their upcoming dilemma more than the potential loss of income to America. The next day in Cordell Hull's office, the secretary of state handed Schacht an envelope with a cool "It's from the president." It contained a note from FDR, which said that Schacht's statement "had shocked him." Schacht noted wryly that it obviously took twenty-four hours to develop this shock. The journalist in Schacht made him describe Hull as stiff, pinched-lipped, slim, with a slightly tilted head and a totally disinterested manner, dressed in ancient frock coat, stiff collar, and slim tie. He seemed an anachronism, from Lincoln's day.

On his part, Cordell Hull described Schacht as "simple, unaffected and thoroughly approachable" and "one of the shrewdest persons with whom I came in contact among the delegations visiting this country prior to the London Economic Conference." He thought that "some leading Americans are convinced that Schacht was not at heart with Hitler and the Nazi program."[159]

The other side of the story is given by Herbert Feis, one of the Roosevelt brain trust. He joined the meeting in Cordell Hull's office, where he saw Schacht "speaking with the voluble assurance of a schoolmaster lecturing to his pupils. His gray, mean face was pinched above his high stiff collar and his pale eyes gleamed

158. Schacht, *76 Jahre meines Lebens*, p. 391.
159. Cordell Hull, *Memoirs*, p. 237.

sharply behind unrimmed spectacles, as his glance darted about from person to person."

Roosevelt's thigh-slapping *Schadenfreude* about the Wall Street bankers is explained by Feis's comment that "Roosevelt in his campaign speeches had criticized the reckless way in which foreign securities had been purveyed to the American people with exorbitant profits for the bankers who sold them." Certainly, FDR wanted to remove the impression that he had given his consent to any German moratorium on payments. The word *shocked* came after Jimmy Warburg, of the German-American banking family, who was part of the American advisory team, had wanted to substitute *disappointed* and was overruled.[160]

On taking his leave, Schacht was asked to join Roosevelt on the president's couch. Then Roosevelt told Schacht he had made an excellent impression because he spoke openly and frankly.

This was Schacht's version of the farewell meeting, a form of press manipulation that was in character. In all probability, he overstated Roosevelt's cordiality so that FDR would have appeared to give his tacit approval to Schacht's antipayment maneuvers.

Actually, Roosevelt was less friendly than Schacht reported. At his most puckish, he said to Warburg, "You know, Jimmy, it would serve that fellow Hitler right if I sent a Jew to Berlin as my ambassador. How would you like the job?"[161] Warburg, knowing that the family's parent bank in Hamburg was in a precarious position, probably decided that it was not the right moment for such a confrontation.

Considering Schacht's new employer, there was a curious farewell dinner given in New York for Schacht. It was hosted by David Sarnoff, the head of RCA and a member of the American delegation to the Young Conference. The event was held at Sarnoff's beautiful townhouse. Most of the participants, with the exception of Owen Young, Governor Al Smith, and the head of the YMCA, were prominent American Jews, among them Rabbi

160. Herbert Feis, *1933: Character in Crisis*, p. 137ff.
161. Chernow, *The Warburgs*, p. 391.

Stephen Wise, the internationally known American Jewish spokesman. Schacht reported that he spoke "carefully but honestly," that there were no controversial questions from the floor, and that Sarnoff thanked him and said, "Dr. Schacht, you have been a good sport!" Supposedly, Schacht had assured the audience that he would try to convince the Nazis to treat the Jews more leniently.[162]

A few weeks later he joined the German delegation at the World Financial Conference in London. The Germans were led by Foreign Minister von Neurath. Hugenberg, Keppler, and Mayor Krogmann of Hamburg were also there.

The conference was a failure. Opinions on how to solve problems were too fragmented; delegates were unable to reach decisions. Still, the British did things with their usual flair for pomp and circumstance, including a royal garden party at which Schacht was presented to the king and queen.

During the actual working sessions, Chancellor Engelbert Dollfuss of Austria received an ovation. It amused Schacht that "the only functioning European dictator at the conference" was enthusiastically applauded by the assembled representatives of the democracies.

Though the London financial meetings had produced nothing of value to world financial recovery, it paid a personal dividend for Schacht. To his delight, the antagonist Hugenberg scuttled himself by sending a memo directly to the chairman of the conference without consulting his own delegation. On his return to Berlin, he was dressed down by Hitler and promptly resigned. The new minister of economics was Kurt Schmitt, former chairman of a major insurance company, who quickly donned an SS uniform to fit in with his new associates. Hugenberg's other portfolio, agriculture, went to a devoted Nazi, the romantic theorist Walter Darré.

And Schacht was finally rid of Hugenberg.

It now became his lot to live with his new associates, the Nazis,

162. Ibid., pp. 389–91.

not an easy task. He was not a member of their party. To make Schacht's presence more familiar to the Brown establishment, Hitler invited him to two of his private luncheons with old cronies. It was not the sort of company Schacht found interesting, and he was less than charmed. He also avoided Nazi evening functions because they often became drunken brawls. Only Hitler was abstinent. Schacht found that the only similarity between the Nazis and their fancied Teutonic ancestors was their love of alcohol.

His hauteur did not go unnoticed. According to Hitler's recorded table conversation, Hitler put up with Schacht's undisguised anti-Nazi snobbery only because "Schacht was one Aryan who could outswindle the Jews," pointing out that Schacht was obvious proof that an intelligent Aryan could easily outthink a clever Jew. [163]

A strange dispatch in August 1933 showed that traces of the anticapitalist faction among the old-line Nazis still existed. The Prague German refugee newspaper *Sozial Demokrat* reported that a group of storm troopers were plotting to assassinate Schacht. It was to be the first blow struck in an upcoming fight against capitalism. Supposedly, three storm troopers were arrested by the Berlin police after Schacht complained that he was being followed. [164] The item never appeared in the German press.

While waiting for the measures that would revive Germany economically, with a special eye on Schacht's plans, the Nazi hierarchy's machinery took complete and sweeping control of the nation. Under the Weimar Republic, Germany had been a federation of sovereign German states. These individual states were now virtually disenfranchised, and a grid of Nazi party *Gauleiters,* or regional Nazi leaders, was superimposed on them. *Statthalter* (state representatives) were also appointed for each state, and all the strings were held by Berlin.

German courts were reorganized so that they would be en-

163. Henry Picker, *Hitler's Tischgespräche,* p. 233.
164. *New York Times* (August 25, 1933), p. 1:2.

tirely responsible to a new Nazi-dominated supreme People's Court. There was no appeal against the judgments of this high court, except to Adolf Hitler himself. Judges wore swastika badges embroidered on their robes.

All other parties were abolished. The National Socialist Party became Germany's only political party. It described itself as a national "movement," a *Bewegung,* rather than a political entity.

On July 20, 1933, any doubts Schacht may have had about the world of the "new" Germany were given a slight measure of relief. The Catholic von Papen justified his vice chancellorship by finalizing a concordat, a treaty, with the Vatican. The senior Vatican official behind the agreements was Cardinal Eugenio Pacelli, the former papal nuncio in Berlin, then papal secretary of state and eventually Pope Pius XII. In essence, the concordat agreed with the Nazi government that "if you don't touch our church people, we will not complain about the way you run things."

At the time, it was rumored that the concordat was already being negotiated at the time of the Reichstag fire and that the Vatican had persuaded some key Catholic Reichstag delegates not to oppose the *Ermächtigungsgesetz,* the Enabling Law.

The concordat was a great international coup. It helped legitimize Hitler's rule. Like all of Hitler's international treaties, he was ready to break it whenever the need arose. Several years later, the mock gift of a magnificent jeweled case was given to Joachim von Ribbentrop, his foreign minister. It contained copies of all the treaties that had been broken by Hitler. Eventually, concordat or not, hundreds of parish priests were arrested by the Gestapo and thrown into concentration camps for trying to protect victims of Gestapo and SS terror. But in 1933 relations between the Roman church and German state seemed benevolent and cooperative.

Hitler managed another religious endorsement of sorts, though it was obtained by chicanery and threats. In May 1933 Friedrich von Bodelschwingh, a distinguished evangelical cleric, was elected as head of Germany's Protestant church. Since von Bodelschwingh was a man of principle and unwilling to give blanket endorsement to Nazi dogma such as the "Führer principle" and the prejudicial racial views, a monstrous campaign was launched against him, involving threats and blackmail. By the end of the year Ludwig Müller, a puppet cleric of the Nazis, was appointed Reich bishop. Like the judges, these newly minted Nazi Protestant clergymen wore swastika badges on their vestments. Now Hitler had both Christian religions under control.

Between his Washington trip and the London conference, Schacht had called a meeting of Germany's foreign creditors, at which he warned them of things to come. Claiming to lay the cards on the table, he told the foreign bankers that once again the Reichsbank lacked the foreign currency because of new foreign import tariffs and the devaluation of their national currencies. This caused an imbalance of German trade. Germany might have to suspend interest payments on Dawes, Young, and other foreign loans. The settlement of all foreign debts must now fall under the control of the Reichsbank. It caused much consternation, though it was probably seen as nothing more than a Schachtian threat. However, according to Schacht's report, the creditors agreed that it was necessary to replenish the Reichsbank coffers. Further, there was general agreement to accept full repayment of the remaining small balance of the Dawes loans but to impose a temporary moratorium on half the interest due under the long-term Young loans.

But Schacht was by no means through. The next move needed the full backing of his new master. On June 9 a law was enacted allowing him to form the so-called Conversion Fund, the *Konversions Kasse,* to be administered by the Reichsbank. All foreign debts — no matter whether private, business, state, or municipal — had to be paid directly into this Conversion Fund. The amount and manner of the repayment of these foreign debts would then be administered solely at the discretion of the Reichsbank, meaning Schacht.

The Reichsbank then offered to pay foreign debts, but at a 50 percent discount, and at a rate lower than the original 5½ percent to 4 percent interest.

Half would be paid in cash, and the remaining half would be in so-called scrip issued by the Reichsbank — but in marks, not in foreign currency. This scrip could be converted into various forms of "special" marks, all to be used with enticing discounts:

The *Reisemark,* or travel mark, for trips to or inside Germany.

The *Registermark* for investments in Germany or purchases of German goods to be exported into the creditor countries.

The *Askimark* for special purposes, such as the support of people or causes, all within Germany.

Naturally, Berlin's wags had a wonderful time, suggesting that there be *Bordellomarks, Beermarks, Homomarks.* Foreign creditors were less amused.

German debtors were officially cleared of their foreign debts after paying the full amount of their indebtedness directly into the Conversion Fund. Foreign creditors were faced with the option of either immobilizing half their money or using it the way Germany wanted. One can imagine the strained relationship between Germans who had done years of business abroad and their suppliers, or between Germans and foreign friends whom they owed money. There were Germans, private individuals and businessmen, who felt ashamed when they paid their debts into the Conversion Fund. They knew that people abroad who had trusted them were getting an unfair deal. Others were delighted to be rid of their debts by getting a certificate from the Reichsbank clearing them of their debts.

While the principal stayed intact, the interest was another story. The *New York Times* ran the following headline on its October 16, 1933, financial page:

GERMANY PROFITS BY TRANSFER PLAN

SCHACHT HAS NO INTENTION OF MODIFYING MORATORIUM ON FOREIGN BONDS

AMERICAN HOLDERS LOSE

CALCULATIONS SHOW THEY ARE DEPRIVED OF 50% OF THEIR INTEREST[165]

---

165. *New York Times* (October 16, 1933), p. 25:6.

And on December 12:

SCHACHT OFFERS CREDITORS CHOICE

BIDS THEM SELECT "INTEREST OR DIVIDEND" AS HE WARNS OF CUTS

IN GERMAN TRANSFERS[166]

If Schacht had been arbitrary about loans and interest, an even harsher measure lay ahead.

In an article on German debt in the December 30, 1933, edition of *Newsweek*, Schacht was called "abrupt" and "ministerial looking" and then accused of casting gloom among Germany's creditors. Schacht had just announced that instead of the 50 percent arrangement of the last half of 1933, Germany's creditors could expect a change to 30 percent cash and 70 percent scrip during the first six months of 1934.[167]

Using the full authority at his command, Schacht began his sweeping ways of tackling foreign debt, mobilizing the mark, and boosting exports. Naturally, there were protests abroad. In a speech at Basel, Switzerland, to the German chamber of commerce, he insisted that foreign debtors must think of themselves as investors. He implied that they had to share the problems of their investments. [168]

Next came the task of cranking up industry and consequently, employment. Although the autobahn, railway, and river projects brought a certain rudimentary form of work, Schacht had disdain for what he called "ditch digging." It was one of the things he found to criticize about FDR's Civilian Conservation Corps and other publicly administered work projects. Schacht preferred to see workers producing finished goods for export. "Ditch digging" produced neither income nor taxes. But first came the task of building employment, which equaled exports in importance. In 1933 Schacht believed in the rearmament of Germany, and so did Adolf Hitler. Schacht always insisted that their

---

166. *New York Times* (December 12, 1933), p. 12:4.
167. *Newsweek* (December 30, 1933), p. 23.
168. Mühlen, *Schacht*, p. 46.

reasons differed radically, but in 1933 their thrust was parallel. During the Nuremberg war-crimes trials, he testified, "I'd even join the devil for a big, strong Germany." [169]

To prime the manufacture of armaments and to slice away at unemployment, he founded a small shell corporation, strangely named the Metallurgical Research Company, or Mefo corporation (short for *Metallurgische Forschung GmbH*). Mefo was capitalized with a paltry 1 million marks, but its bonds were immediately consigned in equal shares to four leading industrial companies: Krupp, Rheinstahl (steel), Gutehoffnungshütte (coal), and Siemens. Mefo bonds paid 4 percent interest and matured in five years, but were redeemable at any time, guaranteed by the Reichsbank. The purpose of Mefo was to finance large government contracts for armaments. Some estimate that there was 21 billion marks in orders. Payment was guaranteed by the Reichsbank. Some of the money came from what had been requisitioned by the so-called Conversion Fund. It was ironic that a portion of German rearmament was paid for with foreign money.

All subcontractors were also paid in Mefo bonds, which were really IOUs. They would then present their bills to the Mefo corporation, which took them to the Reichsbank, to be paid in marks. At the same time, manufacturers earned 4 percent interest on the bonds for as long as they held them before presenting them for payment. Because payments were guaranteed by the Reichsbank, corporate capital reserves, which had been salted away for emergencies, came out of hiding. The project began with the four Mefo owners and then was joined by other important manufacturers, who were also paid in Mefo bonds guaranteed by the Reichsbank. During the next four years, the value of Mefo bonds grew from the original 1 million marks to 12 billion marks, and half of them were traded on the open bond market. The Mefo bonds became a very desirable investment, with their rising value and guaranteed 4 percent interest. The Reichsbank

169. *International Military Tribunal,* vol. XVI, p. 248.

was even willing to purchase any unsold Mefo bonds for its own portfolio.

Schacht called it an inventive way of priming industrial production and wiping out unemployment. Many others considered it a well-camouflaged ruse for cranking up armament production without much visible accountancy or unduly alarming the outside world.

Normally, the manufacture of goods for other than export seemed to go against every economic principle Schacht held dear. He would usually have called it a shameful waste because it did not generate taxes or bring in foreign currency. However, massive production for purposes of rearmament was another matter. Schacht admitted his full commitment to rearmament from the day he was accused at the Nuremberg trials of building the machinery for war until the day of his death. He was firmly convinced that no nation could be taken seriously in its dealings with other nations unless it was a mighty military opponent.

In a retrospective letter to Hitler on January 7, 1939, the year that Hitler went to war, Schacht wrote: "From the beginning the Reichsbank has been aware of the fact that a successful foreign policy can be attained only by the reconstruction of the German armed forces." [170]

In today's nuclear age, this seems an obsolete notion. Two of the most powerful modern nations, Japan and Germany, have only miniscule military establishments.

One of the factors that seemed to confirm Schacht's insistent efforts to finance the rearming of Germany was the failure of every disarmament conference of the postwar period. Many Germans believed the harsh postwar military restrictions imposed on their country would be accompanied by the voluntary disarmament of the victors. This was not to be. Britain's navy shrank and her army and air force atrophied, but only because of budgetary problems, not out of a decision to disarm. Besides, Britain was still a vast empire, with all its members as self-understood al-

---

170. NCA document 3726-PS VI, p. 473, ex Simpson, *Schacht in Perspective*.

lies. France maintained an enormous military establishment. The postwar United States withdrew to the other side of the Atlantic. Its military establishment suffered from sheer inattention because America's attitude was isolationist, bolstered by the Great Depression. But American participation in World War I had been numerically small and chronologically late (1917) compared with the French, British, and Russians, who had begun their war three blood-soaked years earlier.

Although the size of armed forces decreased, there was no specific set of worldwide disarmament decisions. It was therefore no surprise to most Germans when Germany announced its withdrawal from the useless disarmament conference sponsored by the League of Nations, followed by its total withdrawal from the league. In the November 12, 1933, Reichstag elections, the Nazis won 92 percent of the seats, and 93 percent of the electorate approved of Germany's departure from the League of Nations. Surprisingly, although there were no political parties other than the Nazis, about 3 million Germans still cast votes against the overwhelming majority. However, their ballots, without any party affiliation, were declared invalid.

By the end of 1933 unemployment had decreased by about 2 million. This was more than adequate to convince hope-filled Germans to trust Adolf Hitler and to persuade Hitler to trust the ideas of Hjalmar Schacht.

12

POWER

THE YEAR 1934 began with a tightening of Schacht's harsh financial regulations. In late December 1933 the British had protested against his repayment rules, so on January 2 Schacht offered them 77 percent of their interest debt and promised to pay this amount in full. But the British failed to respond, so Schacht let the offer drop.

His single-minded aim was to find any hidden German capital and put it to use. In a speech to the Central Organization of German Banks in Berlin on February 22, he pointed out that there were 21 million savings accounts in Germany and that this money had to be put to work. He chided the savings bankers for their inaction.[171] He also rejected any suggestion of devaluing the mark, no matter how much it would accommodate exporters.[172] He had no intention of seeing foreign debts paid with devalued marks.

On March 15, 1934, in a banquet speech to the German-American Chamber of Commerce in Berlin, he was again back on the attack.

"Only when foreign countries have written off their German losses can they do business with us again."[173]

Meanwhile, an American Nazi named Carl Nicolai called for

171. Simpson, *Schacht in Perspective*, p. 87.
172. *New York Times* (February 23, 1934), p. 32:1.
173. Mühlen, *Schacht*, p. 47.

a boycott of those Americans who boycotted German goods. He was speaking at the Yorkville Casino (210 East Eighty-sixth Street in New York) in front of twenty-five hundred members of the so-called United German Societies. Nicolai had taken over from the former leader, Heinz Spahnknoebel, who had disappeared while the FBI was on his trail. Yorkville was in full support of the "great Leader" of Germany. Another pro-Nazi booster was one Reinhold Walter, of 308 East Eighty-sixth Street, who blamed the "Jewish influence" for the "great Leader's" difficulties in making the "new" Germany's aims understood by foreigners. The meeting ended with hearty "Heil Hitler!"'s.[174]

The so-called Transfer Conference was convened in Berlin in April 1934. It was meant to settle payments owed foreign creditors by an increasingly truculent Germany. Schacht opened the proceedings by stating forcefully, unequivocally, and dramatically that July 1 was doomsday, the deadline when Germany would have to declare bankruptcy. He then subtly addressed the various individual problems of each debtor country, offering preferential treatment to some if they accepted more German exports, and better settlements to others in return for discounts. He handled Britain and France differently from the rest because they were concerned mainly with repayment of the Dawes and Young loans. The conference resembled a bankruptcy committee meeting, and any chance of combined decisions by the creditors was wrecked. Eventually, and to Schacht's joy, the creditors began to fight among themselves.

In the midst of the conference, on May 5, Schacht presided over the laying of a cornerstone for a new Reichsbank building, on thirteen acres and at a cost of 40 million marks. Hitler was in attendance, as were battalions of parading SA Brownshirts and a crowd of ten thousand spectators.[175] These crowds were induced to attend through twisting their employers' arms to give workers time off. Friedrichstrasse, where most of Hitler's foreign visitors

174. *New York Times* (March 28, 1934), p. 19:5.
175. *New York Times* (May, 26, 1934), p. 26F.

were paraded, was known by irreverent Berliners as "Via Spon-
tana." During the cornerstone dedication, Schacht spoke rever-
ently of Frederick the Great's careful management of Prussia's
finances, hinting not so subtly at the Nazi wish to splurge.

Meanwhile, the conference was still faltering.

On June 14 large newspaper headlines all across the globe announced that the Reich was suspending all payments on foreign
debts, beginning with the same July 1 date Schacht had called
"doomsday."

The British finally offered a moratorium on all debts, to begin July 1, 1934. Payments were then to resume through bonds issued with a 3 percent coupon, with annual installments until
1945. Schacht accepted the terms. Germany had the option to retire the debt before 1945, but in September 1934 Schacht opted for
the 1945 date. After much protest, the United States, which was
the biggest holder of Dawes and Young bonds, was willing to negotiate a similar deal.

Schacht also renegotiated the terms of an old-time "standstill
agreement" from 1931 for the repayment of earlier short-term individual loans incurred by communities and municipalities. These
were typically loans made by opportunistic American banks, the
sort that FDR had condemned during his campaign. German
debtors had usually paid excessive interest to American bondholders. Schacht now forced an agreement to lower their sky-
high interest to 3.5 percent, thus saving the Reich 60 million
marks per year. When German businesses grew healthy through
Mefo orders, Schacht told them to make *blitz* payments on American bonds at this new low interest rate,[176] while small debtors still
paid interest at the full rate into the Reichsbank's Conversion
Fund.[177] Schacht's attitude seemed to be that all foreign capital
could be held captive (or at least hostage).

Meanwhile, Schacht put fifty-one German banks to work by
trying to float a new German Reich bond to be sold abroad at 4

176. Mühlen, *Schacht,* p. 54.
177. Ibid., p. 55.

percent interest. Fifteen of the banks were still run by Jewish management. No wonder Schacht was trying to protect them. Their connections were of great value.[178]

These were profitable financial months for Hjalmar Schacht and his client, Adolf Hitler.

But Hitler had new problems. His authority was being challenged, and his plans were interrupted by two men. The first was Germany's vice chancellor, Franz von Papen, one of Hitler's original boosters for the chancellorship. The other was Ernst Röhm, almost Hitler's closest Nazi comrade.

It all began with a strange and totally unexpected protest against Adolf Hitler and his doctrine. On June 17, 1934, Vice Chancellor von Papen was a speaker at the University of Marburg, the twelfth-century Hessian town. To the shock of an audience of distinguished academics, his address was a ringing protest against the National Socialist regime, its terror, its anti-Christian totalitarianism, its refusal to consider monarchist restitution, its "faceless" and throttled press, and the "substitution of vitality with brutality." He asked for a "return to responsibility."

In his memoirs, von Papen recalled that he was rewarded with rousing applause, which drowned out the dissent of the few Nazis in the audience.[179]

The speech was prepared by Edgar Jung, one of the vice chancellor's associates, a former wartime pilot and right-wing intellectual who was deeply troubled by the vulgarity and brutality of Adolf Hitler's rule. Somehow, he convinced von Papen, usually a judicious and opportunistic man, to speak out.

The reaction from Berlin was instant and predictable. The speech was banned from the press, although the distinguished *Frankfurter Zeitung* had already printed excerpts. There were no radio reports. Von Papen's office in the Voss Strasse was raided by the SS and Gestapo, and a young assistant, Herbert von Bose, was shot to death at his desk. Jung, the man who had written the

178. *New York Times* (June 16, 1934), p. 16:2.
179. Franz von Papen, *Der Wahrheit eine Gasse*, p. 346ff.

speech, was arrested. Von Papen rushed to Berlin and protested to Hitler, who tried to mollify him and complained about Goebbels's "bad handling" of the situation. Von Papen offered his resignation to von Hindenburg, but it was refused.

A few days later von Papen was put under house arrest but was soon freed. He retreated to his country estate, where he and his son awaited their fate. But Hitler used people or discarded them as he saw fit, and for the time being he decided to do nothing. He would soon have urgent need for his suddenly rebellious former associate.

The other cataclysm involved Captain Ernst Röhm, one of Hitler's oldest and closest fellow fighters, a former Bavarian World War I officer, and head of the SA, the corps of 2 million brown-shirted storm troopers. There was little of the elegant Bavarian officer about Röhm. He looked like a feisty, scarfaced, and porcine drill sergeant, and his conduct matched his appearance. Ever since Hitler was appointed chancellor, Röhm had raged and intrigued against the army, which was still led by the descendants of old-guard aristocratic officers. Röhm felt that the Nazi revolution had gone flabby and that the "new" Germany's armed forces should now be manned and commanded by men of the people. He despised the careful, precise, and judicious ways of the professionals on the General Staff and insisted that he, Röhm, should be appointed the army's chief of staff. He wanted the huge army of roustabout SA storm troopers superimposed onto the professional army. Hitler's plan was to use the tiny Versailles-imposed Reichswehr of 100,000 men as a cadre for the vastly expanded force. He needed every skilled professional soldier. In the future German army, these Reichswehr lieutenants would be colonels, and the colonels would be generals. He saw the SA for the hooligans they were, good for street brawling, but otherwise of no military value.

In February 1934 there was a confrontation between Röhm and General von Blomberg, the minister for war. Röhm was insistent. Von Blomberg appealed to Hitler, and on February 28 a tenuous compromise was patched together. On leaving the room where they had been negotiating, Röhm immediately declared that he "would not stick to this ridiculous agreement." He yelled that "the corporal will now have to go on leave!" and that "if we can't get there with him, we'll get there without him."[180] Viktor Lutze, an SA general, then denounced Röhm to Heinrich Himmler, head of the SS, which was an elite part of the SA but totally loyal to Hitler. Lutze insisted that Röhm was planning a rebellion. Himmler decided to get rid of the rebellious and dangerous Röhm. A plan for his removal was put into the hands of Reinhard Heydrich, a brilliant and cold new SS staff officer who had recently been cashiered from the German navy. Himmler also enlisted the cooperation of Hermann Göring. Goebbels needed no persuading. He was always slavishly devoted to Hitler. Hitler was not yet informed of the alleged Röhm mutiny.

There were several more stormy meetings between Hitler and Röhm. Then the party newspaper, the *Völkischer Beobachter*, suddenly announced that Röhm would go on sick leave to Bad Wiessee, a Bavarian spa, and that the entire SA would be furloughed beginning July 1. Hitler seemed to have prevailed, and Röhm's days of rebellion appeared over.

Now Hitler could no longer play his favorite game, one entity against the other, the SA against the SS, the SA against the army, Röhm against Himmler, Röhm against the generals. But at least he thought he had curbed a potential rebellion, and without bloodshed.

Then on June 30 he was given no choice. He received a report that despite his seeming submission, Röhm and his SA were planning a massive insurrection the next day, before their enforced furlough. A white-faced, shaking Hitler flew to Munich that very night, and all SA chiefs in Munich were immediately arrested. A caravan of Mercedes limousines then took him and a company of SS through the misty night to Bad Wiessee, where they arrived at 6:30 A.M. They pushed their way past a startled innkeeper, and Hitler, pistol in hand, gave the order to arrest Röhm. Other SA chiefs were rousted from their beds, some with their male lovers,

---

180. Heinz Höhne, *The Order of the Death's Head: The Story of Hitler's SS,* p. 88.

and rushed back to Munich and jail. Röhm was taken to Munich's old Stadelheim Prison, shoved into a cell, handed a pistol, and told to kill himself. He shouted, "Let Adolf shoot me himself!" The half naked, sweating man was finally shot by a group of Himmler's SS men.

The killings set off a countrywide wave of SS murders of SA chiefs, and any and all old enemies of Hitler. Former chancellor General von Schleicher and his wife were assassinated in their Berlin residence. Gregor Strasser, who almost deserted Hitler, was murdered in Berlin. Edgar Jung, who wrote von Papen's Marburg speech, was executed in the Oranienburg concentration camp. In all, eighty-three people lost their lives.[181] Newspapers and radio stations poured out a flood of vilification about the moral decay of Röhm and his SA clique and their homosexual debauches.

Everyone, including Hitler, had known for years that Röhm was homosexual. In the past there had been several lawsuits and scandals involving the SA chief. There was even a denunciation by the cardinal of Cologne. Hitler had always insisted that these were vicious lies and, anyway, Röhm's sexual preference was his own choice. Now, times had changed.

Hjalmar and Luise Schacht heard about these grim events and the murders that followed after they had been stood up for dinner. The night of June 30 they were expecting Dr. Joseph Goebbels and his wife, Magda, to dine à quatre at Gühlen. Schacht knew that Dr. Goebbels detested him and "was not about to surrender his place as the regime's number one intellectual to some economist." So he had invited the two Goebbelses for an intimate evening to find a modus vivendi. Their guests failed to appear. The reason for this rudeness soon became clear. The propaganda chief was part of the events surrounding the raid on Bad Wiessee.

Schacht wrote that he shuddered when he first learned all the brutal facts. "Once again, I was confronted by important decisions." He concluded that "he was dutybound to fight against the

181. Ibid., p. 117.

excesses of the regime *from the inside* [italics added]."[182] Nevertheless, he went to see Hitler.

He asked the chancellor, "How can you take the responsibility to decide the fate of human beings without legal procedures? You really should have convened a court of law, even if it was summary."

To Schacht's surprise, Hitler was quite meek and gave evasive answers. Shortly thereafter, Franz Gürtner, the minister of justice, whom Schacht had always admired as a man of honor, declared Hitler's actions as "rightful."

Then once more "it became clear to me that I had to use my official place to fight for right and justice wherever I had the chance to do so."[183]

On July 25 Engelbert Dollfuss, Austria's dictatorial and anti-Nazi chancellor (he was so tiny that he was nicknamed the *Millimetternich*) was murdered by Austrian Nazis. Though the deed was not unwelcome to Adolf Hitler, the assassination was premature from his point of view. It was not yet on the schedule of things he had planned for Austria. For the moment it was also an international embarrassment because he seemed to be behind the assassination. He had given broad hints for months that he would help to "liberate" his former homeland, so the impression was quite understandable, particularly after the murderous events that had just taken place in Germany. He immediately fired the German ambassador to Vienna and then contacted the shaken Franz von Papen.

The night after the Dollfuss murder, several SS men suddenly appeared at von Papen's estate. He and his son greeted them with drawn pistols, because they fully expected to be arrested. But instead, the SS officers persuaded von Papen to pick up the phone for a call from the Führer. Hitler had need of him. He was to go as ambassador to Vienna, where he was to calm the troubled waters. Von Papen was gentlemanly, diplomatic, and, above all,

182. Schacht, *76 Jahre meines Lebens,* p. 404.
183. Ibid., p. 407.

Catholic (as was most of Austria). Besides, Mussolini, who had a proprietary and paternal interest in the fate of Austria, was said to be furious, and Hitler was more than anxious to calm his fellow dictator. To receive his briefing, von Papen was ordered to Bayreuth, where Hitler was attending the annual music festival. (Mussolini proved hard to mollify. A month later he canceled a planned visit to Hitler's Berchtesgaden mountain home after Hitler had visited Rome in June. The beginning of what would eventually become the Axis was anything but smooth.)

Schacht had also received a phone summons to join Hitler at Bayreuth. On Schacht's arrival, SA General Lutze, the man who had denounced Röhm, greeted him at the villa reserved for Hitler. He saw von Papen, who was waiting for the details of his Vienna assignment. The next morning, on the twenty-seventh, it was Schacht's turn to have an audience.

They met in the sitting room of the comfortable house. Hitler calmly informed him that Economics Minister Schmitt had resigned "due to the state of his health." "I have to fill the post. Would you be prepared to add the Economics Ministry to the presidency of the Reichsbank?"

Schacht was quite aware that Schmitt, despite camouflaging himself in SS uniforms, had found himself under constant pressure and interference from Nazi bigwigs and was at his wits' end. It was also rumored that he took issue with the treatment of the Jews. Obviously, Schmitt had not resigned for reasons of ill health.

Schacht was ready to take the ministry, but he was not about to be trapped like Schmitt. He wanted a free hand, with no party interference, and to clear up one other point. "Before I accept, I want to know how you wish me to handle the Jewish question."

Hitler answered, "In matters which concern the economy, Jews can participate as they did in the past."[184]

Schacht claimed that he made frequent use of this statement whenever the need arose to protect someone Jewish. While Schacht wrote about this conversation after he was arrested for

184. Ibid., p. 404.

war crimes, it was probably factual. His memoirs also contained his anti-Semitic views concerning Jewish participation in German cultural matters; however, he usually helped Jews, possibly to protect German credit and exports and his self-appointed place as the international guardian of German finance. He occasionally got his way by persuading Hitler that an anti-Semitic act or decree would make Germany look bad in foreign eyes and would hurt its financial standing.

1. Schacht's paternal grandfather, a local physician from Friedrichstadt and curmudgeon.

2. His father, William Schacht: teacher, journalist, businessman, general accountant, and naturalized American citizen.

3. Schacht's beautiful mother, the Baroness Constanze von Eggers, as a young bride.

4. Schacht seeing off Owen D. Young at a Paris train station following the Young Conference on reparations in June 1929.

6. Schacht in 1930 reading a financial report, wearing his trademark high collar.

5. Schacht and Albert Vögler, head of United Steel Works, at the Young Conference in Paris. Vögler later infuriated Schacht by walking out in protest and returning to Germany.

7. At this Königsberg conference in 1935, Schacht chastised the Nazis for their brutal and illegal acts.

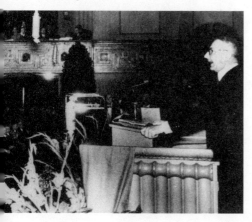

8. Presiding over a meeting of the Reichsbank board of directors in 1936.

9. Visiting Franklin Roosevelt in 1936. On the other side of Schacht is German ambassador Hans Luther, whom he replaced as Reichsbank president.

10. A 1938 newspaper photo of Schacht with his first wife, Luise, along with two of their grandchildren, Harold and Helga van Scherpenberg.

11. Schacht and Montagu Norman, governor of the Bank of England, during Schacht's trip to London to solicit support for his scheme that would enable Jews to emigrate.

12. The three acquitted Nuremberg prisoners —
Fritzsche, von Papen, and Schacht — receiving
their documents of release from Colonel
Burton C. Andrus on October 4, 1946.

13. Von Papen, Schacht, and Fritzsche at the
raucous news conference later that day.

14. Schacht with his faithful Manci (left)
and his devoted daughter Inge on the day
of the acquittal.

15. With his Nuremberg defense attorney,
Dr. Rudolf Dix, on October 8, 1946,
in the Schachts' rented Nuremberg apartment. The German police arrested him
early the following morning.

16. Schacht as a prisoner in a German internment camp during the 1947 German trials that followed his acquittal by the Allies.

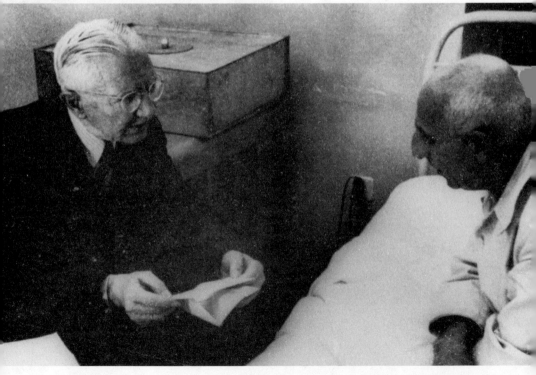

17. Financial advisor Schacht with ailing Iranian prime minister Mohammed Mossadegh, September 14, 1952.

18. The Schachts visit newly installed Egyptian prime minister General Naguib in Cairo, September 25, 1952.

19. Schacht (right) at a 1960 memorial reunion of former Dachau inmates, held at the former concentration camp.

20. A 1927 cartoon from *Kladderadatsch,*
a German satire magazine, accuses Schacht
of bringing down the economy by shaking
the Berlin stock exchange to its roots.
("Dr. Schacht, the Samson of the Stock
Exchange.")

21. From *Ami du Peuple,* Paris, April 1929.
A comment on Schacht's attempt to avoid
reparations. Moreau, the French delegate,
asks, "All right, Excellency, how much do
we owe *you?*"

22. From *Petit Provençal*, Marseilles, May 15, 1929. Churchill to Poincaré: "Astonishing fellow, this Schacht. Writes tons of memoranda but forgets that Germany lost the war!"

23. From the *Philadelphia Record*, August 6, 1934. Industrialist Fritz Thyssen, Finance Minister Schacht, and Führer Adolf Hitler, the way many saw their relationship.

13

CABINET MINISTER

HIS APPOINTMENT as minister of economics began on August 2, 1934. Not long thereafter, he also received the pro forma title of plenipotentiary for *Wehrwirtschaft*, "war economics." Luise Schacht was now *Frau Reichsminister*. It must have caused her fasciophile heart to rejoice.

Schacht began by assembling the ministry's entire staff. He told them that he wished them to be factual, to act justly, and to rebuff all interference from Nazi Party operatives. He promised his full personal support if they followed his guidelines. "My ministry will be a tower of justice."[185]

His fight against party officials began safely enough with his dismissal of Gottfried Feder, once Hitler's pet economist and now a ministry official. Schacht knew that Feder was long out of favor with Hitler because of his sympathies with Gregor Strasser's socialist interpretation of the Nazi creed. His dismissal was sure to bring joy to Hitler.

"But, Herr President," said Feder, "I am perfectly prepared to work with you!"

"That may be so, Herr Feder, but I am not."[186]

Schacht also had to face the jealous inner world of the Nazis.

185. Schacht, *76 Jahre meines Lebens*, p. 409.
186. Ibid., p. 410.

One of SS chief Himmler's senior aides called on the new minister to express Himmler's disapproval of Schacht's appointment. Himmler suggested that Schacht resign at once.

Schacht replied, "I shall resign at once if I am asked to do so by the chancellor. The only other way to remove me is to shoot me, but from the front. You won't get me from the back."

The flustered officer then warned Schacht that his attitude would bring him the enmity of the SS.

"Regrettable," said Schacht, "but can you ask your chief to do me a favor? Have you noticed those two SS guards outside my office? Ask that they be withdrawn."[187] They were withdrawn.

His early battles with the Nazi eminences were usually a mixture of snobbery and arrogance. He detested "these people" and felt sure of Hitler's backing. His disagreements were not necessarily with the Nazi program but with the sort of people chosen to carry it out.

He also prohibited Keppler, the Nazis' old fund-raiser, to enter the ministry building, after Keppler told one of Schacht's subordinates to ignore his directives. "The Führer will soon get rid of Schacht."

Interior Minister Wilhelm Frick, the man Hitler used to rewrite Germany's laws to suit the Nazis, sent Schacht a directive that all Masons in the Reichsbank, past or present, were to be removed from positions of trust. Schacht informed Dr. Frick that he could not carry out the directive "as long as the head of the Reichsbank is a Mason." He meant himself, of course. There was no change of assignment for any of his ministry's officials with Masonic connections.

By coincidence, the shaky presidential signature on the document appointing Schacht to his new position as minister of economics was President Paul von Hindenburg's last official signature. The towering old field marshal, the last link to the kaiser and the Weimar Republic, died at his estate at Neudeck on August 2 at the age of eighty-four. His death brought profound changes.

187. Ibid., p. 411.

On August 1, in anticipation of von Hindenburg's imminent death, Hitler's cabinet voted to combine the offices of Reich president and Reich chancellor. Now Hitler would no longer need any presidential approval, no matter how perfunctory, for his actions. An eventual national plebiscite on August 19 brought him the rubber-stamp approval of the German people. In a mawkish address to the nation, Hitler said that "no one could ever fill the place of the late, great field marshal" and that the position and title of president would now be permanently retired. Instead he, Adolf Hitler, would be known as the "Führer and chancellor" of the German Reich.

Schacht's position was now brutally clear. The only way he would survive Hitler's dictatorship was by giving constant proof that he was one of the world's uniquely gifted masters of the art of economics and an irreplaceable cog in the machinery of Hitler's ambitious plans. Even for someone of Hjalmar Schacht's self-confidence, this must have been an icy and danger-filled realization. Because of Adolf Hitler's urgent need for him, Schacht had so far won a certain independence from Nazi rules and attitudes. He was sure it would last as long as he continued to provide a good balance of trade and available foreign currency.

On August 17, two days before the plebiscite that ratified Hitler's takeover of all leadership, Schacht gave an interview to Berlin's newspaper, the *Lokalanzeiger*, in which he urged the nation to vote 100 percent for the new centralized post. He also said, "Chancellor Hitler understands economic and financial problems with that great unpretentiousness and simplicity which always astonishes us and which conquers all theoretical objections. . . . There is not one economic law, not one deed, not one bond that does not bear the stamp of Adolf Hitler's personal collaboration."[188]

By such statements, Hjalmar Schacht made it eminently clear that he had no interest in national leadership. He might have taken some old-time pleasure from the fact that the old Hanseatic

---

188. *Lokalanzeiger* (August 17, 1934).

port of Hamburg, by voting 20 percent no, cast the largest number of anti-Hitler votes, but there was no doubt about Hjalmar Schacht's allegiance to Adolf Hitler. With a certain steady-as-you-go self-deludedness, Schacht still clung to the notion that Hitler was a man whom he could influence and who could be manipulated despite the stupidity of his paladins. At the same time, the interview in the *Lokalanzeiger* demonstrated his allegiance and loyalty.

Hitler also received support from outside Germany. The *New York Times* reported with some mischievous glee that William Randolph Hearst had given newspaper space to Ernst "Putzi" Hanfstaengel, Hitler's Harvard-educated press chief. Hearst called the plebiscite the "unanimous expression of popular will."[189] According to Hanfstaengel, Hearst promised to attend the next party rally at Nuremberg.

Schacht continued to gather power. A new regulation was passed that the chairmen of business associations, such as ones organized by heavy industry or the financial groups, could be appointed only with the approval of Schacht or Dr. Frick, who could also dismiss them. Schacht also maintained his intransigent image on the international scene.

From a newspaper interview:

> "I will say," and here Dr. Schacht's jaws snapped, "if the United States does not buy more, we will see to it that she sells us less!"

Armed with his new powers, Schacht now took revenge on Goebbels for the snub handed out earlier in the year. From an AP dispatch, Berlin dateline of September 4, 1934:

> It was reported that Dr. Hjalmar Schacht, Minister of Economics, had notified Paul Joseph Goebbels, the Propaganda Minister, that in the future no public money would be available for propaganda in other nations. It was understood that Dr. Goebbels had been spending not less than 200 million marks annually for the purpose. German professors and other prominent persons making visits to other nations frequently have received handsome allowances

189. *New York Times* (August 23, 1934), p. 10:3.

for spreading the Nazi gospel abroad. It was said that Dr. Schacht's position in the Cabinet has been strengthened materially by his decision.

In a similar report, London's *Daily Express* told of Schacht's "ultimatum" to Hitler, that extremists who interfere with his efforts abroad to create a more favorable view of Germany should be "gradually eased out." Both newspaper stories combine to tell a tale of Schacht's aggressiveness. He seemed willing to take chances, although it is unlikely that he lacked a fallback position. He was right, of course. The bloodthirsty German year 1934 had alarmed many Western nations. It shifted old fears of Communism to new worries about Nazi Germany and was undoubtedly one of the reasons why on September 18 Soviet Russia was elected to membership in the League of Nations.

Probably as a hedge against the harm done by his consistent criticism of the party, Schacht, who had become a favorite author for several foreign political publications, contributed an article to the American monthly *Foreign Affairs*. In an article dated October 1934, he uses the following strange rationale for a moratorium on all German debts still payable to the United States:

> It was the great King of Prussia [Frederick the Great] who first proved his sympathy for the American movement in word and deed. It seems to me unworthy of the American people to oppose the new *Weltanschauung* [political view] which has been built up in Germany today, the more so as this new conception of life rests on the noblest human sentiments: fidelity to duty, national unity without differences of class, contempt for all privilege of birth, rank and position, but recognition of all personal achievement.[190]

Sometimes Schacht waffled and wavered. On November 17 the Jewish Telegraphic Agency reported that Schacht had protected several Jewish firms which wanted to sell Christmas gifts to the German public. His "hands off" order quoted a strangely apolitical rationale for the land of Adolf Hitler. "Jews should not

190. *Foreign Affairs* 13, no. 1 (October 1934), p. 4.

be molested in commerce, since any hampering of Jewish-operated trade brings unemployment for German employees."

Hitler gave him a free hand, but there was no such freedom in his home. Luise Schacht was devoted to Nazism and would brook no criticism of the Führer. The Schachts' daughter, Inge van Scherpenberg, and her husband, Hilger, an attaché at the embassy in London, were equally troublesome, because both were strongly anti-Nazi. Schacht feared his wife's besottedness for the Brown masters and was equally afraid of the open political opposition displayed by his daughter.

Another person who shared Inge's disdain for Germany's new ruling clique was Schacht's crusty old secretary, Clara Steffeck, the formidable woman who had once given such a laconic report about his 1923 activities as the inflation-fighter. Frau Steffeck was nicknamed "SS." In 1924, during a financial conference in London, she gave an interview to a tabloid, which then described her as a "smiling slave" and the initials SS stuck. Now "SS" had come to mean something that made Clara Steffeck cringe.

One day an important Nazi called her when Schacht was in London attending a conference. The Nazi chieftain claimed that he "had to fly to London at once to deliver an important message to the minister." He demanded a substantial sum in British pounds to pay for the trip. Steffeck was unimpressed. She refused. "You can send him a telegram for five German marks."

"Impossible. It's much too secret."

"Then," said Steffeck, "send it in code via the German embassy. It's quicker and cheaper than a plane."

She knew that all the man wanted was a quick pleasure trip to London, and she remained unshakable. He finally gave up.[191]

In September 1934 Schacht introduced his "New Plan," a financial strategy that put the reins of German commerce and industry, including every minute detail, into his hands. In order to hoard and enlarge Germany's fund of foreign currency, virtually nothing could be bought and sold by German firms in interna-

---

191. Schacht, *76 Jahre meines Lebens,* p. 413ff.

tional commerce without Schacht's permission. It was complete economic dictatorship, with a new bureaucracy of twenty-five separate "control" organizations. Since no foreign debts could be paid directly, the "blocked" currency left available for foreign dollar, pound, or franc creditors were in the form of scrip or one of the "special" marks. These were accounted against newly devalued foreign currency at the mark's old value. It explains Schacht's constant opposition to all moves to devalue the mark, which would have helped German exporters. Certain weaker supplier nations, such as some Balkan and South American countries, got manhandled. Their shipments were credited to them totally in blocked German marks, which could be used only for the purchase of German goods. About a fifth of all German imports in 1935 were paid for in this arm-twisting manner.[192]

The New Plan had the German economy on a controlled life-support system, and Schacht discarded all the notions of free trade and individual entrepreneurship that he had always cherished. There were understandable howls of protest from abroad, which could not have pleased German businessmen (but, just as understandably, they muffled their complaints).

Why had Schacht strayed so far from his own economic ideals? Probably because he could maintain his independence within the Nazi machine only by producing definitive results, and quickly. Also, his demonstrated vanity probably would not allow him to slide from his high place, even if it meant using atypical and draconian measures.

His frequent capacity for rationalizing was astounding. He claimed that his New Plan was good not only for the commerce of Germany but also for that of many of Germany's foreign trading partners. His reasoning was that the plan allowed nations to enlarge their German market, but he failed to point out that this was because they had the choice of doing it the Schacht way, losing their money, or giving up Germany as a customer.[193] At the

192. Mühlen, *Schacht*, p. 77.
193. Schacht, *76 Jahre meines Lebens*, p. 417.

inception of the New Plan, foreign suppliers were either willing to accept discounted or bartered dealings for the sake of preserving the large German market or too rattled to cut off shipments.

But sooner or later, foreign creditors learned that two could play at this game. The first creditor nation to do so was Switzerland. In August 1934 the Swiss government ruled that all debts owed to German exporters would have to be paid directly into the Swiss National Bank. The bank then retained any amounts owed Swiss exporters or debts for Dawes and Young bonds in Swiss possession, as well as interest owed to Swiss creditors.[194] What remained was transferred to German creditors.

Within eighteen months, similar clearing systems were instituted by France, Argentina, Austria, Bulgaria, Czechoslovakia, Denmark, Estonia, Finland, Greece, Holland, Hungary, Iran, Italy, Latvia, Lithuania, Norway, Portugal, Romania, Spain, Sweden, Turkey, and Yugoslavia.

Later, a different kind of financial self-protection was instituted by Britain, Belgium, Canada, Ireland, Luxembourg, Manchukuo, New Zealand, South Africa, Syria, and Lebanon. Any debts for foreign goods imported by Germany were prenegotiated, with the exact terms and manner of prepayment and payment spelled out before each transaction. France, having found the earlier clearance system insufficient, also instituted this method.

French industrialists became particularly angry when they found out that German importers had been placing the lion's share of their orders with suppliers in the industrial Saar region. The former German Saar was under a fifteen-year mandate to France by virtue of the Versailles Treaty. The year 1935 was the end of that term, and the Saar's citizens had the right to vote to become part of France or to return to the German Reich. Schacht gambled that the Saar would vote to rejoin the rest of Germany. Saarlanders had never been made to feel that they were part of France, and they admired the new industrial élan now being dis-

194. Mühlen, *Schacht*, p. 118.

played by their old home country. With 24 percent of the Saar's labor force out of work, they were dazzled by Germany's newly increased employment. On January 13, 1935, 90 percent of the population voted to rejoin the Fatherland, and on March 1, 1935, Hitler, standing in his long black Mercedes, drove into gray, drizzly Saarbrücken past crowds of miners and steelworkers hysterically yelling, *"Heil!"* to welcome the Saarlanders "back to the Reich." Now those German orders that had been placed when the Saar was still under French domination were filled by industrial companies that were once again German. No francs were needed. Cheated out of much revenue, the French then limited all permits for imports from Germany.

Another blow soon fell. Czechoslovakia, one of the great suppliers of ore, coal, machinery, weapons, automobiles, and shoes, suddenly shut down all trade with Germany.[195] The Czechs were tired of their poor treatment.

A look at the numbers displays some Schachtian arithmetic of the period. Most Western currencies (including the dollar, pound, franc [both Swiss and French], and the Dutch guilder) were devalued between 1933 and 1936. The mark, which Schacht had refused to devalue, then climbed from 4.20 marks for the dollar, to 3.40 marks for the dollar, to 2.46 marks for the dollar.

The mark was being artificially pegged to its old gold value, although it was actually traded in the open market at a 50 percent discount. However, because of the mark's artificial strength against the devalued dollar, Germany could now settle American debts at a massive discount. This changed nothing for the individual German debtor, who still had to pay the full amount of his indebtedness into the Reichsbank's Conversion Fund in marks. It was Schacht's Reichsbank that then turned the discount into profit for the national treasury. The same technique applied to all foreign debts. Schacht saw to it that they were paid in artificially maintained marks against newly devalued foreign coin.

His constant threats that Germany would stop paying interest

---

195. Ibid., p. 121.

had so depressed the value of Dawes and Young bonds that between 1935 and 1936, Dawes bonds slipped from $79.18 to $37.00, and Young bonds from $59.50 to $28.63 using their overvalued German marks. Schacht urgently advised German bondholders to redeem these bonds through the Conversion Fund.

Later, after the 1936 Olympic Games, in a typical act of Nazi chicanery, visiting "Aryan" foreigners of German descent could pay their German bills, such as for hotels or other purchases, in marks, but visitors to Germany who were "non-Aryans" (Jewish or part Jewish) or were Slavic (Polish, Russian, or Czechoslovak) had to pay their bills in foreign currency.[196]

Schacht's mania for conserving foreign currency reached such extreme levels that eventually German citizens were threatened with the death penalty if they settled any foreign debts directly, for the "crime of high treason by robbing the Fatherland of its financial lifeblood."

These fierce dealings with Germany's Western trading partners brought reprisals, and Germany was soon forced to increase its imports from Brazil, Chile, Mexico, Peru, Colombia, and Bolivia — all countries that had not yet instituted protective clearance systems for trade with Germany. They supplied poor quality at higher prices but were never paid on time. Nevertheless, they kept shipping, because none of them wanted to lose a market the size of Germany. In the summer of 1935 Brazil finally stopped supplying Germany, and Argentina refused to advance any central bank funds to Argentinean businessmen who wanted to sell to Germany. The flow of Latin American goods and raw materials soon turned into a trickle.[197]

The Balkans became the next target, specifically Bulgaria, Greece, Hungary, Romania, and Turkey. Schacht made the rounds of each capital on a lumbering Ju 52 passenger plane, the workhorse of Lufthansa. He was struck by "the wide influence

196. Ibid., p. 67.
197. Ibid., p. 128ff.

German culture had in the region." There were dinners with royalty and prime ministers, and Regent Prince Paul of Greece and his wife spoke only German at table. Schacht was quite aware that he was on an emergency mission. Each Balkan country already had its clearing system in place, but it was Schacht's job to tempt them into accepting vast new German orders. As usual, he counted on greed. He was willing to offer premium purchase prices for certain goods that Germany desperately needed, such as soybeans from Bulgaria and Romania, bauxite from Hungary and Yugoslavia, oil from Romania, and magnesium from Yugoslavia. Again, the supplier nations did not get paid and were offered German goods in barter, usually not of the most salable kind. Even these barter goods were often shipped after long delays. Germany gathered an army of creditors as if massive debts were a badge of honor. Schacht's Lufthansa Ju 52 also made stops in Baghdad and Tehran, where Reza Shah Pahlavi ran his bully pulpit. The Shah's frightened ministers warned Schacht to keep strict protocol, such as three bows when greeting and three bows when leaving the imperial presence. Instead, he was greeted with warm informality, and the Shah gave the fascist salute when wishing him farewell after the audience. The eighteen-year-old heir to the throne, Mohammad Shah Reza Pahlavi, attended the meeting. This side trip to Iraq and Iran was probably part of his hunt for oil, but it was also a venture into foreign affairs and was sure to displease Dr. Joseph Goebbels and Foreign Minister von Neurath.

Meanwhile, Germany's earlier trading victims were still trying to recover. Denmark, a leading supplier of livestock, butter, lard, and foodstuffs, found itself as one of Germany's hapless creditors. A newly established Danish-German chamber of commerce in Berlin asked the Danes "to show utmost consideration" for Germany's export needs. The Danes eventually became customers. They had to accept cologne and Dresden china in barter and soon found themselves in temporary financial trouble. The Bank of England bailed them out with a loan of 1.5 million pounds sterling, or the equivalent of about six months of butter exports to Germany.[198] Brazil had sold Germany 100,000 sacks of coffee, which the Germans then traded at discount prices in exchange for goods they desperately needed. In order to avoid the collapse of world coffee prices, the United States was forced to grant Brazil a loan of $60 million so it could afford to cancel another German order of 100,000 sacks of coffee.[199]

The Turks reluctantly continued to do business by bartering for older-model German cars.

Schacht was ruining his reputation as a reliable figure of international finance. His way of importing foreign capital was to import foreign goods and then to block payments or negotiate in barter. It was the way of the financial brigand, but his mind was focused on the Führer in the Chancellery on the Wilhelmstrasse. Schacht wanted to feel sure of a safe landing platform at the end of his wind-whipped tightrope. [200]

Sometimes his best-laid plans fell flat. A large effort to promote barter of American goods for German goods was mounted at one of the big Leipzig trading fairs in March 1934. Three hundred ninety-two American buyers were reported as attending, but none cared to discuss barter arrangements. Nor was there a single American manufacturer or wholesaler showing at the fair. The news report called it "a fiasco."[201]

By the beginning of 1935, Germany's armament industry was in full swing, and Hitler was ready to recruit German soldiers to man these rifles and guns. On March 9 he declared that an air force, a Luftwaffe, would be built. Then on March 16 the German government issued a terse three-paragraph law, signed by Adolf Hitler and the full cabinet:

> The Reichs government has decided on the following law which is hereby proclaimed:

198. Ibid., p. 142.
199. Ibid., p. 144.
200. Ibid.
201. *New York Times* (March 5, 1935), p. 3:4–6.

1. Service in the armed forces will be based on universal conscription.
2. Germany's peacetime army, including military police, will be organized into twelve army corps of thirty-six divisions.
3. The full laws governing the rules of military service will be submitted by the Army Minister to his Reich Ministry.

This law scrapped Article 173 of the Versailles Treaty, which limited Germany to a 100,000-man army. The thirty-six divisions amounted to about 550,000 men. Britain protested two days later, but asked whether a state visit to Berlin by Lord Simon, the British foreign secretary, and Privy Seal Anthony Eden was still acceptable. It had earlier been postponed because Hitler had a "cold."

France, which had lengthened its time of military service to two years, seemed oddly passive. Hitler had used France's new extended term of conscription as an excuse for his March 16 decree, which marked the beginning of a pattern. No matter which act of aggression Hitler committed, he invariably used the pretense that it was "retaliatory." Even his eventual attack in 1941 on his treaty partner, the Soviet Union, was "to prevent an offensive by Soviet troops, massed at the border."

Armed with the arrogance of a man who was sure of his abilities, Schacht continued to have countless major and minor skirmishes with the party and its functionaries. He tells of seeing a painting at Hermann Göring's palatial manor, Karinhall. The picture was a gift from Hitler. Schacht saw that it featured a well-known Jewish society woman from Vienna, and he told Göring so, not endearing himself to his host.

As a birthday gift from the Führer, Schacht received a painting in a lavish frame with an inscription from Hitler. Schacht knew the painting was a fake, so he returned it with his deepest thanks "for the thoughtful choice," but threw doubt on its provenance and kept the frame.

Field Marshal von Blomberg received another fake as an anniversary gift, and Schacht pointed out the forgery. The party leaders who had arranged the present got into trouble.

He battled Labor Chief Robert Ley, who wanted to squelch the traditional ceremonies in which certain apprentices in medieval guilds were promoted to masters. He forced Ley to give in by threatening to resign.

These constant acts of opposition, sometimes expressed directly to Adolf Hitler, were a strange phenomenon, since he frequently and publicly voiced admiration and support for the Führer and his program. Were they his way of restoring his vanity for these acts of obeisance? Or did he feel the need to soothe his conscience? On May 3, 1935, he had another chance to voice criticism. As usual, it was done in a memo and handed over during a public occasion. The new German liner *Scharnhorst* was on a trial run with Hitler and several of his top cabinet ministers aboard. Schacht's memorandum complained about the party's attacks on the church, the ill treatment of the Jews, and the illegal excesses of the Gestapo. He admitted that Jews were disliked all over the world and quoted Schopenhauer's plaint that "if you step on a Jew's toes in Frankfurt, the international press from Moscow to San Francisco breaks into howls." His criticism of the regime's anti-Semitism was not based on its immorality. He reasoned that it was internationally counterproductive for Germany.[202] "If you wish, you can mark the Jew as a citizen with limited rights, but you must grant him official protection against the fanatic and the ill educated."[203]

Hitler read the entire memorandum, asked Schacht to meet with him, and gave him some soothing explanations.

In June, during the 1935 British royal family's Silver Jubilee celebration, Hitler sent Joachim von Ribbentrop, his new personal advisor on foreign affairs, to London. Conducted outside the usual diplomatic channels between the German foreign ministry and the British foreign office, von Ribbentrop's mission began as soon as the parades and ceremonies for the royal pair ended. The task of the German "special envoy and plenipotentiary," a designation on which von Ribbentrop insisted, was to reach a naval agreement with Great Britain. Hitler wished to ar-

202. Schacht, *76 Jahre meines Lebens*, p. 438.
203. A. Fischer, *Hjalmar Schacht und die Deutsche Judenfrage*, p. 155.

rive at a formula of thirty-five tons of German naval shipping for every one hundred British tons. By accepting a diminished German naval role, he was offering to let Britannia rule the waves if the British would give Germany a free hand on the Continent. At the same time, even 35 percent would be a large increase over the few German coastal vessels allowed under the terms of Versailles. Von Ribbentrop's approach was crude and undiplomatic, quite out of character for a former officer and a wealthy international businessman. He was determined to show the British gentry that he was representing a new German style, quite different from the elegant aristocrats who had conducted international policy for the Weimar Republic. He would also prove his worth to his patron Adolf Hitler, given that a previous Nazi mission to England, led by Nazi guru Alfred Rosenberg, had failed to convert the British into admirers of Hitler.

He opened the negotiations at the Foreign Office by immediately demanding the 35:100 formula — "take it or leave it." His bumptiousness so infuriated Foreign Secretary Sir John Simon that he excused himself and left the discussions to others. Within days, to von Ribbentrop's total surprise, the British accepted his terms. The British policy of appeasing the Germans had arrived. Hitler was impressed by the quick success of his new expert on foreign policy, and Joachim von Ribbentrop's star was on the rise. The agreement was signed on June 18, to the discomfort of the French, who saw it as an act of British perfidy. Since von Ribbentrop had reported his combative style to his patron, it seemed to reinforce Hitler's belief that successful foreign policy was a matter of ultimatum, threat, and the presentation of a fait accompli.

On August 18 Schacht was the keynote speaker at the opening of the annual trade fair at Königsberg in East Prussia, an important event for German industry and agriculture. Obviously feeling sure of his ground, he decided to press home the points he had made on the *Scharnhorst* in his memorandum to Hitler. The Führer's tepid response had probably encouraged Schacht to speak out once more, so he launched into the identical list of complaints, but this time from a podium, in front of a large audience of Nazi chieftains, press, foreigners, and representatives of industry, agri-

culture, and banking. What's more, the speech was being nationally broadcast by German state radio, the Deutschlandsender.

When Schacht complained about party attacks on Masons
and Jews, the very prominent SS general Erich von dem Bach-
Zelewski stood up and stalked toward the exit, his spurs jingling.
Schacht claimed that he was ready to direct him to the men's
room ("To the hallway, then second door on the left"), but instead he finished his speech. It included an indictment of the
party newspaper, the *Völkischer Beobachter,* for its amateurish
economic views and its use of slogans, such as "The nation comes
before the economy" and "The flag is more valuable than the
bank account." He pointed out that to "face serious problems
with cheap slogans was dangerous." He even took to task those
people "who smear anti-Semitic slogans onto store windows by
night and treat Germans who work for Jewish companies as trai-
tors." He also chastised chauvinists "who boost their self-esteem
by belittling others, when only competition can prove one's
worth, rather than brutality."

When Schacht returned to his seat, Erich Koch, East Prussia's
Nazi chieftain, leaned over and said, "Little monk, little monk, thou
settest out on a hard road!" — an admonition given to Martin
Luther when he launched his protest against Rome. Schacht "knew
that from then on I would be seen as an enemy of the Party."[204]

As a preemptive attack, Schacht immediately dictated a letter
to SS chief Himmler, complaining about von dem Bach-
Zelewski's "unseemly conduct toward a Cabinet Minister of the
Reich." The SS general, so Schacht claimed, was not punished but
was soon transferred to remote Silesia.

An apoplectic Goebbels was informed about Schacht's rebellious speech. The broadcast could not be aborted, but newspaper
reports of the speech were "sanitized." Schacht countered by having 250,000 copies of the unabridged speech printed by the
Reichstag Press, which he controlled.

Eight days later at a meeting with Hitler on other business,

204. Schacht, *76 Jahre meines Lebens,* p. 441.

the Königsberg speech was barely mentioned, except for an enigmatic "Herr Schacht, in Königsberg you said, quite rightly, that we are all sitting in the same boat."

While Schacht seemed bent on protecting Jews from arbitrary attacks, he managed to protect his own flank from accusations of Jew-pampering with a sentence he did not emphasize in his memoirs. According to an August 18 report by American correspondent Otto Tolischus, who was present in Königsberg, Schacht said:

> Jews must reconcile themselves to the fact that their influence among us is over, once and for all. We want to keep our people and our culture pure and our own, just as the Jews have put up this demand for their people since the Prophet Ezra. But the solution of these problems must take place under State leadership and cannot be left to unregulated individual action, which constitutes a grave disturbance of the national economy and therefore is constantly forbidden by the State and party organs. [205]

The massive annual Nuremberg party rally in September 1935 became the launching platform for the anti-Semitic laws known as the Nuremberg Laws, although they were actually written in Berlin. Proclaimed on September 15 and designated as the "Laws for the Protection of German Blood and German Honor," these new commandments officially classified each German with Jewish ancestors as a full-, half-, or quarterbreed and limited every phase in the lives of these designated "non-Aryans," including marriage, residence, employment, and even unmarried heterosexual intercourse. It declared such intercourse between Aryans and non-Aryans to be a crime called "racial shame," or *Rassenschande*, and made it severely punishable. The 1935 Nuremberg Laws were superimposed on all previous punitive anti-Semitic measures and became the platform for all increasingly brutal anti-Jewish measures to follow. They eventually became the so-called Final Solution, a term first used by Göring. In a letter of July 31, 1941, he urged National Security and Police Chief Rein-

205. *New York Times* (August 18, 1935), p. 1:4.

hard Heydrich in writing to find a final solution to the Jewish problem. The fat *Reichsmarschall,* who had been brought up on the bounty of a wealthy Jewish noble, Dr. Hermann von Epenstein, demanded an end to this bothersome and even boring matter.

(On January 20, 1942, Heydrich convened a dull, bureaucratic conference at Wannsee Lake, near Berlin. Frustrated by their failure to force every German Jew to emigrate and saddled with Jews from all the conquered countries, the Nazis faced the excessive task of housing and feeding these millions in concentration and forced-labor camps. Their Final Solution to this dilemma was systematic extermination.)

Schacht's way of dealing with the official new 1935 "racial" laws was an attempt to trivialize them while seeming to maintain the Nazi credo. He was invited to attend a meeting of senior cabinet members and party functionaries to discuss the way in which the law should deal with marriages between non-Aryans with only 50 percent Jewish blood and full Aryans. He listened quietly while many opinions were voiced and was then invited by the minister of the interior, Dr. Frick, to give his views. His response was that he could not understand their inferiority complex! After all, Germanic blood was so strong that a mere 25 percent of Jewish blood could never dominate the union between a full-blooded Aryan and a half-Aryan. Besides, the percentage of Jewish blood would be even further diluted during generations to come. Why not be patient instead of building the Thousand-Year Reich with such "Jewish haste" (*jüdische Hast,* the pejorative expression used by German anti-Semites to describe Jewish pushiness)?[206]

After his controversial speech at Königsberg, Schacht held a series of lectures, including one at the Kriegsakademie, the army staff college, in which he wanted to make it clear that Germany was unable to continue rearmament unless it conducted a sane and careful economic policy.

Buoyed by the seemingly good reception to his admonitions, he asked Hitler for the opportunity to speak to the party leader-

---

206. Schacht, *76 Jahre meines Lebens,* p. 449.

ship and, surprisingly, was granted his request at the Nuremberg party rally. He spoke to the Brown hierarchy on September 17, two days after the publication of the Nuremberg Laws. Once more, he outlined the severe problems of rebuilding Germany's fighting forces without the income from international trade, pointing out that instead of "a display of turbulence in the racial wars," all such actions must be "conducted within a legal and controlled framework and coordinated with the country's economic necessities." The meaning was clear. "If we are perceived to behave like savages, it will cost us income, because foreigners will not do business with us."[207]

His appeal to the Nazi chieftains was not based on moral imperative but on economic necessity. He probably had to improvise on the spot. The two-day-old Nuremberg Laws could have left no doubt about the party's future direction and gave him little choice. This time he did not speak out against "those who smear anti-Semitic slogans onto store windows at night." After Schacht had finished, Hitler asked to meet privately with the party's leaders, and Schacht left the room. He heard later that Hitler had ordered his angry cohorts not to interfere with the much-needed Schacht.

In an attempt to distance himself from any connection with the party rally, Schacht explained later that he left Nuremberg at once, having gone there only for the purpose of the speech. [208]

His daughter, Inge, and her husband, Hilger van Scherpenberg, had returned to Berlin after seven years at the German embassy in London. In his diary, Sir Bruce Lockhart, a British political commentator, told about lunch with van Scherpenberg on September 11 in London. Schacht's son-in-law was worried about something Sir Bruce had published about Schacht. Lockhart thought that van Scherpenberg "is now a Nazi," which was most unlikely. (He was later jailed by the Gestapo.) The sentence that disturbed van Scherpenberg was said by Schacht during a

207. Ibid., p. 444.
208. Ibid.

dinner in Berlin: "Now I am going either to [climb a pedestal to become] a monument or to [climb] a scaffold [to be hanged]."

In a meeting held at the German Academy of Laws on November 29, 1935, Schacht rose to deliver a rousing endorsement of capitalism and the private entrepreneur. The audience was composed of high government officials and diplomats, including William Dodd, the American ambassador. Schacht was defending the capitalist system, which both he and German heavy industry favored, versus a new school of Nazi economists who believed that capitalism and the public-stock corporation were "instruments of a Jewish conspiracy." The Ministry of Justice had just declared that more than half the existing public-stock companies "would have to be liquidated," and Hitler had just made a speech in which he poured ridicule on "bourgeois heads," the public who bought stocks.[209]

Schacht seemed to be quite aware of his increasingly precarious place in Hitler's world. Yet, he insisted on attending services in Pastor Martin Niemöller's fashionable church in the wealthy Berlin suburb of Dahlem. Niemöller, a former World War I submarine commander, was an avowed anti-Nazi on purely religious grounds. His politically dangerous sermons were the talk of Berlin. He was arrested by the Gestapo a number of times and finally sent to Dachau concentration camp. To listen to a Niemöller sermon during the time of the Nazis was an act of open defiance. For a cabinet minister to do so was unheard of. To attend the sermon while the Reich minister's official limousine, with its swastika flags flying, waited outside was sacrilegious. It was typical of Schacht.

As usual, Schacht liked to use the Christmas holidays to bring matters to a head. On December 24, 1935, he wrote to War Minister General von Blomberg that he was no longer in a position to supply foreign currency that the War Ministry had requested for certain armaments. Schacht claimed that beginning in 1936, he tried systematically to limit expenditures for further armaments; but 1936 was also the year when he lost some of his omnipotence.[210]

209. *New York Times* (December 1, 1935), p. 35:1.
210. Schacht, *76 Jahre meines Lebens*, p. 457.

14

THE TIGHTROPE

THE YEAR 1936 began with an enormous boost to the prestige of Adolf Hitler. At dawn on March 7 a contingent of German troops marched into the demilitarized German Rhineland. It was a political gesture with sweeping implications. Hitler called it the most exciting time of his life, and there were eyewitnesses who saw him walk the floor of the Chancellery office all that night, waiting to hear whether the French would block his precipitous action with their own troops. It is generally believed that the course of history would have been changed if the French had done so, since Hitler had left orders for the German units to withdraw at the first sign of French military opposition.

Schacht had been talking about the return of Germany's colonies, though this was more his own view than a demand of Hitler's, who had made himself clear in *Mein Kampf.* Hitler believed that colonies were useless unless one controlled the seas, and he was willing to concede that portion of the world to Britannia. His attention was focused on continental Europe, particularly the east.

His Rhineland entry was the final breach of the Versailles Treaty and the subsequent agreement at Locarno between German and Allied statesmen. The French complained but did not respond in kind. Official London saw "no attack." Foreign Secretary Anthony Eden stated that Britain would come to France's aid only in the case of an attack on France itself.

Hitler had presented another fait accompli and had dealt another unanswered slap in the face of the Allies. Even Schacht's threat that there might be French sanctions against Germany had not deterred the Führer. Schacht was wrong. Hitler was right.

He was not the only dictator to flaunt his soldiery. Mussolini's troops squashed helpless Ethiopia, and the League of Nations would and could do nothing. Then Spanish general Francisco Franco, a fascist, launched a rebellion against the democratic Spanish government, gaining the complete sympathy of Adolf Hitler. Later that year, based on German initiative and egged on by advisor von Ribbentrop, the so-called Axis was formed, bonding together Germany, Italy, and Japan. After years of denigrating all Mongoloid races, Berlin proclaimed the Japanese "honorary Aryans of the Orient." Though not a formal international treaty, the Axis was meant to be an alliance against the *Comintern,* the Communist International based in Moscow, but distanced itself from being an actual coalition against Soviet Russia.

For Hitler, 1936 was the beginning of a time of triumph. It was also the year of the Olympic Games. The winter contests took place in Bavaria's Garmisch Partenkirchen. The Summer Games were held in a magnificent new oval stadium in Berlin, embellished by Arno Breker's Hitler-pleasing neo-Greek, uncircumcised statuary. Hitler or his chieftains appeared daily in special box seats, forcing all eyes to jump from athlete to Führer-box. It seemed as though all Germany had been briefed, groomed, and trained to greet the flow of foreigners who arrived, all curious to see Hitler's creation, the "German miracle."

"Are you going to the Olympics?" became 1936's haut monde alternative to "Will you be in Venice?" The Goebbelses gave a lavish party for foreign visitors on an island near Berlin, and the von Ribbentrops, at their villa in Dahlem. Official anti-Semitism was temporarily suspended. The ever present banners and posters proclaiming that THE JEWS ARE OUR MISFORTUNE were nowhere in sight, and the NO JEWS signs on guesthouses, hotels, and resorts were temporarily removed. Towns like Magdeburg, which had even banned Jews from its streetcars, canceled the regulation.

Von Ribbentrop was appointed ambassador to Great Britain. He had no intention of using the normal channels to von Neurath, the foreign minister. Instead, he made frequent flights on his assigned official plane to Berlin, where he paid obeisance to Adolf Hitler. London's wags called him Germany's "part-time" ambassador. He committed unending faux pas while trying to ingratiate himself with the London circle of Germanophile King Edward VIII, who would soon abdicate for the love of his American divorcée paramour. Poison-tongued members of London society soon nicknamed the German ambassador "Herr von Brickendrop."

He shook off his personal setbacks. His earlier negotiations with the British government over naval parity had bred his disrespect for them, and his total attention was focused on his master in Berlin. His dislike for the British would eventually return to haunt him and the whole world.

Before assuming his post in London, von Ribbentrop had invited a large number of prominent British visitors to the Olympic Games. They were most impressed, and "Chips" Channon, a famous London society gossip, even thought that the Nazi anthem, the "Horst Wessel Song," had "a nice lilt." The world seemed dazzled by Nazi achievements.

The very idea that this clumsy clique of unskilled Nazis could achieve such international acclaim and so many political triumphs must have infuriated Schacht. However, as the year opened, he was still sure of himself. His many barbs at the Nazis still remained unpunished, as did his frequent skirmishes with party officials. In October 1935 a New York political journal, *The Commonweal*, had speculated that Schacht would be forced to devalue the mark and that he was in imminent danger because of his opposition to Nazi ideology. "He may be ejected forcibly or [sic] it may even be a concentration camp, before many weeks have passed."[211] But as 1936 continued, Schacht still seemed an

---

211. *The Commonweal* (September 18, 1935), p. 610.

unlikely target for destruction. He was widely quoted among Berlin insiders as having told Hitler, "You need me and you'll continue to need me for two or three years. After that, you can shoot me if you want to, but you can't shoot me yet!" Headlines all over the West's financial pages said, as did the one of February 23, 1936, in the *New York Times,* that Schacht was winning the export battle (AT GREAT COST GERMANY HAS TURNED TRADE DEFICIT INTO BIG SURPLUS BY MEANS OF SCHACHT'S "NEW PLAN").

But like so many others, he had misjudged. Hitler was indeed fed up with Schacht but had no intention of eliminating him. Schacht was much too valuable, and his reputation abroad seemed undiminished in spite of his years of outrageous international machinations. Perhaps to establish some perspective, Hitler began to apply certain measures limiting his sharp-tongued economics minister's displays of self-importance and opposition.

From *Newsweek,* May 9, 1936:

> Dr. Hjalmar Horace Greeley Schacht slammed his hiking clothes into a suitcase last week and rushed back to Berlin from a Bavarian holiday. Reason: Adolf Hitler had given the Assistant Nazi-in-Chief, Air Minister Goering, absolute control over raw material imports and foreign exchange. Since this cut away much of his power, the disgruntled Economic Minister handed in his resignation. The Fuehrer handed it back — and reminded the doctor that Adolf Hitler is Germany. Four days later the Chancellor soothed his money expert with a three-hour interview and a luncheon.[212]

The true reasons for the sudden withdrawal of Schacht's responsibility for foreign currency were obscure. Schacht claimed that he was tired of seeing the party ignore the nation's laws by dealing in foreign currency. He had discovered that bundles of marks were sold abroad by the party at large discounts and that the foreign currency was then used for Goebbels's propaganda. He suggested to Hitler that Göring could "shoulder the responsi-

---

212. *Newsweek* (May 9, 1936), p. 20.

bility" for dealing in foreign currency.[213] Actually, there was more than currency concern to his disagreements with the party activists, led by archenemy Wilhelm Keppler, the man whom he had helped in the early days of Hitler's rule and then summarily banned from the Economics Ministry. Keppler's wing of party radicals wanted to devalue the mark, increase taxes, and postpone a balanced budget.

Göring happily assumed the burden and, according to Schacht, used it as the stirrup for swinging himself into the saddle of power, a curious metaphor, considering Göring's girth. Nevertheless, upon hearing the news of the shift in responsibilities, the Berlin stock market took a tumble and foreign newspapers wrote about the end of Schacht as a powerful factor when dealing with Germany, also implying the end of a voice for moderation.

Hitler's May 1 speech in Berlin at the annual parade for the Day of German Labor included a lengthy passage that, according to Frederick Birchall of the *New York Times,* went over the head of the audience. It was aimed straight at Schacht, reminding him that even if a man "is a genius, he cannot succeed unless he makes millions [of people], consciously or unconsciously, into his followers."

Later in the same speech Hitler said:

> Lies are spread that tomorrow or the day after Germany will invade Austria or Czechoslovakia. I ask myself who are these elements [which have spread these lies]? Who are the elements which want no quiet, no peace, which constantly agitate and throw suspicion, which want no understanding?

The well-trained crowd automatically yelled back, "The Jews!" although the actual required answer was "the Bolsheviks."[214]

Only a week before Hitler's protestations about Czechoslovakia, a New York headline declared that Konrad Henlein, leader of

213. Schacht, *76 Jahre meines Lebens,* p. 464.
214. *New York Times* (May 2, 1936), p. 3:1.

the Sudeten German population of Czechoslovakia, had denied that his movement had any ties with Hitler. He discouraged any talk that Hitler would invade and "bring a German paradise." He lamented that the German minority in Czechoslovakia was being mistreated and in distress, a claim that G. E. R. Geyde, correspondent for the *New York Times,* found later "to be very real."[215]

While teaching Schacht a lesson, Hitler kept him available because he could not afford to lose a powerful salesman for German industry. In one of the famous luncheon conversations recorded later by his Boswell, Henry Picker, Hitler proclaimed how much he had admired Schacht for deducting half a billion in interest for the Reichsbank from the German government before handing out 8 billion for armaments. "You know," he said, "Schacht was very good at *bescheissen* [screwing people]."[216]

In June 1936 Schacht was in Belgrade to calm angry creditors and to resume the flow of grain needed by Germany. On the same trip, he sold arms to Bulgaria, to settle money Italy owed the Bulgarians. In return, Italy was about to become Germany's debtor, a state of affairs not unwelcome to Hitler, who was anxious to gain some leverage over his fellow dictator. Mussolini still thought of himself as the protector of the Balkans. He also kept a proprietary eye on Austria. Schacht went on to Hungary, which was becoming leery of its very deep trading involvement with Germany. He tried to reassure the Budapest government and bankers. By July Schacht was in Greece, where he landed a $13.5 million order for armaments from dictator General Ioannis Metaxas. In August he took Krupp's sales agents to Bulgaria and Turkey to arrange barter transactions.[217] Taking full advantage of the League of Nations' sanctions against Italy over its invasion of Ethiopia, Schacht quickly grabbed the Italians' market in the Balkans.[218] Schacht was playing with empty pockets. An apoc-

215. *New York Times* (April 25, 1936), p. 9:1.
216. Picker, *Hitler's Tischgespräche,* p. 233.
217. *Great Britain and the East* (August 27, 1936), p. 296.
218. *The Fortnightly* 383 (June), pp. 432–34.

ryphal story was told about a conversation between Schacht and a leading American banker.

"Dr. Schacht," said the American, "you really ought to come to New York. We've got lots of money. That's real banking."

Schacht answered, "No. Come to Berlin. We have no money at all. *That's* real banking!"

Late in August Hitler doubled the time of compulsory military service, and Schacht paid a call on the Jewish premier of France, Léon Blum. The result of that meeting was a curious game of camouflage. André François-Poncet, the suave French ambassador to Berlin, was invited to the German Foreign Office and informed by Foreign Minister Konstantin von Neurath that Germany would join the Western powers in not sending arms to Spain. While Hitler sent no arms, his volunteer *Condor* Legion of fifteen thousand German Luftwaffe men and their planes provided transport for Franco's troops. The following year, in supposed retribution for a Spanish government air attack on a German ship, *Condor* planes bombed the Spanish town of Guernica.

Despite his invaluable work as a trade emissary, Schacht was dealt another blow to his vanity and powers a few days before the 1936 Nuremberg party rally, which was scheduled for September. Hitler informed Schacht from his Berghof retreat that a brand-new economic program would be introduced at Nuremberg, but he refused to tell Schacht any details. Schacht immediately contacted War Minister von Blomberg, recently promoted to field marshal by Hitler, and expressed his fears that the party radicals had taken over. Blomberg listened to Schacht's complaints and said, "I am sure you are right, but I believe that the Führer will certainly straighten things out."

Schacht bid him good-bye with a cynical "May God preserve your capacity for belief!"[219]

The other shoe fell with a painful thud. At the Nuremberg party rally, from the podium under the vast, wreathed stucco swastika, high above the assembled uniformed mass formations,

219. Schacht, *76 Jahre meines Lebens*, p. 465.

Hitler declared a new Four-Year Plan, to be administered by Hermann Göring. Göring's task was to make Germany independent of all foreign imports by launching a program of autarky. To achieve this euphoric idealized state of self-sufficiency, the new administrator of Germany's Four-Year Plan would create fuel, textiles, rubber, and other industrial necessities through new technology. He would reactivate certain long-abandoned mineral and coal mines inside the Reich's borders. The official order launching this autarkic enterprise followed on October 18, 1936. It was everything Schacht had deplored earlier. He had warned in a memo on May 27 that any artificially created *Ersatz* raw materials must never be priced above the world market. Schacht also pointed out that autarky created a state of mental isolation.[220]

Germany's *Ersatz* period had begun. Autarky flew in the face of Schacht's hopes for Germany as one of the world's great trading nations. Obviously, his way was too slow and cumbersome for Adolf Hitler.

---

220. Simpson, *Schacht in Perspective*, p. 129.

15

THE OUTSIDER

Göring's four-year plan seemed to illustrate opposing fundamental views held by Hitler and by Schacht. Hitler needed the threat of armed German might for his ambitious plans, while Schacht declared expensive rearmament necessary to return the nation to international equality. It could be scaled back as Germany returned to economic health. Whereas Hitler wished every ounce of attention and energy to be devoted to armaments (to the exclusion of most other products), Schacht believed that the only purpose of industry was profit and the collection of taxes through the sale of products. He distrusted a long period of armament production because it brought neither tax revenue nor sales.

Hitler had his timetable, and his minister of economics was beginning to create obstacles that could no longer be tolerated. Still, Hitler decided to wait. The talented curmudgeon at the Ministry of Economics had shown too much salesmanship and influence abroad to be discarded yet.

On October 28, in front of a massive audience at the Sportspalast, Berlin's Madison Square Garden, Göring shouted, "Germany's men of science, go to work on autarky!"

On December 17, 1936, he told some major industrialists, "I don't care how costly the production, just produce!" and "I don't care how illegal it is to get foreign currency. Just get it! I'll justify the illegality."[221]

This triggered a series of combative exchanges between Göring, the new economic czar, and Schacht, the old one. Industry was on Schacht's side when it came to autarky. The high cost of artificial raw materials would raise prices to such an extent that products would be uncompetitive in the world marketplace. However, neither Hitler nor Göring focused on production for international export. They needed planes, tanks, and guns for a different agenda.

Meanwhile, Schacht had to stem a wave of demands to devalue the mark from the same industrialists who resisted autarky. Schacht was obdurate. He wished to maintain the official value of the mark, even though it was only fictitious. Everyone abroad could buy the mark at bargain prices.

To bolster his new fiefdom as head of the Four-Year Plan, Göring quickly constructed a large bureaucratic machine of several hundred officials, who were assigned dozens of special categories of *Ersatz* products. In December he swore in twenty-four military economics "expeditors." His most immediate aide was Colonel Georg Thomas, an army economist who would become a key player in the year to come. Although Thomas was in favor of autarky, he supported Schacht's stiff-necked opposition to party radicals who wanted to nationalize and socialize German industry and to dismantle all traces of entrepreneurship. They aimed at the end of the profit motive. After all, they were still the *National Socialist* German *Labor* Party, with all the hidden bolshevization that implied.

Thomas had become a proponent of a Nazi-invented cult described as *Wehrwirtschaft,* or "war economics," to which Schacht had originally been assigned as a plenipotentiary. It was more a frame of mind than an actual economic program. Each German was supposed to think in daily terms of building the country's

---

221. Schacht, *Abrechnung mit Hitler,* p. 66.

armed might. The German *Staatsbürger* was to act, breathe, and dream rearmament. It was a vague term and mainly propagandistic, but Colonel Thomas saw it as the very soul of German rearmament. Eventually, he and two other colonels, all three economists for the army, were promoted to major generals by Göring and formed the *Wehrwirtschaftsrat,* or Council for Armaments Economics. [222]

Schacht was courageous but not foolhardy. It became clear to him that the time had come to curb his assault on the party. According to Berlin's political pundits, Schacht's new discretion explained his new approach:

> *Martin Luther sagte was er geglaubt hat,*
> *Hitler glaubt was er sagt,*
> *Goebbels glaubt nie was er sagt,*
> *Schacht sagt nicht was er glaubt.*

> Martin Luther said what he believed,
> Hitler believes what he says,
> Goebbels does not believe what he says,
> Schacht does not say what he believes.

He was skating on ever thinning ice, which must have caused some problems with Luise. In his memoirs, Schacht spoke of an increasing estrangement. He hinted rather pointedly that he and Luise Schacht, who was not a well woman, spent the last years of their marriage in separation. Her increasing infatuation with Adolf Hitler and his cause seemed to differ sharply with her husband's increasing disgust. Schacht was never disillusioned with Hitler, as he had no illusions. From the beginning he valued the man's boundless determination and his ability to gather support from the populace. But he was no admirer. He accepted Hitler as a powerful ally for some of his own national aims:

The discarding of the Versailles Dictate.
The return of Germany as a powerful factor among nations.

222. Mühlen, *Schacht*, p. 204.

The return of a Germanistic morality, based on Christianity.
The battle against Communism in all its manifestations.

Eventually, Schacht found Hitler naive and simplistic, surrounded by an army of despicable Nazi Party paladins.

He thought the anti-Semitic part of the Nazi program to be counterproductive and downright harmful to Germany, and he detested the extralegal excesses and brutalities of the Nazis. Still, he was quite willing to accept the exclusion of Germany's Jews from all opinion-shaping activities. He wished to see them treated as honored strangers in the midst of the German *Volksgemeinschaft* (national community). He would no more allow a Jewish associate or friend to be mistreated by the Nazis than he would have allowed a foreign friend to be arrested arbitrarily. But he saw Jews as a foreign element with a different cultural heritage, even though he readily acknowledged their worth to Germany as soldiers, bankers, and industrialists.

Apparently, Luise shared none of his reservations about Adolf Hitler and his circle. Schacht blamed her stolid background for her unwillingness to see the dark side of National Socialism. They were no longer a team.

A very different picture emerges from the memoirs of Martha Dodd, daughter of the American ambassador to Germany, William E. Dodd, who saw a great deal of the Schachts. Schacht was at the American embassy so frequently that Mrs. Dodd, the embassy's hostess, had learned not to worry if a dinner guest had to cancel at the last minute. "We can always count on Dr. Schacht."

Martha Dodd's description of Luise, who was then a towering middle-aged woman, differs from the austere picture frequently painted by her husband.

"Frau Schacht was witty and delightful, with a big swastika pendant among her enormous breasts [sic] a huge, simple, motherly type, with sparkling eyes, a comic counterpart to her lean, owl-like husband, over whom she kept vigilant watch. She took the role of mother, embracing both her husband and her family."

Martha Dodd had a talent for biographical sketches. Her description of the ever present Dr. Schacht, the constant guest at the embassy: "A tall, sinewy, wiry [man], an ugly clown mask of a face, curiously alive and attractive, resembling somewhat the bald, tough shrewdness of an old eagle, celebrated far and wide for his wit."

She described Schacht as "a show in itself." He became "one of the intellectual shows of the embassy," known for his "cutting and devastating humor and his sarcastic poems in guest books." [223] Schacht obviously stayed close to the American embassy because he considered America to be the key player in the game of international economics, and William Dodd, though amused, was under no illusions about the tall minister's attentiveness. His daughter warned against thinking of him as anti-Nazi. He "is very helpful to the Nazis."

The battle with Göring and his Four-Year Plan continued. After a speech by newly promoted Field Marshal Göring on December 17, 1936, in which he told German business leaders that he failed to see any reason to punish someone for bringing illegal foreign currency into the country and assured his audience that it was more important to have full production than to make profits, Schacht responded. On the occasion of his sixtieth birthday on January 22, 1937, in a speech to the same audience, now assembled to pay him tribute, Schacht hit back at Göring. Without mentioning the field marshal's name, Schacht threatened prison for anyone breaking the currency laws and called anyone manufacturing goods without wishing to make profits harmful to Germany. A few days later Göring confronted him, saying, "You were extremely critical of me and contradicted my ideas." Schacht replied, "And I shall contradict them even more harshly if you persist!"

He finally sent a long letter of economic explanation to Göring and directed a copy to Adolf Hitler. The letter to Göring ended with "I have been telling you for months to add the portfolio of Minister of Economics to your other responsibilities, since I disagree with your policy on foreign currency and cannot

223. Martha Dodd, *Through Embassy Eyes*, pp. 234–40.

allow myself to share your decisions." This virtual resignation caused the Führer a substantial dilemma. In a dictatorship one cannot just quit an office.

In a report from Berlin, Schacht was described at sixty as "having the appearance of a lean, slightly stooped schoolmaster. His stand-up collars are inches too high. His hair is sandy and sparse, and carefully brushed back to conceal a bald spot. Nazi colleagues, with whom he is constantly at war, dislike and distrust him, take no pleasure in his clammy handshake."[224]

On the last day of January, to emphasize their position as employees of the state, Hitler decided to decorate several of his top cabinet members with the Golden Party Badge, an award of extreme importance in the Third Reich. It looked like any of the small enameled party badges but was surrounded by a gold wreath. On the list were several men who were not party members, among them Schacht and Minister of Transport Paul von Eltz-Rübenach. Von Eltz-Rübenach decided to retire rather than accept the badge. Schacht kept his, which came to haunt him later. It seemed to signify his entry into the party, but he never actually joined. When Ambassador Dodd's wife and daughter saw him wearing the new insignia and congratulated him, he "just rolled up his eyes," according to Martha Dodd. Still, Schacht admitted that it made things easier for him in everyday life. Men with the Golden Party Badge were treated with great deference and courtesy and could find good theater seats or tables in crowded hotel dining rooms when others had to stand in line. Oskar Schindler eventually used his to save Jewish lives, because most SS authorities were impressed.

Meanwhile, Hitler used 1937 to execute plans that had been delayed by the propagandistic Olympics in 1936.

Anti-Semitic laws were extended and became even harsher. Chicanery followed chicanery, and the Gestapo ruled. There was an end to the careful treatment of the Catholic clergy. On January 22 Germany's Catholic bishops issued a Pastoral Letter, com-

224. *Literary Digest* (February 27, 1937), p. 36.

plaining of party interference with the conduct of church affairs. It was only the beginning. Fourier's definitive *Lexikon der Päpste* estimates that four thousand priests, mostly German, were murdered by the Nazis.[225]

Rearmament boomed, and Göring's Luftwaffe had a chance to test its mettle in Spain. German airmen were rotated frequently to give the greatest number possible a chance to bomb, shoot, and fly in combat, although Schacht claimed that he collaborated with the army's generals to block a full-scale expeditionary force.[226]

Schacht was sent on two new missions for his complicated master. The first was to Brussels in an attempt to create strong economic bonds with tiny Belgium. Hitler suddenly decided that Belgium would be a perfect platform for all sorts of political initiatives — a place like Switzerland, to be kept protected and neutral. Although he reported a friendly reception and lengthy, pleasant conversations with the king, Schacht met with resistance from the Belgians.

The other task was to open the German Pavilion at the World's Fair in Paris at the end of May 1937. Schacht was there in loco Hitler and used the occasion to chide the press for "not being helpful." He explained that he had much to discuss with the premier of France, Léon Blum, and that "if you fellows" would only let them, they could "do things to help the world's economy."[227] Since Blum was Jewish, one could not blame the press for being cynical.

He was also singled out as uniquely qualified for other international duties. When Thomas J. Watson, president of IBM and head of the International Chamber of Commerce, was decorated by Adolf Hitler with the Order of the German Eagle, Schacht was asked to make the presentation. Watson was the first American to receive the Nazi-invented decoration, which was awarded to foreigners only. The same award was later bestowed on Henry Ford and Charles Lindbergh, though it was given to Lindbergh as a

225. Werner Classen, *Fourier*, p. 379.
226. *New York Times* (January 17, 1937), p. 33:2.
227. *New York Times* (May 26, 1937), p. 12:4.

surprise by Göring during a luncheon at the American embassy. The surprise later cost Lindbergh dearly.

After many forced appearances at various police precincts, on July 1, the same day Watson received his decoration, Pastor Martin Niemöller was finally arrested by the Gestapo. It must have been a harsh signal for his parishioners, including Schacht.

Schacht spoke again on July 8 at the ceremony celebrating the completion of the roof of the vast new Reichsbank building. He compared the slow but solid construction of the edifice with "the building up of the National Socialist Party." He had laid the cornerstone in May 1934.[228] "We are all working on the same building of a master builder."[229]

In 1937 Hjalmar Schacht also lost his indomitable Danish mother, the young aristocrat who had once followed her love across the ocean. She died in Berlin, ever the American, ever the democrat, one of Schacht's anchors to the world of his boyhood. They often spoke Danish with each other. He went to Italy for a few days and was spotted by reporters in Genoa on September 16. The Associated Press was startled that there were none of his usual meetings, no conferences. He was mourning his loss.[230]

On October 6, 1937, Schacht was bid to Hitler's Berghof in the mountains of Bavaria for a long discussion. Schacht was probably unaware that back in September 1936, before Hitler declared the Four-Year Plan and designated Göring's place in it, Hitler had written a confidential memo about Schacht's future role. It was circulated to a very few intimates. Schacht never learned the actual details until much later, but he heard occasional bits and pieces from Göring.

Part of the memo was an obvious reference to Schacht's disdain for autarchy, its vast cost and inefficiency.

1. Production methods are none of the Economics Minister's business.

228. *New York Times* (July 9, 1937), p. 12:3.
229. Mühlen, *Schacht*, p. 182.
230. AP (September 16, 1937).

2. The Economics Minister has no business limiting the purchase of raw materials, and thereby hampering rearmament.

3. The Economics Minister has no business stating that Germany's smelting industry is antiquated.

At the mountain retreat Hitler urged Schacht "to make every effort to get along with Göring. I cannot afford to lose you." When Schacht expressed his doubts, Hitler heaped praise on him and flattered and reassured him. Schacht remained unconvinced. Finally came the bizarre moment when, as Schacht described it, Hitler, with tears in his eyes, protested, *"Aber Schacht, ich liebe Sie doch."* ("But Schacht, don't you realize how fond I am of you?")[231]

Schacht was unyielding. Even Hitler's unusual expression of personal devotion had failed to change his view. Schacht tried once again to drive home his points in a lengthy letter dated October 8, two days after the Berghof meeting. As a gesture of conciliation, he even used the unaccustomed and Nazified *"Mein Führer!"* instead of his usual *"Herr* Chancellor!"

He wrote that only one man could run the economy of the nation and that it was impossible to do so with interference from the party and from Göring. He pointed out that he had taken official leave since September 5 and had not been at his desk. He asked to be released from his post as minister beginning November 5, exactly two months after his departure from his regular daily duties at the ministry.

He ended his letter by quoting a popular verse he claimed was making the rounds in Berlin:

> *Gebt mir, sprach Göring, vier Jahre Zeit*
> *Bis ich die Wirtschaft vom Gelde befreit.*
> *Ich lasse den Schacht Euch als Bürgen,*
> *Ihn möcht Ihr, entrinn ich, erwürgen.*

> Said Göring, in four years I will have proved,
> Economics can work with all money removed.

---

231. Schacht, *76 Jahre meines Lebens*, p. 471.

As hostage I'll leave you Schacht. You can poke
 him,
and, if I'm not there, well then you can choke
 him!

Schacht finished his letter with "Since I am personally not inclined to accept this fate, I remain, my Führer, as always, your still
devoted . . ."

To satisfy Hitler's request, he had one final meeting with
Göring on November 1. After a total stalemate, Göring protested,
"But surely I should be able to give you my instructions?"

Schacht replied, "Not me, but my successor."

Their next meeting would be as fellow prisoners at the Nuremberg war-crimes trials, when they were led to a bathroom with two
tubs, and Schacht commented, *"Sic transit gloria mundi!"*

On November 26, 1937, Schacht was finally released from his
post as minister of economics and plenipotentiary for the war
economy. At Hitler's insistence, he accepted the meaningless title
and task of minister without portfolio, supposedly in order to remain at the disposal of the head of government for advice and
guidance. It was a sham. Hitler was not yet ready to announce the
dismissal of a man of Schacht's international reputation.

Schacht could not have known that on November 5, his
Janus-headed chief had held a very secret meeting with a select
group of top people, from which he was excluded. Assembled in
the Führer's elaborate private office at the Chancellery were
Göring, Foreign Minister von Neurath, General von Blomberg,
and the commanders of the army and navy, General Werner von
Fritsch and Admiral Erich Raeder. The meeting was recorded by
Colonel Friedrich Hossbach, Hitler's army aide, and it became famous later as the *Hossbach Protokoll,* the Hossbach Memorandum. It played a vital role in Nuremberg during the war-crimes
trials because it tended to prove conclusively that there was a
conspiracy to wage war, one of the causes for indictment.

At the secret meeting, Hitler informed those in attendance
that sometime before 1943, when Germany's armament advan-

tage over other countries might have shrunk, an invasion of Czechoslovakia had to be risked to protect Germany's flank, and then a German military attack mounted toward the east, probably in alliance with Mussolini. It was the plan he had outlined much earlier in *Mein Kampf,* and it dealt with his theory of needed *Lebensraum,* or "living space."

Von Neurath, the foreign minister, later claimed he was deeply shaken. Von Blomberg, von Fritsch, and Raeder objected on military grounds. They would all soon regret their opposition.

Meanwhile, Göring became the temporary minister of economics. When he entered Schacht's old office, he was quoted as asking, "How can anyone have big ideas in such a small office?" He then called Schacht and told him gleefully that "I am now sitting in your chair." Schacht hung up and thought, "Don't fall off!"[232]

On November 24 Hitler made his choice for a permanent minister to replace Schacht. The man he appointed was Walther Funk, the financial journalist Schacht had sent to Hitler in 1931 to teach him the rudiments of economics. Hitler must have remembered the lessons. He saw Funk at the opera one night and appointed him to the ministry during intermission.[233] Funk was presented as the new minister at one of Hitler's rubber-stamp cabinet meetings on February 4, 1938. A complaisant man and easy to deal with, he left his job as *Reichs Pressechef* and chief of staff in Goebbels's Propaganda Ministry. This was the last cabinet meeting of Hitler's regime.

Schacht remained in place as president of the Reichsbank.

At a Berlin cocktail party, sometime before the official announcements, a *Time* correspondent asked Schacht about all the rumors.

"What rumors?"

"Well, many of your countrymen say you are resigning."

232. Ibid., p. 474.
233. Fest, *Hitler,* p. 543.

"If they say that, it is right," barked Hjalmar Schacht. "I have resigned. It may be announced officially today or tomorrow. I have not been at my office at the Ministry since August 11."

"Are you resigning as president of the Reichsbank, too?"

"Not yet!" snapped Dr. Schacht.

Time punned that "Der Führer has fired the Schacht heard 'round the world."[234]

His resignation from the post of minister of economics and its disturbing implications and possible consequences completely dominated the international press news coverage of Germany. Among other things, a visible increase in German anti-Jewish activity was immediately blamed on his departure. An Associated Press story later that year from Berlin concluded that "the policy of Dr. Hjalmar Schacht, sponsor of the slogan 'Leave the Jew undisturbed in his economic life,' has been abandoned since his resignation as Minister of Economics was accepted."[235]

President von Hindenburg had appointed Schacht as president of the Reichsbank for four years, beginning in 1933. Originally, the Reichsbank presidency had been for life, but Schacht had felt even in Weimar days that this was dangerous; and the term was changed to four years. When Hitler wished to renew Schacht's presidency in 1937 for another four years, Schacht insisted that the renewal had to be accompanied by the Führer's assurance that all bonds in Mefo, Schacht's razzle-dazzle stopgap invention, would be paid off in 1938, as originally agreed. According to Schacht, he was already reluctant to trust Hitler, having "learned the unreliability and untruthfulness" of the man.[236] Schacht therefore advised Chancellery Chief of Staff Hans Lammers that he would resign the presidency after one year if Mefo bonds were not retired by 1938. He saw no sense in paying interest on bonds in a shell corporation that was no longer needed. Besides, Hitler's reappointment was accompanied by a request-

234. *Time* (November 8, 1937), p. 23.
235. AP (December 30, 1937).
236. Schacht, *76 Jahre meines Lebens*, p. 457.

demand for an extra 3 billion marks of Reichsbank credit for the military, which would have complicated the retirement of Mefo bonds.

Hitler gave in, and Mefo bonds were finally retired. Schacht then granted the request for the 3 billion, with the proviso that this would be the last military credit. Later in 1938, after Schacht was no longer in the ministry, the government floated two enormous national loans and tried for a third with little success. The banks underwriting these loans got stuck with 500 million marks, or about a third of the final offering. As Schacht pointed out, the day of financing armaments through bond issues was over.

Göring's measures took forceful hold. Armament factories were working full speed ahead. Yet, although the original unemployment was down by 5 million to 1 million, the standard of living had not risen. Twenty-five percent of all Germans were on *Winterhilfe,* the social assistance program instituted by the party to provide food, clothing, medical care, and fuel for the needy. Germans lived an *Ersatz* life, with hard-to-get and expensive artificial gasoline, scratchy synthetic wool, and inelastic artificial rubber. Foodstuffs, particularly butter, margarine, and shortening, were in short supply; the government had initiated the national custom of eating *Eintopf Gerichte,* so-called one-pot meals of various fat-free vegetarian stews. To show the populace that everyone participated, there were newspaper photos of Adolf Hitler and his paladins dining on *Eintopf Gerichte.*

Henry Luce's *Fortune* magazine published an article about the curious phenomenon of Hitler's Germans. Their lot had not improved markedly, but they seemed satisfied nevertheless: "Strange fact that a sausage-loving nation can be reasonably placid eating sausage made by stuffing fish into ersatz casings."

Obviously unaware that Schacht's influence was waning, *Fortune's* editors saw Schacht "reaching the bottom layer of his hat full of white rabbits." Their cynical conclusion was that "National Socialism, in the final analysis, exists as compensation for the great German inferiority complex; it is a Teuton prescription for healing the wounds of the Versailles Treaty."

16

ALONE

BY THE BEGINNING of 1938, Hitler had made his decision. He was quite prepared to go to war, and until then, he would accept all the diplomatic blood-free victories he could gain by bluff and by threat. His readiness to risk a fight influenced his opponents. The French and the British were not cowards, but it had been only a short twenty years since the brutal World War and the enormous loss of their finest young men.

Many chroniclers agree that in 1938 the average German was equally reluctant to face a bloody war, a fact that eventually infuriated their martial Führer. When he was ready to sound the trumpet later in 1938, he came to the angry conclusion that his Germans were not ready. Many witnesses attest that when he ordered an elite new armored unit from nearby Potsdam to parade through the center of old Berlin, the man in the street showed little enthusiasm. Hitler, who viewed the parade from a Chancellery window, noted the apathy and occasional aversion displayed by the Berliners. It infuriated him.

But in early 1938 he had not yet faced the need for war and there were other obstacles to be removed. To take full charge of Germany, he needed absolute control over its foreign policy and its military strategy and to rid himself of the deadweight inheritance of the von Hindenburg days.

He would never be able to carry out his mercurial and threatening foreign ploys unless he removed Foreign Minister Konstantin von Neurath. Von Neurath still tried to practice the external ritual of old-time diplomacy, a kind of noblesse oblige to camouflage the crude new Germany. Many of his Foreign Service officers were members of Germany's old nobility. Von Neurath, a tall, corpulent southern aristocrat, was an opportunist. He was quite willing to accept the rewards and trappings of high office and to play along with the party, including its anti-Semitic laws. But when foreign policy was involved, he preferred to avoid confrontation, and whenever his Führer demanded decisive action, von Neurath usually stalled and waffled.

Control of the military was even more important.

Hitler was now the master of Germany and had demonstrated his superior judgment from the Rhineland to Austria. He no longer felt abject respect for the generals and their grand seigneur attitudes. Once they were the objects of his reverence; now they had become his subordinates.

At the head of the military stood War Minister and Field Marshal Werner von Blomberg, another inheritance from von Hindenburg. Hitler's bowing and scraping Day of Potsdam lay far behind. He had discovered new and younger military men like Erwin Rommel and Friedrich Paulus, dedicated professionals without family titles. They could be politicized but also had great tactical and strategic talent. These young officers became *his* generals. He still used the elder fellows where they could have some prestigious impact.

Von Blomberg was sent to London to lead a small German military contingent during the lavish international military parade for the coronation of George VI in May 1937. Reinhard Spitzy, an aide to von Ribbentrop who was there to watch the festivities, described the impact of the field marshal and his men, all in field gray and wearing their characteristic World War I steel helmets. In the breathless present tense that was fashionable in Germany, he called them "tall men, walking with dignity, spurs clinking and a slight rattling of sabers, their uniforms decorated only with world war medals." They were a sobering contrast to the peacock-parade uniforms of other nations. The group in field gray was a cold and ruthless reminder of Germany's new military might. The raucous crowds along the parade route suddenly fell silent. Certainly, von Blomberg had been useful in this and many other ways. It was von Blomberg whom Hitler usually delegated to approach Schacht with requests for more credit for armaments.

Yet, these elder military men had expressed their doubts about Hitler's every plan, from the occupation of the Rhineland to a full-scale expeditionary force for Franco. Even the key ideas Hitler had outlined in the *Hossbach Protokoll* met with their opposition. True, von Blomberg had helped plan the details of the Rhineland action, but he did so with marked reluctance and was rewarded with a marshal's baton for his cooperation. Hitler learned quickly that generals were not above bribery, subtle or otherwise. His confidential talk with von Hindenburg's son at the von Ribbentrop villa during those last days before becoming chancellor had even thrown some doubt on the integrity of the lofty old field marshal, that icon of Prussian respectability. Like an emperor of old, Hitler kept rewarding his military leaders with promotions, land, and cash until the final collapse. But he had also discovered that they were not indispensable and that he could always find talented young replacements.

Von Blomberg was the first target. At a youthful sixty, the field marshal, a widower, was tall, handsome, and somewhat of a ladies' man. On January 12, 1938, after a long period of bachelor-hood, he finally married the woman of his dreams, his secretary Eva Gruhn, a charming and attractive girl. Although she was of simple background and not really a suitable match for the titled bridegroom, everyone was delighted. Fräulein Gruhn had several previous affairs, and there was even talk that one of her lovers had been paid off by Göring to keep silent.[237] The Führer and Göring were in attendance for the military wedding, which was celebrated nationally as a romantic event.

Shortly thereafter, Gestapo records revealed that Eva Gruhn was a well-known call girl who had posed in the nude for several of her lovers. A Belgian military attaché was said to be in posses-

---

237. Author's interview with Reinhard Spitzy.

sion of such photos. Adolf Hitler gave an angry demonstration of affronted righteousness. To his disgust, he had been misled into blessing this alliance by his very presence at the ceremony. He spoke about von Blomberg's "besmirching of the noble German military spirit." He protested to high heaven that if this sort of thing could happen with a Prussian general, whom could one trust?

He summoned the field marshal and informed him that "our ways must part."

Von Blomberg shrugged his shoulders and retired in comfort with his new beloved. He was lucky.

General Werner von Fritsch, chief of staff of the army, was the next victim of a blow struck at Prussia's military nobility. Von Fritsch was tackled in a more ruthless way and sustained more damage. He was accused of soliciting a male prostitute on a suburban railroad platform near Berlin. His accuser was a blackmailer who was serving time in jail. Once more, Göring became the conduit, since the Gestapo dossier landed on his desk. On the way to Hitler's presence in the Chancellery, Colonel Hossbach, who had been ordered to escort von Fritsch, warned the chief of staff of what lay ahead. Hossbach, who was still Hitler's army aide, was then censured and reassigned.

Von Fritsch, a rational man, did not shout his disgust or break his sword over his knee and throw it at his faithless master's feet, which was probably a mistake. Hitler dismissed him at once instead of waiting for the eventual findings of a military court of honor, which later acquitted him. The case dragged on and finally collapsed as a proved case of mistaken identity. Von Fritsch's career lay in ruins, but it was too late for redress. News of his acquittal was drowned out by the rush of international events that followed.

Schacht learned the details of the stage-managing that preceded the von Blomberg–von Fritsch dismissals from Count Helldorf, the Berlin police commissioner. Von Helldorf, a black sheep aristocrat, became an avid Nazi when Hitler became chancellor. He was a playboy and a gambler, and he thought that a pact with Göring and the Nazis would restore his fortunes. He was probably the only man who knew the true story of the Reichstag fire. By 1938 he was disillusioned, disgusted, and anxious to find rehabilitation by seeking connections with "better people" like Schacht.

Finally, Hitler was rid of the two top military men he had inherited. He promptly appointed himself commander in chief. Generals Walther von Brauchitsch and Wilhelm Keitel became his subordinates as army commander and army chief of staff. They were both malleable and complaisant men, and Hitler could count on them to do his bidding. Keitel became widely known among army cynics as *Lakeitel,* a German wordplay on *lackey.* Von Brauchitsch immediately moved into the Continental Hotel in Berlin to be at his new chief's beck and call.

The Foreign Ministry came next.

Next came the civilians. On February 2, 1938, Minister Konstantin von Neurath celebrated his sixty-fifth birthday, and his Führer came to congratulate him personally and to present him with a piece of medieval art. On the morning of February 4, the von Neuraths were at the official villa, packing for a short vacation at their estate in the south of Germany, when the foreign minister was asked by phone to meet with the Führer at 3 P.M. Somewhat annoyed at the interference with his plans, he walked to the nearby Chancellery and attended a long meeting on foreign policy with Hitler and von Ribbentrop. When it was over, von Neurath walked the few steps to the ministerial villa to begin his vacation. Once more the phone rang, asking him to return "for a few minutes" to the Chancellery. Hitler met him in the garden behind the building, linked his arm through von Neurath's as they strolled, and informed him that von Ribbentrop was the new foreign minister and that von Neurath was to become president of a special state advisory council that had just been formed. Hitler said, "This is my fondest wish."

The stunned von Neurath realized he had been dismissed. He returned to his villa to tell his wife, who was equally shocked. Not knowing what lay ahead, they canceled their trip. Two days later they were instructed to have their servants report to the von Ribbentrops' villa in Dahlem and were officially reminded that the silverware was government property. The von Ribbentrops also inquired about how soon the ministerial residence would be available.

Joachim von Ribbentrop, the new foreign minister, was the complete and willing servant of Adolf Hitler. He had served as the special and blunt emissary to the naval talks in London in 1935 and as the controversial and clumsy German ambassador in London. His tour of duty spanned the stormy time of Edward VIII's abdication and the coronation of George VI. He had spent much of his time among the British trying to impress London society and the ruling circles, acting out the role of a new style of emissary from the new Germany. He had assured his Führer that Britain's reactionaries toppled King Edward because of his sympathy for Germany and his wish to marry a commoner.

Hitler was outraged. He condemned Britain's snobbish aristocrats for objecting because the king wished to marry "a girl from the people."

When he was in London, von Ribbentrop, who was detested by the party faithful as an outsider and a rich man, was in constant fear of being backstabbed by political enemies in Berlin. Only a few weeks before his appointment to the ministry, von Ribbentrop feared that he had completely fallen out of favor. As usual, Hitler had thrown one of his paladins off balance, the better to control him, which he succeeded in doing.

Now Hitler had unchallenged command of the armed forces, the Foreign Ministry, and the Ministry of Economics. Schacht at the Reichsbank was the only remaining possible source of opposition. Like any country's reserve bank, the Reichsbank needed full independence from the government to create a healthy counterbalance. Its president had to be free to issue credit, set lending rates, and control currency values. Schacht knew that Hitler would have to demand immense sums of money to accelerate the production of armaments and to pay for Göring's costly, autarky-driven Four-Year Plan. Ahead lay an economy for waging war.

Hitler was taking wild gambles because he seemed to fear an early death and had to "flee forward." Whatever demons possessed him drove him and Germany onto a precipitous path, the conquest of foreign territory, beginning with Austria. As he saw it, his homeland was an inseparable part of Greater Germany. He was outraged by the very existence of an independent Austrian state. After all, he had left Austria because of his adoration, love, lust, for all things German and had fought in the losing war in a German regiment after refusing Austrian military service.

An exchange of state visits between Mussolini and the German Führer had strange results. Hitler was less than taken with the Fascist state and infuriated because he had to deal with the "decadent" Italian royal house while Mussolini took a secondary ceremonial place. By contrast, Mussolini was deeply impressed by the sparkling and dangerous new Germany. The Duce brought back many of the things he had learned in Berlin, including a set of anti-Semitic laws, installed by 1938, and the military goose step, renamed the *passo Romano*. He also hinted that he would no longer insist on the sanctity of Austrian independence. The Rome-Berlin Axis was now in full flower, and Hitler was free to indulge his appetite for conquest, bloodless or not.

Austria's chancellor Kurt von Schuschnigg was a lawyer-turned-politician, a reasonable and distinguished man. He faced the unpalatable choice of preparing to defend Austria militarily against its threatening neighbor or surrendering his country, which would then become a German province. As a final attempt to negotiate with Adolf Hitler, he agreed to enter the lion's den, the Führer's Berghof in Berchtesgaden, just across the mountainous border from Austria. The February 12, 1938, meeting between the German Führer, the son of a minor Austrian official, and the aristocratic Austrian chancellor was held in the stormy privacy of an upstairs room. Bullied and threatened, von Schuschnigg finally agreed to some of Hitler's demands, which included the appointment of a senior Austrian Nazi to his cabinet. He then left for Vienna. It was only a stopgap measure. After some thought, von Schuschnigg decided to ask the Austrian people to vote on whether they preferred to lose their independence. He announced a plebiscite, which outraged Hitler, who thought he had settled the matter in Berchtesgaden.

Meanwhile, as Germany's financial and economic needs increased, Hitler had no wish to unbalance the crucial area of commerce. On March 10 he renewed Hjalmar Schacht's appointment as Reichsbank president for another four years. Why did Schacht accept? Was it, as he claimed, that he had to be inside the Nazi machine to prevent disaster? Probably, as well as the chance to confound his enemies in the party.

On March 12, using a list of von Schuschnigg's "provocations," Hitler cast his die. Smiling and cheerful German troops crossed the border into a jubilant Austria. Then on March 15, from the Heldenplatz at the center of Vienna, Hitler triumphantly declared to thousands of his fellow Austrians that they were now part of the great German Reich. It was the *Anschluss*, the joining of Austria to Germany, which then became Germany's *Ostmark*, its "eastern province." Tens of thousands of Viennese cheered their new god.

Within days, Vienna's Jews faced open persecution, with special cruelties reserved for the upper strata. Lawyers, professors, and businessmen were forced to scrub old pre-*Anschluss* anti-Nazi graffiti from the pavement with toothbrushes, under the "supervision" of Austrian storm troopers. Vienna's substantial Orthodox Jewish community was treated with bestiality, while Vienna's street people were gleeful and abusive spectators.

A worried Schacht reserved judgment, but not for long. He eventually considered the *Anschluss* natural, inevitable, and constructive. It became his task to incorporate the Austrian reserve banking system into the Reichsbank's. Although the party was trying to portray the financial structure of Austria as slovenly and uncontrolled, Schacht found this to be quite untrue. He took command of the Nationalbank of Austria without discharging a single employee, except its head, a partly Jewish former minister of finance named Viktor Kienböck, who was retired with full pension and honors.[238]

Austria had substantial debts to Britain, France, Switzerland, Italy, Czechoslovakia, and the United States, on which Germany now refused to pay interest. Sir John Simon and Montagu Norman then negotiated a unilateral separate deal for Britain by lowering interest rates. Other angry creditors of Austria called both the German refusal to pay interest and the selfish British maneuver the "Schacht school of finance."

---

238. Schacht, *76 Jahre meines Lebens,* p. 488.

No sooner had Schacht initiated a smooth transition than he had to fight off an attempt by Hitler, who was listening to his old advisor Keppler, to revalue the Austrian schilling from half a German mark to two-thirds (66.33 pfennigs) in order to make the average Austrian feel richer. The obvious results would have been a derailing of the entire structure of the Austrian economy and a quick decrease of real income for the Austrian worker.

In an oblique reference to himself, Schacht said to Hitler, "Among your collaborators is one of the great experts on world currencies, and you wish to ignore his advice. How can you justify that?"

According to Schacht, Hitler replied in rather a lame fashion, "For political reasons."

Göring nationalized Austria's ore and coal mines and started digging new ones near Linz. Austria's industries were also brought into the armament business by their new government.

Later, in his usual blunt fashion, Schacht debunked the notion of Austria as a "victim of Hitler's aggression." In his memoirs he countered any and all politically convenient revisionism by writing that he "participated wholeheartedly in the enthusiastic happiness he encountered all over Austria."[239]

In Paris and London only the most complacent observers failed to show alarm. Anti-Jewish cruelties, Niemöller's arrest, the von Blomberg–von Fritsch–von Neurath dismissals, Germany's arrogant new foreign minister, its unknown new economics minister, and the enormity of the Anschluss all combined to cause fear and suspicion. It seemed increasingly likely that Hitler's string of bloodless victories would ultimately end with bloodshed. Germany was led by a frightening man who moved unaccountably and abruptly, and then followed each aggression with an offer of reconciliation and peace. Hjalmar Schacht, ever the internationalist, wondered how long the Western democratic world could allow itself to be bullied and bluffed. He put out the

239. Ibid., p. 490.

first feelers toward those in Germany who might help unseat the dangerous man in the Chancellery on the Wilhelmstrasse.

It was quite clear to him that he was part of a small minority. Had they known of his growing disillusionment with Adolf Hitler, most Germans would have disagreed radically. They worshiped the Führer. From Krupp to the janitor, they were enthusiastic about their seemingly infallible leader. For working-class and lower-middle-class citizens, there was even the pleasurable sense of personal superiority, brought on by their governmentally sponsored disdain for Jews, Slavs, Magyars, Poles, and other racially inferior creatures. How *herrlich*, how absolutely *wunderbar*, to be able to look down upon those who did not qualify as documented Aryan members of the German *Volksgemeinschaft*. They lived in joyous, delusive imitation of Wagnerian heroes and heroines — a populist nobility forged by a fervor for "steel and earth," of a blue-eyed, blond-haired, slim-skulled, eagle-nosed superrace. Even the intellectuals, academics, scientists, and artists devised many pages of rationale for what they should have known to be hogwash.

Schacht's views were tied to the conviction that Christianity was the basis for German culture, but he was also an internationalist and a pragmatist who admired many prominent Jews. Besides, it embarrassed him to associate with plebs, with cretins, with the semi-educated Nazi leadership, and he never bothered to hide his distaste. Above all, he was devastated that a man of his proven superiority could be discarded by Hitler, a creature he had helped launch and form.

Luise and he separated in 1938, which was fortunate because her admiration for Hitler continued. As he wrote: "My wife could have sent me to the gallows." They maintained some measure of mutual admiration and old friendship. They saw each other from time to time, until she eventually fell ill. He kept in dutiful touch with her and visited her in a hospital in the south of Germany shortly before her death in 1940. Despite his obvious attachment to her, his memoirs seem to convey a well-hidden sense of relief.[240]

240. Ibid., pp. 154–55.

Schacht continued as head of the Reichsbank. Early in May, while Hitler was on what would be his last state visit to Italy, Schacht paid his debt in return for Hitler's promise to retire the Mefo bonds. He helped float a gargantuan public loan of 1.6 billion marks, his final unhappy contribution to Hitler's martial plans. According to the press, subscriptions from the former Austria "exceeded all expectations."

He cabled his success to the Führer, who was suffering the cool Savoyan courtesies extended to him by the tiny Italian king, and quickly received a telegram of sincere thanks.

Hitler's message found some ready takers in the depression-ridden and paranoid Western world. In Britain and the United States, among other countries, various versions of National Socialism came into being. In America the anti-Semitic, anti-Roosevelt radio priest, Father Charles E. Coughlin, preached his own brand of fascism and isolationism to a wide home audience, as did another clergyman, Gerald L. K. Smith, a protégé of Henry Ford. The German-American Bund, led by former Ford worker Fritz Kuhn, opened its *Hauptquartier* at 178 East Eighty-fifth Street in Manhattan, and "Heil-Hitlering" ersatz storm troopers drilled at Camp Siegfried in Yaphank, Long Island, New York. In 1939 Kuhn was sent to Sing Sing prison in Ossining, New York, for misappropriating Bund funds. In Britain the aristocrat Sir Oswald Mosley formed the British Union of Fascists, complete with raised arm salutes, black shirts, and mass meetings.

Meanwhile, a tawdry display was taking place in Evian-les-Bains, the French spa, where the United States, through Assistant Secretary of State Sumner Welles, had convened an international conference to see what could be done about the problem of Jews who could not emigrate because of the restrictive quotas of many countries, including the United States, Britain, and France. German and Austrian Jews were desperate to leave the countries of their birth but were refused visas by country after country.

At Evian delegates from thirty-two nations assembled between July 6 and 14, 1938, but the conference was a failure. The participating international delegates dared not recommend to their own governments that the drawbridges to their countries be lowered. Most Western democracies were in the midst of serious economic depression, and their ruling politicians lacked the stomach to confront the labor unions or the political opposition. Why allow a flow of immigrants when there were not enough jobs to go around? Like other national leaderships, the Roosevelt administration was unwilling to face American labor unions, reactionary conservatives, and isolationists. There were also old prejudices afoot. When William E. Dodd was about to move to Berlin in 1933 as U.S. ambassador, he was told by Roosevelt's closest advisor, Colonel Ed House, at Beverly Farms near Boston, "You should try to ameliorate Jewish sufferings. They are clearly wrong and terrible; but the Jews should not be allowed to dominate the economic and intellectual life in Berlin as they have done for a long time."[241]

That summer of 1938, according to testimony at the Nuremberg trials, at a dinner given by the Schniewind family in Berlin, Schacht turned to his table partner and said, *"Gnädige Frau, wir sind Verbrechern in die Hände gefallen, wie hätte ich das ahnen können?"* ("Madam, how could I have known that we have fallen into the hands of criminals?")[242]

With Austria in his hands, Hitler continued his insatiable march forward. The sacking of Czechoslovakia, as outlined in the Hossbach Memorandum, could now be launched ahead of schedule. Konrad Henlein, the Sudeten German leader of Czechoslovakia, became Hitler's new and valuable puppet. But Henlein was not enthusiastic about redressing Sudeten German wrongs through a German invasion. Hitler paid scant attention to him. He insisted that the Sudeten Germans were "his" Germans and that they needed defending, if necessary through Germany's armed might. The Sudeten Germans, like the Volga Germans and eventually other foreigners of German descent, be-

241. Charles Callan Tansill, *Back Door to War*, p. 49.
242. *International Military Tribunal*, vol. XII, p. 502, ex Joachim Fest, *Das Gesicht des Dritten Reiches*.

came the first to be nicknamed *Beuteteutonen* (Booty Teutons).

The Czechoslovaks were outraged by the threat to their sovereignty from across the border. They were a young nation, patched together after the war, but well armed and quite able to defend themselves. Their mountain fortifications were powerful, and Czechoslovak engineers had designed and built some of the most advanced military equipment in the world. Their president, Eduard Beneš, was less than conciliatory. He refused to accept interference in the internal affairs of his country and considered Hitler's bombast about "saving our German brothers in the Sudetenland" to be exactly that. A full-scale international crisis of substantial magnitude was in the making.

Meanwhile, the new British prime minister, Neville Chamberlain, instead of supporting the independence of a young fellow democracy, set out to pacify and appease Hitler. It would prove a daunting task, since, as French ambassador André François-Poncet rightly described Germany's Führer, the man was a *Nimmersatt*, the German word for someone insatiable. Schacht was unaware of Chamberlain's intentions. During one of the periodic meetings of the Bank for International Settlements in Geneva, Schacht persuaded his old Bank of England friend Montagu Norman to speak to his prime minister about supporting a German anti-Nazi coup. Chamberlain's response to Norman was "Who's Schacht? I have to deal with Hitler." He was probably unaware that Schacht was not alone. Several Germans of varying influence had made efforts to persuade Britain to call a halt to Hitler's demands and to call his bluff, instead of appeasing him. The brothers Erich and Theo Kordt, both members of Germany's Foreign Service; Ewald von Kleist-Schmenzin, a Pomeranian noble and reserve officer; Adam von Trott zu Solz, a Rhodes scholar and Foreign Office employee; and even Hitler's personal aide Captain Fritz Wiedemann had flown to London under various pretenses to persuade Whitehall to stiffen its stance. Their efforts were in vain.

On May 20 the Czechoslovak government decided to mobilize its army and to man the defensive installations in the mountains facing Germany. On August 11, 1938, Ernest Hemingway wrote in *Ken:* "There has been war in Spain, now, for two years.

There has been war in China for a year. War is due in Europe by next summer at the latest." [243]

The Nazi legal machinery fabricated endless new attacks on German and Austrian Jews. Among much other indignity, every male Jew now had to add the name "Israel" to his given names. Females were forced to add "Sara."

In July, as tensions rose, Chamberlain dispatched former British trade minister Sir Walter Runciman to Czechoslovakia to "ascertain the actual facts of the dispute and to gauge the truth of complaints by the Sudeten Germans." But nobody paid much attention to Runciman, who was roundly ignored and even resented by both the Czechoslovaks and Sudeten Germans. By August even the Sudeten German leader Henlein had met with Hitler in Bayreuth and tried to persuade him to forgo a military attack.

Without knowing the details of other attempts to forestall an attack, Schacht sensed that nothing immediate would be done by France or Britain to oppose Hitler. He reached the inescapable conclusion that the man was pushing and pulling Germany toward war. Sooner or later the Western democracies would give up their attempts to satisfy the voracious man in the Reichskanzlei; then they would have to fight. He made up his mind that Hitler had to be eliminated, probably by force of arms. Civil insurrection was impossible. The Nazi machinery had complete control of the population. Besides, to the vast majority of Germans, Hitler was still an incomparable hero, a man who had gained so much without bloodshed, the savior who had restored Germany.

His first careful contacts with the General Staff were failures. General von Brauchitsch, Admiral Raeder, and General Gerd von Rundstedt all claimed that they could not listen to a word he was saying and would prefer that nothing had ever been said to them.

After weeks of further discreet inquiries, he finally located a circle of senior military men who shared his concerns. They were led by General Ludwig Beck, chief of the General Staff, who first realized what horrors lay ahead when on May 30, 1938, he was

243. Ernest Hemingway, *By-Line: Ernest Hemingway*, p. 291.

briefed by Hitler about "Case Green," the Führer's plan for the invasion of Czechoslovakia.

Beck was convinced that the German army had been rebuilt to create parity with the West, not to set off another World War. He was backed by General Erwin von Witzleben, one of the leading commanders, and by Panzer General Franz Halder.

In August there was a meeting at Gühlen, attended by von Witzleben and the man who commanded the Potsdam garrison near Berlin, General Count Erich Brockdorff-Ahlefeld. A coup was planned. Of all the leading civilians, Schacht probably had the highest reputation among the senior military. They felt some kinship to this tall man, despite his having been disqualified from military service by his poor eyesight. They seemed to sense his courage and his calm, deliberate ways. Later, Schacht would speak of "his" putsch. They were now convinced. Something had to be done to stop "the corporal."

That summer, Hitler had ordered the construction of a line of western fortifications named the West Wall, or as the British would eventually call it, the Siegfried Line. Until the emergence of Case Green, this line of fortresses had seemed to indicate that Germany was in a defensive, not an aggressive, posture. Now it became apparent that the West Wall was just a temporary backstop defense for the German army's thrust southeast into Czechoslovakia. War was in the air.

The coup was planned for October 28, 1938, at noon, the date and hour scheduled for the Case Green invasion. Plans were drawn to take over the Berlin government with a lightning attack by General Brockdorff-Ahlefeld's armor and infantry from the nearby Potsdam garrison. When asked who the targets were, Colonel Hans Oster, an elegant and witty intelligence officer, answered in a cabaretlike singsong, "Hi-Gö-Rib-Hi-Hey," for Hitler, Göring, Ribbentrop, Himmler, and Heydrich.[244] Their hopes were in vain. Leading anti-Hitler Germans had already visited England to feel out the British government's reaction to a coup. They

---

244. Heinz Höhne, *Canaris: Patriot im Zwielich*, p. 329.

had failed to get assurances. It became increasingly clear that no help was forthcoming from London. The tepid British response put an end to the plans of Beck, Schacht, and the others. They realized that they would have had little popular support because most Germans still worshiped Hitler, but the plotters would have been willing to take their chances had they had received some backing from London and Paris. On August 27 a disgusted and miserable Beck obtained permission to retire from the army.

As if to confirm their decision, on the morning of September 14, 1938, a cable arrived at the Chancellery in Berlin from Chamberlain:

> In view of the increasingly critical situation I suggest that I visit you at once in order to attempt to find a peaceful solution. I can come to you by air and shall be ready to travel as of tomorrow morning. Please advise the earliest time when you can receive me and indicate a place for the meeting. I should be grateful for a prompt reply.

Hitler accepted at once.

On September 15, when he heard the news, Schacht walked up and down in his office in a rare display of open fury. Every few minutes he slapped his forehead and groaned, "Imagine! The prime minister of this world power comes to visit this gangster!"[245]

The Munich conference that followed (actually three separate sessions, stretching over two weeks, in three different locations, and also involving French premier Edouard Daladier and Benito Mussolini, who offered himself as a kind of ombudsman) forced the Czechoslovak government to surrender the Sudetenland; the Czechoslovaks who lived there became German citizens. President Beneš and Czechoslovakia were the losers, and the country was carved up by foreign negotiators.

Once more, Adolf Hitler looked like the man who was always right. *Der Führer hat immer Recht.* Yet he seemed far from satis-

---

245. Hans Bernd Gisevius, *BIS ZUM BITTEREN ENDE,* p. 356.

fied. Schacht later related that he had heard Hitler say that Chamberlain spoiled his march into Prague.[246]

Ulrich von Hassell, German ambassador to Italy and distinguished diplomat, sensed imminent disaster, a World War. He, too, was trying to find kindred spirits willing to resist Hitler. In September, following the Munich conferences, while in Berlin for briefings, he visited Schacht, who immediately called Hitler a cheat and a crook (*Schwindler*) and said that in the long run England would never make a deal with him. "Chamberlain made an enormous error. He will not avoid war!"

The following day von Hassell met again with Schacht, who was visiting the Foreign Ministry. Schacht told him, "We're in trouble."

Referring to Schacht's leverage as a cabinet minister, von Hassell pointed out that Schacht's views carried some weight. "You're responsible!"

Schacht shook his head. "No. Today 'minister' means nothing." Obviously in distress, he continued, "Any regime based on immoral principles cannot last."

More pessimisitic, von Hassell disagreed. He cited a list of immoral dictatorships that had lasted for decades.[247]

Later that month, during a birthday dinner at the home of banker Emil von Stauss, Schacht again criticized the Nazi leadership. Schacht's "beautiful and intelligent" niece, the daughter of his doctor brother, told von Hassell that her uncle often frightened her with these outbursts.[248]

The anti-Semitic excesses of the party finally crested on November 9, 1938, in that strange horror known as Kristallnacht, "Crystal Night." The cynical Berlinese nickname referred to the broken shopwindow glass littering the streets and trivialized the massive countrywide burning of Jewish synagogues and attacks on Jewish stores and shops, as Jewish men were beaten, arrested, and sent to concentration camps. The excuse for this "expression

246. Fest, *Hitler*, p. 566.
247. Ulrich von Hassell, *Die Hassell-Tagebücher, 1938–1944*, p. 51.
248. Ibid., p. 57.

of the people's fury," carefully organized by the Nazi Party, was that a minor official in the German embassy in Paris had been shot to death by a Jewish refugee, a teenager. The diplomat, Ernst vom Rath, was himself anti-Nazi, under investigation by the Gestapo. The boy, Herschel Grynszpan, had fled to Paris while his Polish-born parents were trying to hide in the rough no-man's-land between Germany and Poland. Although they had German passports, the senior Grynszpans were expelled from Germany as Polish-born, and the Poles would not let them cross the frontier. Their son, Herschel, whom they had smuggled to safety in Paris, was desperate and crazed. He went to the German embassy to take revenge and shot the first German official he encountered. The whole event was very convenient for the Gestapo and the party leaders.

While Kristallnacht met no resistance from ordinary Germans, they did not support it or show the slightest enthusiasm for it. Some were embarrassed, others turned their back. They were fed headlines in the controlled press and on state radio proclaiming the people's "righteous indignation," but Germans showed little sign of being indignant and certainly were not righteous. Most of the savagery was carried out by SA storm troopers, but some was perpetrated by plainclothes police agents. Local fire departments were alerted to prevent the flames of burning synagogues from spreading to nearby houses. There are many views about who was actually responsible. Goebbels? Himmler? Hitler? Who set off the debauch? Foreign press reporters were aghast and cabled fierce descriptions of the savage events to their papers. One hundred seventy-one synagogues were torched, seventy-five hundred Jewish-owned shops and stores were wrecked, ninety-one Jews were murdered, and twenty-six thousand were arrested and sent to concentration camps. They were held from a few days to many weeks and then released after much ill treatment, without explanation.

Any foreigners who had tried to see some good in the Hitler regime now had to retreat. Pro-Nazi organizations in Western countries knew their days were numbered.

Germany's insurance companies paid out about 100 million marks to Jewish claimants, who then had to turn over their compensation to the government. A fine of 1 billion marks was imposed on the Jewish population as a "penalty" for vom Rath's murder. President Roosevelt recalled Ambassador Hugh Wilson in protest. (The recall was postponed four days while an American public-opinion poll was conducted, which showed only limited sympathy for the victims. Sumner Welles, the assistant secretary of state, then pushed through the recall.) The *New York Times* ran an editorial on November 11, 1938, about "scenes witnessed yesterday . . . which no man can look upon without shame for the degradation of the species."

Schacht was thoroughly revolted. He asked for a meeting with Hitler and told him, "Unless you can assure the Jews that they will be safe, you will have to give them the chance to emigrate." In the Schacht manner, he then proposed a curious financial machination, which he himself described as "not ideal" but which might have been the basis for saving Jewish lives. His suggestion was helped by what Schacht saw as Hitler's "discomfort" brought on by Kristallnacht.[249]

He presented an outline, a quick fabrication of his nimble mind:

> All Jewish holdings in Germany and Austria would go into a trust, administered by an international committee, which would include some Jews.
>
> The trust would then sell twenty-five-year bonds at 5 percent on the world market with dividends in dollars.
>
> Jews all over the world would be expected to buy these bonds.
>
> Part of the dollar dividends (25 percent) would then be paid out to German and Austrian Jews to help them emigrate. Part would be applied to German exports.

To his surprise, when Schacht suggested initiating this plan in London, Hitler agreed.

Late in November 1938 there was an architectural exhibition at the House of German Art in Munich, presided over by Adolf

---

249. Schacht, *76 Jahre meines Lebens*, p. 842.

Hitler. The model of a planned new Berlin cathedral, which would hold one hundred thousand worshipers, was being unveiled. Schacht sat in the second row, in easy eye contact with Hitler. When the crowd clapped wildly, Schacht crossed his arms over his chest and calmly stared at Hitler without applauding. Hitler seemed to catch his censorious gaze and to be somehow taken aback.

Shortly thereafter, in early December, there was the traditional annual Christmas party for the Reichsbank's young clerks and messengers. As was the tradition, the president of the Reichsbank addressed the young men. There were several party leaders in the audience.

Schacht said, "The burning of Jewish synagogues, the destruction and looting of Jewish businesses, the ill treatment of Jewish citizens was so disgraceful that every decent German must blush with shame. I hope that none of you took part in these things. If anyone did, I would suggest that he quickly remove himself from the Reichsbank. There is no room in the Reichsbank for those who do not respect the life, property and views of others. The Reichsbank is built on loyalty and faith."[250]

Another show of disgust came from a surprising quarter. Count von Helldorf, head of the Berlin police, was away from the city on business on November 9. When he returned, he assembled the senior commanders of his force and berated them for their lack of interference with the looting, burning, and personal assaults. He told them they should have ordered the use of firearms.[251]

Despite his open opposition to the party's recent acts, Schacht was still given permission by Hitler to travel to London to launch his scheme for Jewish emigration. On December 14 he met with two of the former heads of the disastrous Evian conference, American lawyer George Rublee and Lord Winterton, both of whom liked his plan. There was also support from Lord Bearsted of the London banking house of M. Samuel, as well as from An-

---

250. Ibid., p. 494.
251. Gisevius, *BIS ZUM BITTEREN ENDE*, p. 369.

thony de Rothschild. Rublee was FDR's "delegate" in matters of Jewish emigration. After the Evian failure, he helped found the Intergovernmental Committee on refugees, based in London. Montagu Norman of the Bank of England was, as usual, more than willing to help his old friend Hjalmar. Roosevelt was less than sympathetic to the scheme proposed by Schacht, his old antagonist, but did not scuttle it entirely. He needed something — anything — to assuage the angry voices in America that sounded their disgust after Kristallnacht. However, a New Year's address to Congress in which he attacked Germany did not help to ease the climate for Schacht's negotiations.

Despite that, the first week of January 1939 was filled with rumor of progress. On January 4 Montagu Norman traveled to Berlin, supposedly to attend the christening of Schacht's third grandchild at the Schacht villa. The actual purpose of the trip was the refugee plan. Rublee was also scheduled to arrive. Everything looked promising.

The urgency was clear. In Vienna Jewish intellectuals, unable to find work, were sweeping the snow from the city's streets each night.

The AP reported that Mussolini fired some prominent Italian Fascists for expressing sympathy for German and Austrian Jews.[252]

At breakfast with von Hassell, Schacht reported that he was optimistic about the London meetings, which von Hassell described as the Warburg Plan. However, von Hassell agreed with others, such as Generals Beck and Fritsch, that Schacht was inclined to do one thing and say another, but Schacht insisted that he would be honorbound to stay at his post until he was handed conditions, such as runaway inflation, that would make his job impossible.

Eventually, Schacht's plan was rejected for many reasons, but primarily because it seemed to be blatant blackmail. After Kristallnacht few were willing to pay ransom money secured by Jewish lives. Besides, once Jewish refugees were given the financial means to emigrate, they would have to be accepted by one of the reluctant Western democracies.

252. AP (January 10, 1939).

There was also a strange resistance on the part of certain British and American Jewish bankers, who felt that by accepting the plan, they would confirm the Nazi notion of the "Jewish world conspiracy" that played power politics with its money. [253]

Schacht, who had been able to persuade Hitler to countenance the whole idea only by promising that it would boost German exports, had failed. It must have given Hitler, Göring, and Goebbels great satisfaction to see him stumble. Hitler had shielded Schacht from the party stalwarts because he had always been sure of Schacht's ability to obtain results abroad. Now he knew he had little to lose by discarding him. He even blamed the Polish concentration camps on Schacht's failure to move Jews out of Germany. (Schacht had even investigated a much-discussed and constantly rejected plan to create a homeland for refugee Jews on the island of Madagascar.) Blaming the Holocaust on Schacht, Hitler said to his associates at lunch that "the first Jewish transports to the East followed Schacht's failure to put emigration plans into the works." [254]

Almost as a gesture of supreme contempt for Schacht's and anyone else's sympathies for the Jews, Hitler authorized that 937 of them, mostly people of wealth, would be allowed to leave Germany on the German liner *St. Louis*. The ship left Hamburg on May 13, 1939, and cruised the Atlantic with its refugee passengers, trying to find a place where they could disembark and be permitted to remain. They were turned away by Cuba and the United States and had to return to Europe. After five weeks at sea, the captain, a determined man named Gustav Schröder, finally managed to obtain permission for his increasingly desperate passengers to land at Antwerp.

England, Belgium, France, and Holland then accepted groups of the refugees, but not before the Goebbels propaganda machine had trumpeted that "no one wants the Jews." The press called the *St. Louis* the "ship of the damned." Later, it became known as the Ship of Fools.

253. Chernow, *The Warburgs*, p. 480.
254. Picker, *Hitler's Tischgespräche*, pp. 305, 340, 456.

17

CLASH

ON JANUARY 7, 1939, Adolf Hitler was handed the following memorandum signed by all eight members of the Reichsbank's board and its president, Hjalmar Schacht:

> The currency is severely threatened by the uncontrolled expenditures of those who govern. . . . Currency and reserve banking are shaken by the bloated expenses of the state, and will cause the collapse of the national financial structure despite vast efforts and ever increasing taxation. . . . No amount of genius can prevent the ruinous consequences on our currency caused by this uncontrolled policy of spending. It is understandable that the Austrian and Czechoslovak actions caused an increase in spending, but there has been no cut-back since then. To the contrary, there seems to be a planned increase. It is our duty to warn against this assault on the currency.
>
> We shall be happy to do our best to collaborate with all future goals, but for now the time has come to call a halt.

After he read it, the infuriated Führer screamed, "This is mutiny!"

Schacht had planned on a meeting with the Minister of Finance to discuss this memorandum and the economic future. He would have to change his plans.

In Schacht's own words:

On the evening of January 19, I returned home very late to find several telephone messages and telegrams that I was to be at the Chancellery promptly at 9:00 A.M. the next morning. In the morning, a telephone call moved the appointment from 9:00 to 9:15 A.M. As soon as I entered the Garden Salon of the old Chancellery, the Führer appeared, and the following conversation took place.

"I have asked you to come here so that I could hand you the official notification that you are released from the presidency of the Reichsbank."

He handed me the paper, which I held in my hand without comment.

"You do not fit into the entire National Socialist framework."

I remained silent. There was a short pause.

"You have refused to let your officials be examined by the party for their political reliability."

I remained silent. Another pause. Hitler betrayed increasing nervousness.

"You criticized the events of November 9 [Kristallnacht] in front of your employees."

I had not answered Hitler's first remark, because I agreed with him that I did not fit into the framework of the party. I had also repeatedly told Hitler that I would not permit my people to be examined. If I was trusted to do a job, I had to have the right to choose my own collaborators. But since he mentioned my Christmas speech to the young boys at the office, I answered with all the sarcasm I could muster. "My Führer, had I known that you approve of events of this kind, I would have kept still."

My answer left him speechless. He exclaimed, "I am too upset right now to speak to you."

"I can come back when you have calmed down."

"And, besides, the thing you fear won't happen. There will be no inflation."

"That would be fine, my Führer."

Without saying another word, he accompanied me through two rooms to the nearest exit, and I bid him good-bye.[255]

Hitler changed his mind. Apparently, he had planned a scathing letter, but it was never sent. Nor was Schacht fired from the meaningless post of minister without portfolio, which he had held since his dismissal as minister of economics. The Schachts moved into a villa they owned in Berlin's exclusive Charlottenburg district. He refused any further government compensation.

Schacht's refugee plan was suspended at once.

All but two of the Reichsbank directors resigned. The two that remained were both party members.

Schacht's view of the economy was not mistaken. In the German world of *Ersatz*, where suits were made of wood-based material, the gag making the rounds in Berlin was "If your suit sprouts in spring, please cut off the shoots and use them for patches."[256]

"Short and chubby" (in the words of the January 21, 1939, *New York Times*) Walther Funk was appointed as the new president of the Reichsbank. When von Hassell met with Schacht on January 25, Schacht seemed deeply emotional. "You cannot believe how relieved I am to be out of this thing!" Von Hassell suggested that he was courageous to resign, but Schacht "thundered" his denial. "On the contrary, he threw me out!"[257]

From Hitler's point of view, Schacht was no longer a hindrance, a brake, a nuisance. Now, with a rubber-stamp minister of economics who was also president of the "National Socialistic–oriented" Reichsbank and Göring's "guns over butter" Four-Year Plan, the Führer could plunge ahead. He felt invincible and infallible, ready to vent his anger and frustration at not being able to attack the despised Czechoslovaks. His police machinery was

255. Schacht, *76 Jahre meines Lebens*, p. 495ff.
256. *Time* (January 30, 1939), p. 19.
257. Hassell, *Die Hassell-Tagebücher, 1938–1944*, p. 80.

omnipresent. Himmler and his right-hand man, Reinhard Heydrich, were in complete control. Every German became part of the vast denunciation network, from miniscule block wardens to powerful *Gauleiters*. Concentration camps all over Germany and in Austria loomed for those who deviated from the standardized customs, manners, styles, attitudes, opinions, or racial prototypes of Nazi Germany. From university professors to shoe salesmen, each German knew that to say anything against the official norm, he had first better look over his shoulder and speak softly to someone he could trust.

It would be wrong to assume that this fully *gleichgeschaltet* ("equalized," a euphemism for "Nazified") way of life caused discomfort, fear, or upset for the average German citizen. On the contrary, there was a certain righteous view that all was as it should be. Everyone had the duty to be part of the effort, to support this newly reborn nation. Who could criticize the Führer, when he had achieved so much in a few years and had done so without war?

There were surprisingly few complaints. Nazi Germany was one of the most highly taxed countries, citizens were forced to donate to various government funds, and there were unending shortages of daily necessities. Many Nazi promises, such as a cheap "people's car" (*Volkswagen*) that could be paid for in installments, never came to be. Yet, they were willing to face it all, hoping for they knew not what. Perhaps it was the sense of superiority that came with unending party emphasis on German racial supremacy and on the racial inferiority of others. Perhaps it was the end of national impotence after the lost World War and the Versailles Dictate. Mostly, it was the mass delusion that he, the Führer, the leader, the one who "was always right," would eventually produce some form of paradise. He would assemble all Germans, even the ones outside the Reich and its new *Ostmark*, the *Volksdeutsche* in Czechoslovakia, Russia, the Baltic, Danzig, and Poland. Then there would be a true Greater Germany, no longer afraid of its jealous and greedy neighbors. Some of the elder people had occasional doubts. Sunday sermons were not always politically acceptable, and parishioners feared for the safety of their priests.

A few insightful people realized that war was only a step away, but had they attempted to remove Hitler, they would have been crucified.

Hitler's next move was to force the Poles to release their hold on the Hanseatic port of Danzig, formerly one of Germany's most important outlets to the Baltic. He also wanted undisturbed access by railroad and road through a free zone to be created in the Polish Corridor, the creation of the Versailles Treaty, carved out of German territory to give Poland access to the sea.

Hitler invited Colonel Josef Beck, Poland's foreign minister, to visit him at the Berghof, and Beck could not refuse. Hitler then outlined his requests, with some arrogant offers of quid pro quo, which Beck refused.

Hitler then sent his foreign minister, Joachim von Ribbentrop, to Warsaw on a state visit. On January 26 von Ribbentrop's train arrived in the Polish capital, and the next few days were filled with empty gestures, superbly drilled Polish honor guards, and lavish dinners and banquets; but there were no results. The Poles refused to discuss Danzig or the Corridor. Hitler's anger increased. In his view, he had been reasonable. He would settle with the Poles one day soon.

Besides, he was not through with Czechoslovakia. The little republic was now virtually helpless. It had been stripped of its defenses by the agreements reached by outsiders during the Munich conferences. In protest, President Beneš resigned and Foreign Minister Jan Masaryk went to England. The Slovak region formed a separate province and installed a governor who was a Nazi sympathizer, a priest named Father Josef Tiso. The Poles and Hungarians had reclaimed and been awarded territories that had become part of Czechoslovakia. Italian foreign minister Count Galeazzo Ciano and von Ribbentrop were the "judges" who had apportioned these vultures' shares during a session of wine, women, and song in Vienna. Ciano, who was Mussolini's son-in-law, was known as a playboy.

The man in the pompous Speer-styled Chancellery on the Wilhelmstrasse still lusted to crush crippled Czechoslovakia. His Hossbach Memorandum plan still held. The pretext came sooner than he expected. Father Tiso launched such virulent anti-Prague propaganda that on March 10 Prague occupied Bratislava, Tiso's capital, thereby precipitating an instant and fierce set of events.

On March 11 Tiso was persuaded to ask for Hitler's help. Then "in order to prevent further violence and to protect Germans living in the area," Hitler agreed to an immediate meeting in Berlin with the incumbent Czech president, a sick old judge named Emil Hácha. There are many versions of the events that took place at Hitler's Chancellery on that snowy winter night in Berlin. The consensus is that the old Czech was threatened and badgered during a session that began at 1:30 A.M. and continued until early morning. His daughter, who was also his nurse, could not help him when he had a seizure. At 3:55 A.M., Hitler's personal "Dr. Feelgood," Dr. Theodor Morell, administered amphetamines, which restored Hácha temporarily. The shaken and battered man then "put the fate of Czechoslovakia into the hands of Adolf Hitler." He was told that German troops would cross the border at once. Pathetically, Hácha felt he had to obtain agreement from the new Czech foreign minister, who had accompanied him, and also from the Czech cabinet in Prague via phone. Considering the situation, he had no problem obtaining it.

On March 15, 1939, Hitler made his triumphant entry into Prague, standing in the front seat of a gray, six-wheel cross-country Wehrmacht Mercedes, license plate number WH 32288. That night he slept in the Hradjin Palace, high above the Golden City. On March 16 he signed the decree creating the Protectorate of Bohemia and Moravia, effectively ending the Czechoslovak Republic.

The following day, on March 17, a grim Neville Chamberlain spoke in Birmingham. He asked bitterly if anyone could ever again believe Hitler. In Paris Daladier told the German ambassador, Count Hans Welczek, that Hitler had betrayed him.

It was the first of the many crucial events that Schacht did not witness from a front-row seat. He had asked the Führer for permission to go on a long trip abroad and received it quickly and with some relief. Hitler was more than eager to be rid of Schacht's constant opposition, rational thought, and political and fiscal conservatism.

Where Schacht could go was another matter. He had to clear

his trip with businessman-turned-diplomat Joachim von Ribbentrop.

"So," said the arch von Ribbentrop to Schacht, "you wish to
make a trip around the world?"

"Not really. Only to East Asia. I want to visit China and Japan."

"But you know, Herr Schacht, that we are closely allied to
Japan, while our relationship with China is sliding. For these political reasons, I cannot agree to a trip to the Far East."

"But, Herr von Ribbentrop, we still maintain diplomatic relations with China. Why can't I visit both countries, particularly because I am traveling as a private citizen?"

Von Ribbentrop remained adamant. He then turned down
Schacht's requests for trips to the Netherlands East India and India
for equally obscure and convoluted reasons. A disgusted Schacht
finally rose and left after saying, "Well, I suppose I'll have to con-
fine myself to the Harz Mountains."[258] No doubt he was subtly al-
luding to the Harzburg rally, long before von Ribbentrop became
a Hitler paladin, when Schacht's very presence had lent prestige to
the Nazis. Using all his remaining connections, he finally got permission to travel to India. Schacht began his journey early in
March, accompanied by his nephew Sven.

Schacht felt he should keep a journal of the trip, though he
had never really believed in diaries. Some of its sections sound
much like a standard travel book, about the Taj Mahal, the
Golden Temple of Amritsar, and the maharajahs. But other passages are salted with anti-Nazi observations. In Calcutta he wrote
about the "curse of the Party" that haunted the German expatri-
ate colony, most of whom were thoroughly frightened of denunciation. The Gestapo had a long arm.

In early August Hjalmar and Sven returned to Berlin and an
ominous atmosphere. Obviously, war was near, propelled by
Hitler's invasion of Prague and his increasingly hysterical verbal
attacks on Poland. Schacht complained that Funk's economic
policies were completely inflationary, a euphemism for ignoring

---

258. Schacht, *76 Jahre meines Lebens*, pp. 498, 499.

trade and export while plunging every resource into armaments.

Soviet Russia now loomed as the key player. If Hitler attacked Poland — and his speeches left no doubt about his willingness to do so — he might have to face an immediate attack by Britain, which had guaranteed Poland's borders, and also by France. Russia could then be drawn into the conflict. Would Russia attack Germany's back while Britain and France launched themselves at Germany in the west to help Poland? The game of national barter that was to follow during the next weeks haunted the world for decades to come. Probably to protect the sensibilities of the German Führer, Chamberlain and Daladier had ignored Stalin during the 1938 Munich conferences over the fate of Czechoslovakia. Now, in August 1939, an Anglo-French delegation was dispatched to Moscow. It was at most a halfhearted effort; the British and French members of the group were only minor officials and powerless to negotiate. They arrived in Moscow by slow boat and train on August 11, 1939, led by retired British admiral Reginald Drax.

The Russians insisted that to defend Poland, and possibly Romania, they would have to enter Polish and Romanian territory. It was soon obvious that Drax could make no decisions without lengthy consultations with London, and he was quickly discounted by Marshal Kliment Voroshilov, the Russian negotiator. The Russians soon broke off the meetings.

Hitler's way was different. Once he had made up his mind to take the thoroughly distasteful step of dealing with the Soviets, he immediately instructed his ambassador to Moscow, a distinguished diplomat named Count Friedrich von der Schulenburg, to make all preparations. It was made clear that no time was to be lost. Von der Schulenburg, who was not devoted to the Nazis but was eager to keep the peace between his beloved Germany and Russia, made the necessary arrangements within a few days. Hitler then rushed von Ribbentrop to Moscow on his personal Lufthansa Condor superplane. Von Ribbentrop landed on August 23 with a bagful of political gifts for the Soviets. Within twenty-four hours, negotiating long into the night in an office deep inside the Kremlin, a deal was struck between Soviet Russia and Nazi Germany, the two blood enemies. At least a degree of honesty was preserved by Stalin. When von Ribbentrop began to toast Germany's new Soviet allies in extravagant terms, Stalin lifted his hand and said, "We have been pouring buckets of manure all over each other for years, so let us tone down the praise."

The Germans gave Stalin what he wanted. They waived any interest in the eastern half of Poland as well as Estonia, Latvia, Lithuania, and eventually Byelorussia. In return, the Soviets committed themselves not to attack Germany. Lines were drawn marking the new German-Russian border in the middle of Poland. Von Ribbentrop returned to his Führer in triumph, and the following day an incredulous world heard the stunning news that Russia and Germany had signed a nonaggression treaty.

Schacht had developed contacts with certain officers close to Admiral Wilhelm Canaris, Germany's chief of military intelligence. Canaris, an enigmatic career officer of great worldliness, had begun to have doubts about his Nazi commander in chief. Canaris's deputy, the sophisticated General Oster, was a true anti-Hitlerite. Surprisingly, General Georg Thomas, the military economist who had been involved with Schacht since the beginning of Göring's Four-Year Plan, became another anti-Hitler ally. Schacht found out on August 25 that Hitler's order to invade Poland was imminent. He then asked Generals Oster and Thomas to arrange a meeting for him with General von Brauchitsch at an army headquarters in Zossen twenty miles south of Berlin.[259] Schacht hoped that he could somehow persuade von Brauchitsch, the man who succeeded the disgraced von Fritsch, to prevent the outbreak of war. Von Brauchitsch refused a meeting. He threatened to have Schacht arrested if he insisted on coming to his headquarters.

Shortly thereafter, Schacht felt reassured when Hitler called off the order to attack. He could not have known that Hitler had received an emergency visit from Italian ambassador Bernardo Attolico, which conveyed the Duce's deep regrets that he could not join his German ally because the Italian army was not yet

259. Ibid., p. 513.

ready for offensive action. At the same time, Chamberlain promised he would persuade Poland to produce a negotiator. On August 30 the Poles mobilized. Hitler was unwilling to wait for their promised emissary. He set an impossible deadline and then drafted a totally reasonable peace proposal to Chamberlain. He also made sure that it was read to Sir Nevile Henderson, the British ambassador, but only after the Polish deadline had passed. It was Hitler's cynical way of demonstrating that on his part, he had been willing to keep the peace. The British and French then mobilized on the evening of August 31.

At 4:45 A.M., September 1, 1939, Hitler ordered the activation of "Case White," the code name for the attack on Poland — with or without Mussolini and his troops.

The German invasion was launched with the army and air force that Schacht's financing had helped create, but Schacht flatly blamed the senior military for going to war. He had envisioned a defensive military establishment, not one to be used for aggressive purposes. He later quoted Field Marshal Milch of the Luftwaffe, who said during the Nuremberg war-crimes trials that on September 1, 1939, the RAF was superior to the Luftwaffe. According to Admiral Karl Dönitz, the German navy had only fifteen U-boats, and General Alfred Jodl testified that the army had only seventy-five divisions, some of them not armed or ready for combat.

Schacht's judgment was quite correct, but the military results showed that he was wrong. Poland's foreign minister, Colonel Beck, had assured his British allies and the world at large that the Polish army could handle any German attack, but the Germans devastated the Poles with dive-bomber attacks and new, combined armored and infantry tactics. The word *Blitzkrieg* was coined. By September 18 the Russians crossed the Polish border and rushed toward the agreed line of demarcation, where they were to meet the Germans. The SS under Reinhard Heydrich and his senior officers organized their famous *Einsatzgruppen,* the killer units that roamed behind the fighting troops, murdering Jews and Poles, burning synagogues, raping and looting.

These SS bestialities would have gone without a word of criticism from anyone in the army, had it not been for the commander of the German forces in Poland, Colonel General Johannes Blaskowitz, a gentleman of the old school. Blaskowitz would not permit himself to remain a silent witness to swinishness and mass murder, rape, and plunder. He expressed his fury at these abominable acts and sent a scathing letter of complaint to Berlin, pointing out that it affected the morale of his men. Hitler saw the memorandum on November 18, 1939. He was furious but did not relieve Blaskowitz of his command. In a second missive, the general stated that "the attitude of troops toward the SD [security detachments of the SS] and police units alternates between abhorrence and hatred. Every soldier feels disgusted by these crimes committed in Poland by nationals of the Reich and representatives of our state."[260]

Army officers at Blaskowitz's headquarters would no longer shake hands with SS officers. Eventually, Blaskowitz was relieved of his command. He was never punished but was never promoted, even though he was a fine field commander and led troops in the western campaign that followed. Ironically, at the end of the war he was arrested by the Allies and charged with war crimes. It was too much for him. He committed suicide in his Nuremberg prison cell in February 1948.

Schacht was in touch with some of the best-informed senior military officers, such as intelligence chief Canaris and his deputy, Oster. It is unlikely that Schacht did not know about Blaskowitz's letters of outrage and, more important, the SS actions that had caused such anger. Every senior German in government, business, and the military had become keenly aware that since the outbreak of war, Himmler, Heydrich, and the SS had grown even more powerful. Himmler's paramilitary Waffen SS had grown into elite military units, and the old Gestapo, a civilian police force, had been swallowed by the SD. Concentration camps were now entirely in the hands of the SS.

Blaskowitz's open complaints were the last of their kind from any senior military officer or official during the war. The SS po-

---

260. Heinz Höhne, *The Order of the Death's Head*, pp. 281, 282.

lice state now reached into every military headquarters, every business office, and even the private offices of Nazi cabinet ministers. Germany became a paranoid country, with every man looking over his shoulder, frightened of being denounced for the slightest criticism. Schacht knew that with his record of open opposition to Hitler and the Nazi Party, he had to be especially cautious. His son, Jens, who had gone to the United States in May 1939 to become an intern at the First National Bank of Chicago, had returned to join the army. This also provided some dangerous leverage. Sons were frequently punished for their fathers' perceived offenses. Wisdom dictated silence.

Despite his obvious fall from power, or perhaps because of it, Schacht was approached by several American publications to write articles about the state of affairs in Germany. It seemed that his name still carried some weight abroad. He met with von Ribbentrop to inform him that he had been contacted by the American magazine *Foreign Affairs*. The foreign minister agreed to let Schacht write but asked him to submit a copy before sending it on to America. It was not an unreasonable request, considering Schacht's history of unpleasant surprises for Germany's leadership, but Schacht turned him down and sent his regrets to *Foreign Affairs*.

On December 20, 1939, Schacht wrote to Hitler that he had once more been asked by an American publication to write about Germany, this time by the *Christian Science Monitor*. He reported his earlier refusal to submit an article to von Ribbentrop for censorship. He was then asked to a meeting with Hitler at the Chancellery, where Schacht explained that it would take much more than an occasional article in an American publication to divert the rising anti-German attitude in America. To be truly effective, an expert who could influence the American press and gauge public opinion, would have to be sent there. Hitler took the broad hint. He immediately asked Schacht if he was prepared to take on the assignment; of course, Schacht gave an affirmative answer. Hitler then said he would take it up with the foreign minister. He knew full well that von Ribbentrop would bury the idea. As expected, Schacht never heard another word.

Early in March 1940 Sumner Welles, American secretary of state Cordell Hull's right-hand man, came to Berlin on a fact-finding mission. He received strange treatment. Göring invited him to Karinhall, his bucolic and pompous hunting estate, but did not even offer him so much as a snack. Next came a meeting with von Ribbentrop, who spoke excellent English but insisted on the presence of an interpreter, obviously to squelch any possibility of a free exchange. Sumner Welles finally arranged a meeting with Schacht at a diplomatic tea party on Sunday, March 3, at the residence of American chargé d'affaires Alexander Kirk. Among the other guests was the beautiful wife of Italian ambassador Bernardo Attolico. Schacht describes her as "ravishing," his way of not mentioning that she was Jewish. Attolico was also out of favor with Hitler because he was the man who had dragged Mussolini into the Munich negotiations over Czechoslovakia as an "advisor."

Sumner Welles, who was startled by the lack of civility he had received at the hands of Göring and von Ribbentrop, seemed delighted to be with Schacht. As Schacht reported, Welles assured him that "[in America] your views on the economy are still held in the highest regard."

Their conversation touched on some proposals for peace but was inconsequential, and Schacht would have had no way of transmitting them and putting them into action. He was completely hors de combat.

Shortly before the American tea party, Schacht had received a call from the Foreign Ministry's chief of protocol, suggesting that he use an official interpreter for his meeting with Welles. Obviously, von Ribbentrop was desperately anxious to prevent an intimate meeting with the American. Schacht explained that he did not feel the need for one.

Hitler later told his chronicler Picker that Schacht's "Freemason methods" prevented him from continuing to use him, but that he did use him for the Sumner Welles meeting.[261] But Sum-

261. Picker, *Hitler's Tischgespräche*, p. 234.

ner Welles's trip to Germany could have done little to reassure Washington. Peace was clearly not at hand.

In the weeks following Welles's trip, Schacht became the subject of several strange rumors. He was reported as being "in India, on a mission for the Bank of England." He was "an incognito passenger en route to the U.S.A. aboard the Italian luxury liner *Conte di Savoia*."(Sumner Welles was aboard, on the way home, and the ship was held and searched in Gibraltar for more than twelve hours.) Schacht had always captured the attention of the American press. His unusual looks, his strange Americanized name, his fluent English, his great wit, and his occasional temper tantrums were "good copy," but none of this explained the rumors, or their source.

On May 27, 1940, Luise died, convinced to the very end that Hitler was Germany's savior. Schacht's memoirs hint at some regret for the loss but could not hide his sense of relief.

Politically, Schacht, as minister without portfolio, was a man without a presence in the ruling hierarchy. His status was best described in a newspaper report of January 1942:

> Dr. Schacht, who has been out of the spotlight since his retirement from public office, has been the occasion for considerable speculation recently. While retaining his seat as a member of the Cabinet, he was rarely seen in public. Inquiries as to his whereabouts were invariably met with statements that he was being "held" for special assignment.[262]

Meanwhile, Adolf Hitler's successes mounted. The Poles were crushed out of existence. His back was secure from Russian attack. Danzig and the Polish Corridor were in German hands. Using the excuse that Churchill, who had replaced Chamberlain as British prime minister, was planning to land Allied troops on the coast of Norway to grab the iron ore and armaments factories in neutral Sweden, Hitler's army, navy, and Luftwaffe swept through

262. *New York Times* (December 1, 1942), p. 13:4.

Denmark on April 9 and then north into Norway. Norway surrendered within sixty days, and a Norwegian Nazi named Vidkun
Quisling became a household word, although he was eventually
replaced by a German Nazi, Josef Terboven.

While Schacht was flushed with anger to see his old German-
Danish boyhood homeland in Nazi hands, much more humiliation lay ahead.

On Friday, May 10, 1940, from the Oberkommando, the High
Command of the Wehrmacht:

> In view of the widening of the war by our enemies onto Belgian
> and Dutch soil and the resultant threat to the Ruhr area, the Ger
> man army attacked at dawn across the western German frontier on
> a wide front.

Once more, a preemptive attack — this time aimed at the
heart of France. The Franco-British forces crumbled and had to
be evacuated from the beaches at Dunkirk. Paris was occupied on
June 14. The Italians finally came into the fight on June 18, though
with minimal success.

On June 22 the Germans forced the French to sign a surrender in the same railway car, 2419 D, formerly Marshal Foch's salon car, that had been used at the end of World War I. It was
shipped from its museum place to a clearing in the woods of
Compiègne so that the Germans could have their gleeful revenge.
Finis the Versailles Dictate!

At dawn the next morning, Hitler was driven to a silent Paris
of empty streets, part conquering hero, part architectural pilgrim. He would never visit Paris again.

He returned to Berlin by train. The leading Nazis and cabinet
ministers were ordered to attend his arrival at Anhalter Station,
where the victorious Hitler would be smothered with adoration
and adulation. Since Schacht was still a member of the cabinet, it
was understood that he would be among the worshipers. He simply could not afford to be notable by his absence. He offered a
ride in his limousine to the strange Alfred Rosenberg, the Nazi
Party's ideological guru. At the station they joined dozens of gold-

braided and booted leaders of the Reich. The Führer's private train came to a halt, and the new man of the century walked down the line of uniformed well-wishers in tan, gray, navy blue, and light blue, shaking hands and chatting euphorically. Then he stopped in front of Schacht, the only man in civilian clothes, and held out his hand. Smiling broadly, Hitler taunted, *"Na, Herr Schacht, was sagen Sie nun?"* ("Well, Herr Schacht, now what do you have to say?")

Schacht, in a quandary, shook Hitler's hand and said, "May God protect you!"

A caravan of official cars then followed Hitler's large black Mercedes parade car through walls of cheering Berliners to the Chancellery for a victory celebration. It was the last time Hitler was to drive through Berlin in triumph, standing next to his SS chauffeur Kempka, left hand on the windshield, right one saluting.

When they arrived at the Chancellery, Rosenberg got out of the car, but Schacht shook his head, saying, "It's not for me!" and was driven home.

The German press called the conquest of France "an easy victory." On June 5, Wehrmacht headquarters reported the cost in its daily bulletin.

Heldentot (hero's death): 10,323 officers, noncoms, and simple soldiers
Missing: 8,463
Wounded: 42,523 officers, noncoms, and simple soldiers
Aircraft lost: 432

Schacht continued to speak openly against the war, a tiny voice in a storm of admiration for the Führer who seemed invincible. In December Schacht was bid to the Foreign Ministry, where the chief of staff, Ernst von Weizsäcker, said that he had been instructed by his chief, von Ribbentrop, to warn Schacht against further "defeatist talk." He had been overheard making antiwar statements. When Schacht asked for a source, he was told it was Funk.

He immediately wrote to Funk:

I was called to the Foreign Office to warn me, because of reports that I had given you a pessimistic estimate of the situation. I can recall one or two conversations about the economy in which you asked for my views. I told you that the fight against England would last a long time and that we were economically ill prepared for a long war. I cannot understand the basis for Herr von Ribbentrop's warning. If he wants to change my views, he will have to give me proof. On the other hand, he cannot expect me to be silent or to falsify my views. I would consider that a breach of loyalty toward the Führer.

I asked Herr von Weizsäcker to inform Herr von Ribbentrop that I am a Minister at the request of the Führer and that it is my duty to answer truthfully whenever I am questioned by a fellow Minister.

A copy of the letter was sent to von Weizsäcker for transmittal to von Ribbentrop.[263]

On January 30, 1941, the eighth anniversary of Hitler's appointment as chancellor, the party newspaper, *Völkischer Beobachter,* published a detailed chronicle of all the achievements and events of the preceding eight years. There was no mention of Schacht.

Schacht's vanity refused to let him understand why he had been excluded. He was obviously furious. He wrote that "this sort of 'silencing out of existence' is the vital instrument in the hands of a dictatorship." He lamented, "There were many martyrs in the fight against Hitler, and they disappeared into the silence of graves and concentration camps. What good is martyrdom in the fight against evil, if it is not known and therefore cannot help to encourage others?"[264]

Schacht considered his economic achievements acts of patriotism for Germany, not for the Nazis. He was also afraid that if his name was ignored, it would downgrade his importance as a

263. Schacht, *76 Jahre meines Lebens,* p. 519.
264. Ibid., p. 520.

critic. He was protecting his international status as a voice of the opposition.

Schacht saw Hitler one final time, in February 1941, to inform the Führer of his wish to remarry. As a minister, he felt it his duty to inform his chief. Hitler reached for Schacht's arm as he was about to leave and stopped him, asking if he would still be prepared to go to America to handle press relations. Schacht discouraged the notion.

"Impossible, not after Lend-Lease [the device through which Roosevelt supplied the British with ships and other war matériel]. It is too late."

It was his last face-to-face meeting with Hitler.

When he was finally dismissed as a minister by Hitler in January 1943, not a word appeared in the press.[265]

265. Ibid.

SECOND LIFE — MANCI

FROM THE Associated Press, April 4, 1941:

SCHACHT WEDS SECRETLY

BERLIN, 65-year-old Dr. Hjalmar Schacht, Minister Without Portfolio, is honeymooning in Switzerland, friends of the former Reichsbank President said today.

They said he was married secretly and unostentatiously to a young Munich lady whose name they did not know, but who was connected with the *Haus der Kunst* (House of Art). The first Mrs. Schacht died on May 27, 1940.

The marriage occurred about March 28, it was said, but no notices were sent even to the most intimate friends.

Two days later, the *New York Times,* under the headline RE-VEALS NAME OF SCHACHT BRIDE, ran an AP report from Berne, Switzerland, that identified Schacht's wife as " . . . the former Mauzika Vogler, born in Lipuk, Hungary [then Yugoslavia], thirty-three years ago. The Schachts are spending their honeymoon in Switzerland."

Schacht still managed to fascinate people all over the globe. And he still fascinated women.

Eventually, an AP photo of the honeymooners was published in newspapers worldwide. It showed Schacht and his bride breakfasting in the dining room of a hotel in Vevey, Switzerland. They looked embarrassed, as if they were aware of the photographer but were trying to ignore him. The bridegroom was dressed in his usual somber businesswear. They probably had good reason to look preoccupied and even worried. As Schacht put it, "The honeymoon trip became an oasis from the heart-wrenching events of the time. It made me forget the risk of marrying a young woman, when I might have been arrested for high treason at any moment. But my wife dealt with it all calmly."

He was obviously very much in love, and he sang the praises of Manci (her nickname): her charm, her warm nature, her splendid figure, her classic face and blond hair, her love of the arts, and her hunger for knowledge. He also singled out her wit and her generosity. She was a curator in Munich's Haus der Kunst museum and had apprenticed in Thuringia at another museum.

They had first met in the Bonbonnière, a fashionable Munich cabaret. Schacht, who actually loved partying and nightlife, knew that, like everyone else, Manci thought of him as a coldhearted rationalist. Quite obviously, he gave her good reason to change her mind, but it took time. She was thirty years his junior and courted by many men. Besides, she loved her work and was very involved in her career. He also worried that his own precarious position might disqualify him from making a commitment. But Manci had made up her mind and never wavered through all the hardships that lay ahead.

Schacht was a man who adored women, and women sensed it. His frustrating final years with Luise had not left him without other companionship. A reference to a wedding present given the duke and duchess of Windsor mentions that the gift was a statue entitled "Love," the work of Anny Hoefken-Hempel, "the lover of Hjalmar Schacht."[266]

During his honeymoon, some leading Swiss bankers asked Schacht for his views about the German government's recent requests for credit. For years, the Swiss had supplied armaments

266. Charles Higham, *Trading with the Enemy,* p. 180.

and raw materials to Germany. Schacht, who certainly must have known that any shortage of war matériel would have acted as a brake on Hitler, told the Swiss that "he tried to see things from the point of view of the Swiss economy." He argued that a denial of credit to Germany would cause financial hardship to Switzerland's workers and might bring social unrest, which could be exploited by Adolf Hitler, their powerful neighbor.[267] It was the most specious of arguments and probably entirely self-protective. Schacht reasoned that if his presence in Switzerland had coincided with a suspension of credit by the Swiss, Hitler would probably have blamed him. The newlywed Schacht was not about to let that happen. For the moment, he wished to distance himself from the dangerous man in the Chancellery. The Schachts returned to Germany in early April and went straight to Gühlen.

While the Schachts were on their honeymoon, Adolf Hitler made the decision that eventually sealed his doom. On April 6, 1941, on his private train, the *Adler* ("Eagle"), he told von Ribbentrop that he had decided to attack the Soviets. Schacht was still well informed. He found out early that Hitler intended to invade Russia, "through my political and military connections," probably General Oster in the Abwehr. According to General William Donovan of the American Office of Strategic Services (OSS), Schacht predicted the attack to Donald Heath of the U.S. embassy in Berlin.[268]

For Hitler, other problems came first. Ignoring Hitler's advice, Mussolini had invaded Greece, and his troops were floundering. The Duce also mounted an offensive against British troops in North Africa, driving east from Libya. Here, too, the Italians were bogged down. A furious Adolf Hitler, in an "I told you so!" mood, was forced to bail out his fellow dictator. German troops swiftly occupied Greece, and an expeditionary force called the *Afrikakorps* under the command of General Erwin Rommel, a Hitler favorite, was sent to North Africa. In both cases, German

267. Schacht, *76 Jahre meines Lebens,* p. 524.
268. Peter Przybyski, *Täter neben Hitler,* p. 325.

troops did brilliantly, which was encouraging and took some of the nuisance out of Hitler's need to brace the back of his boastful Italian ally.

On March 26, 1941, Yosuke Matsuoka, the foreign minister of Japan, Germany's Axis ally, had visited Berlin. Both von Ribbentrop and Hitler hinted to the Japanese minister that they were distrustful of their pact with Russia. They hoped to encourage Japanese participation in any joint military action against the Soviets. Nothing could have been further from Japanese intentions. The men from Tokyo had their own agenda of conquest, and a fight with the Russians was not on it. They considered Soviet Russia an enemy to be avoided. The USSR was not the czarist Russia of the days when the Japanese mauled them at Port Arthur. Japanese troops had tangled with these new, fierce Soviet Russians as recently as 1939 in Manchuria, and the Russians under a new young commander named Zhukov had given them a beating. Ironically, instead of strengthening the alliance, Hitler pushed Matsuoka into an immediate effort to form a nonaggression pact with the Russians. Matsuoka stopped in Moscow on the way home to Tokyo and made sure the Russian bear remained tame. Stalin accompanied him to a farewell ceremony at the train station, which was quite unusual. Probably to reassure Hitler, Stalin then made a demonstrative show of friendliness to von der Schulenburg, the German ambassador, and within hearing of everyone told him, "We must stay friends, no matter what."

Britain was being pounded by Göring's Luftwaffe, but there was still no sign of surrender. German U-boats did their best to starve out the British, who just tightened their belt and carried on. On May 11 Rudolf Hess, one of Hitler's closest and oldest comrades, the man to whom he dictated most of *Mein Kampf* while they were both jailed in 1923, took it upon himself to fly a fighter plane to Britain and then make a parachute landing. He was trying to bring his personal message of peace.

Adolf Hitler was apoplectic. Schacht always claimed that the very idea of an attack on Russia caused Hess to fly to England.

Then on the morning of Sunday, June 22, 1941, came "code name: Barbarossa; German troops crossed the border and attacked in the direction of Moscow, to "preempt an attack by Stalin."

All these events were witnessed by a frustrated and helpless Schacht, who could neither interfere nor advise. For the next year he would see his every assumption go awry. Hitler, the corporal, the semi-educated parvenu, was fighting his war with great success. The Germans soon dominated the Balkans and began to conquer the Mediterranean after a parachute attack on Crete. They drove the British almost to Cairo and sliced across Russia at an astonishing rate of speed. They took hundreds of thousands of prisoners.

To Schacht, who considered the world a large arena for trade and profit, war was the ultimate ruination of all he held dear. As he saw it, he had been disappointed by those who believed in the monarchy, let down by those who practiced democracy, and betrayed by those who believed in nationalism and dictatorship. The "world according to Hjalmar Schacht" did not exist.

And still, he could not resist the temptation to get involved. As German troops were achieving their extraordinary early successes in Russia, Schacht chose to send a letter to Adolf Hitler. He argued that now, while the German war effort was at its absolute zenith and the Western allies were still inclined to overestimate German strength, was the perfect time to make peace. He suggested that such an overture must not be done through speeches and offers to meet with the enemy. Instead, the initiative could be launched in America, which was still not at war with Germany.

A letter of acknowledgment arrived from Lammers, the Chancellery's chief of staff. "The Führer has read your letter and wishes me to transmit his thanks." Schacht heard later that Hitler's reaction was that "Schacht still does not understand me." Schacht was right. It would have been the perfect time for negotiations.

Despite this latest rebuff, Schacht continued to argue with Hitler. When an astonishing order was issued that even cabinet ministers were prohibited from listening to foreign broadcasts, he protested in writing. "Prohibiting me from hearing foreign broadcasts puts into doubt both my loyalty and my judgment, and I feel no shortage of either." [269] He asked to be relieved of his last official post, the meaningless ministry without portfolio.

He received no reply.

In December 1941 the Japanese attacked Pearl Harbor, and America was in the war. No more appeals to America as a broker of peace were possible.

Hitler had hoped to finish the Russian campaign long before Christmas 1941, but this time the blitzkrieg tactics failed. The steppes were too vast, the supply lines too long, and nearly all needed military matériel was in short supply. Schacht's warnings were becoming reality. Germany was not equipped for a long global war. By mid-1942 German troops were stalled fifteen miles from Moscow. They were blocked at Leningrad to the north and at Stalingrad to the south. The German *Landser* had barely survived the first winter in Russia, and the next one lay not too far ahead. The medal issued to troops fighting in the Russian campaign was already nicknamed the "Frozen Meat Medal" (*Gefrierfleischmedallie*). Appeals were made in the Fatherland for contributions of furs and winter clothing. People could reach into their closets for clothes, but not for gasoline and machine gun cartridges.

Hjalmar Schacht was deeply worried. Jens Schacht was an infantry officer on the eastern front. Schacht had been wrong about German capabilities in Poland, Belgium, Holland, France, North Africa, and the Balkans, but now — when he least wanted it to be — he was right. German troops were in deep trouble.

Failure suddenly became the norm. After seesaw battles in North Africa, Field Marshal Erwin Rommel and his Afrikakorps could not reach Cairo and had to face a new enemy, General Bernard Law Montgomery and his refreshed, reequipped, and reinforced British Eighth Army. Like the troops in Russia, Rommel was hampered by a lack of supplies and the Wehrmacht's inabil-

269. Schacht, *76 Jahre meines Lebens*, p. 527.

ity to deliver them. In Russia, German troops survived a mud-locked spring and a stalemated summer but faced the prospect of a second fierce winter. The Russians seemed to have revived miraculously. They produced an endless flow of reinforcements from the eastern Soviet Union, in large part because they did not have to defend their back against the Japanese. Stalin had abandoned his usual antifascist political appeals. It was no longer the survival of Communism that he touted. Like the czars of old, he asked his people and his troops to save Mother Russia. He counted on old-fashioned patriotism, and his people responded. German field generals were dazzled by the outpouring of Russian tenacity, both civil and military.

In World War I, not a single foreign soldier had crossed the Rhine or the Elbe Rivers. In Hitler's war, the German *Vaterland* was no longer safe. Since early 1942 British air attacks against targets, both military and civilian, inside Germany had begun in earnest. Göring's Luftwaffe attacks on Britain were repaid with interest by the RAF, and in May 1942 the U.S. Air Force launched its Flying Fortresses from fields in southern England. Clearly, Göring had failed to shatter British morale. Worse, he had boasted that if a single Allied plane were ever to appear over Germany, his fellow Germans could call him "Meier," a name as common in Germany as Jones is in Wales. It was his way of saying, "My name will be mud." Now he was "Herr Meier." While men fought for their lives in Russia, their wives, children, and parents in Germany's cities spent their nights in air-raid shelters or in freezing apartments and offices. Many were burned out. Many lost their lives.

The fragility of the German war effort began to show in 1942. From then on, the few German successes could be credited to the dedication of German soldiery and the talent of the field commanders. Most of their air and armored equipment was now outdated, and increasingly scarce. Far from being a fully mechanized army, the Wehrmacht in Russia started to slaughter its valuable draft horses. Russians were better equipped, often with American transportation. Even basic German vehicles like the *Kübelwagen* version of the Volkswagen were inferior to the American jeep.

The Germans still depended on the same motorcycle and sidecar *Krad* units they had used three years earlier in Poland. The fierce dive-bombers of 1939 and 1940, the Stukas, were now slow and cumbersome compared with British, American, and Soviet fighter planes. There were no German long-range heavy bombers like the B-17 Flying Fortress or Lancaster. New German tanks were few and far between, and panzer divisions lacked necessary spare parts. At sea, the U-boat fleet was dated and decimated. There were no capital warships to give battle to the combined Anglo-American fleet. The Luftwaffe had the first jet fighters in the history of air warfare, some built by Messerschmitt. They appeared at the end of the war but were still experimental and had minimal range. The only part of Germany's weaponry that was in full supply and stayed dominant until the last day of the war was the astonishing 88mm antiaircraft, antipersonnel, antitank multipurpose gun. Every Allied soldier could tell tales of admiring horror about its efficiency.

The true credit for avoiding an early collapse went to Germany's troops. Any knowledgeable military man could see that the fortunes of war had shifted, with a massive Anglo-American invasion across the Channel or the Mediterranean still to come. Most of Germany's talented strategists and tacticians were stuck in the midst of the Russian cauldron. Only a few leading generals supervised the western defenses.

By 1942 being a German general had become a risky business. Whereas Hitler had once relied on his military leaders, he now took complete charge. Irreverently, but never openly, he was soon dubbed the *Gröfaz,* a derogatory acronym for "The greatest field commander of all time" (*Grösster Feldherr Aller Zeiten*). From his Wolf's Lair headquarters in East Prussia, he issued detailed tactical instructions and troop dispositions, but his expertise was that of the corporal he had once been. He allowed no opposition from his professional soldiery, and each Führer order was accompanied by the open threat of dismissal, demotion, or worse. The word *traitor* was quickly applied to any field commander who wished to extricate his troops from an untenable situation. Part of Hitler's disrespect for his generals was due their to acceptance of bribes, such as decorations, promotions, and cash. He had handed them gratuities, as if they were his servants. Now he saw them as his incompetent servants.

To retain internal control, Hitler gave carte blanche to Heinrich Himmler and his ever growing SS empire. The Gestapo's power increased with every fictitiously optimistic military report. Dozens of concentration camps and subcamps held millions of slave laborers from the conquered territories. Since the January 1942 Wannsee Conference, newly built extermination camps in Poland administered the "Final Solution" for dealing with Jews who had not been able to escape German invasions and with those remaining German Jews who were too weak, too old, or too young to work as slave laborers.

In April 1942 justice of sorts was finally meted out to Reinhard Heydrich, Himmler's chief of police, who had convened the Wannsee Conference. He was in Prague to replace the former foreign minister von Neurath as governor of conquered Czechoslovakia. Von Neurath was considered too lethargic to force full cooperation from the Czechoslovaks. Heydrich was assassinated by British-trained Czech agents who were parachuted back into their home country. They threw a bomb into his open Mercedes while he was on his way to his Prague office. As punishment, the population of an entire Czech village, Lidice, was executed. Heydrich was given a hero's funeral in Berlin, though it was said that neither Himmler nor Hitler was overly pained. Heydrich was highly intelligent but thoroughly ambitious and dangerous.

On November 2, 1942, Montgomery launched the attack at El Alamein that began the destruction of the Afrikakorps. Rommel was in Germany on sick leave, and his successors were not up to the task. On November 8 the Americans landed in western North Africa, behind the Afrikakorps, and on the eleventh, German troops ended the sham of an "independent" and sovereign French zone, run by Pétain and his Vichy government, by rushing through the *Zone Libre* toward the south to face the Allies across the Mediterranean.

Newly promoted Field Marshal Friedrich Paulus, who was Hitler's favorite commander on the Russian front and one of the few generals who had fully approved of the SS cruelties in Poland in 1939, was running out of courage. Since November 1942 he and his frozen men had been surrounded and battered at impenetrable Stalingrad, while his supreme commander at Führer headquarters in East Prussia insisted that he hold his ground. On February 2–3, 1943, he finally surrendered to the Russians with his entire vast command of ninety thousand men. Hitler branded him a coward and an archtraitor. Having only just handed Paulus his field marshal's baton, Hitler yelled, "The man should have shot himself!" The captive Paulus promptly organized a committee of fellow prisoners into a somewhat suspect "anti-Nazi" group.

It is very likely that many of the sophisticated initiates within reach of the Hitler circle in Berlin had heard about the extermination camps, what later became known as the Holocaust, or *Shoa* (the Hebrew term).

The first U.S. newspaper reports were in the *New York Times* of June 30, 1942 (page 7) and July 2 (page 6). On August 28 a cable reached Rabbi Stephen Wise, the American Jewish leader in New York, from Gerhardt Riegner of the World Jewish Congress in Geneva about the existence of extermination camps. Belsen had been open since March 16, and Himmler paid an official inspection visit to Auschwitz on July 17. The first deportation train to Treblinka arrived on July 23.

The cable to Rabbi Wise had actually been sent on August 8, 1942, but was held up in American diplomatic channels for twenty days. A copy finally reached New York because it was transmitted by Sidney Silverman, a British Labour M.P.

More reports of extermination camps appeared in November 1942. There was still widespread disbelief, even among Jewish groups. The whole thing seemed too monstrous, even for the Nazis. Jews in Palestine could not believe the reports, and there were doubts voiced in the Histadruth executive meetings of November 25–26, 1942.

American OSS reports about the killer camps were viewed with reserve by Allen Dulles, brother of Schacht's old protagonist from the Versailles conference days, now undercover OSS chief in neutral Geneva.[270] At great personal risk, in September 1942 the

German industrialist Eduard Reinhard Schulte informed several key people in Switzerland about the mass deportations. Dulles saw it as "a wild rumor, inspired by Jewish fears."[271] American Jewish organizations were still sending parcels to people who no longer existed. [272]

If these stories circulated everywhere in the world, they certainly had to be known among leading Nazi and government sources in Berlin. Hitler's "court" was a rumor mill, a kettle of infighting, backstabbing, and whispers, which did not upset the Führer. He liked dissension among his followers.

Knowledge that the SS was systematically massacring human beings in mechanized abattoirs might have horrified many leading Germans, even leading Nazis, but no one protested. The sight of SS uniforms with the threatening diamond-shaped SD (*Sicherheits Dienst,* or Security Service) of the secret police on the left lower sleeve made even army generals quake. The penalties for any statements that might be interpreted as "diluting the German people's will to fight" (*Wehrwillenzersetzung*) ranged from long prison sentences to death.

For the average German, the very remoteness of the extermination camps in conquered eastern Poland removed a sense of reality, which was exactly why the SS had built them there. If the Jewish lawyer, doctor, or businessman who had "lived downstairs in the apartment house" until 1939 had been slaughtered in an eastern camp three years later, who was to know? Lists of victims were not published. If Jewish people were arrested by the police, it was usually explained by euphemisms like "resettlement," "reapportioning," "relocating." No one could doubt that it was dreadful to be marched toward a railroad station with hundreds of others, guarded by armed SS or police. To a status-conscious

270. OSS report nos. 2896, 88254, 24736, 24728.

271. A. Kraut and R. Breitman in *Commentary* (September 1, 1993), ex *New York Times* (September 28, 1993).

272. Walter Laquer, Leo Baeck Memorial Lecture 23 (1979), pp. 3–28.

middle-class German, this was the ultimate degradation. But most people did not necessarily conclude that the deported families were on their way to extinction. Germans, like other Europeans, thought of themselves as normal churchgoing human beings and were convinced that organized mass murder was not the German way. Such brutalities were "the Soviet way," like the mass executions of Polish officers at Katyn. Obviously, Germans had witnessed many anti-Jewish brutalities and abuses such as public beatings, synagogue burnings, and the denunciation of Jewish neighbors by *über* Nazis for minor offenses. They were not pleased with a storm-trooper neighbor who had beaten up a Jew when he was drunk. Their reaction to these events was generally *"Wenn das der Führer wüsste!"* ("If the Führer only knew!") Obviously, the Führer could not know about the neighbor's drunken debauch, and no one was going to send a letter to Herr A. Hitler in the middle of a war.

They had other, more immediate worries. They faced nightly air attacks, which grew in intensity and frequency. Their menfolk on the eastern front were fighting for their lives. Casualty lists were long, and most families had their dead and wounded. The official Wehrmacht reports spoke of "defensive triumphs." The rumor mill told another story, but no one grumbled openly. It was too dangerous. The SS and its informers were everywhere. The SS also guarded the concentration camps, both the forced labor ones and those in faraway Poland.

And then there were also SS men who were fighting alongside the army, Waffen SS, first-class troops. The average German civilian was too confused, frightened, bomb-scared, and sleepless to make judgments, and the Wehrmacht in combat often welcomed the presence of a dedicated SS panzer division. As they said, "*In der Not, frisst der Teufel Fliegen.*" ("In an emergency, the Devil feeds on flies.")

No one blamed the Führer. Adolf Hitler, the man "who was always right" and who had won so many bloodless victories through bluff and bluster, was still sacrosanct, even in the midst of a brutal, losing war. He still held a paternal place in their lives.

If cruelties were being committed, they were "not his fault." The "people around him" were to blame. He "received bad advice." His lieutenants "lied to him."

At a more sophisticated level, it seemed clear that the real culprit was Heinrich Himmler, the colorless former chicken farmer with the rimless glasses. His black-tabbed, gray-uniformed SS policemen and their leather-coated Gestapo brethren were known to be capable of almost anything. Everyone wanted to avoid "that bunch." After the dangerous Heydrich had been laid to rest with pomp and ceremony, Fritz Kaltenbrunner, a towering, chain-smoking Austrian lawyer, was appointed to take his place, and there was no letup in the constant and pervasive presence of the secret police. But Himmler would have been powerless without his Führer.

Against this background of danger, it was astonishing that Schacht launched yet another protest, this time to Göring. When he heard in November 1942 that fifteen-year-old high school boys were about to be drafted for antiaircraft duty, he was outraged. His letter to the *Reichsmarschall* outlined an eight-point list of reasons why the war was lost and why it was time to seek peace:

1. The chance of a quick war has long gone.
2. The chance to subdue England through air attacks has gone.
3. The promise that Germany would not be attacked by enemy aircraft is broken.
4. The repeated statements that Russia's resistance is crushed are untrue.
5. The flow of Allied supplies and Russian men to the eastern front has brought forceful counterattacks against our forces.
6. The victorious march against Egypt has foundered.
7. The "impossible" Allied landings in North Africa have taken place.
8. Our U-boats could not prevent this seaborne invasion.
   In addition to all this, there are visible shortages of civilian supplies, transportation, raw materials for armaments and in the labor force. The drafting of fifteen-year-olds should strengthen the view that it is time to put an end to this war.

He waited seven weeks for a reaction. It began when Hitler's chief of Chancellery, Lammers, sent one of his flunkies with a document discharging Schacht from his Ministry without Portfolio. A letter from Lammers that accompanied the firing conveyed the following message: "In view of your attitude toward the German nation in the midst of its fateful struggle, the Führer has, first of all, decided to discharge you from the office of Minister of the Reich." The wording promised that more was to follow.

Next came a letter from Göring, accusing Schacht of being defeatist and of undermining the fighting will of the people. This time Schacht was dismissed from membership in the Prussian state council, a meaningless organization.

Then a letter from the all-powerful Martin Bormann, the Führer's tiny, fat, and crude personal secretary, instructing him to return the Golden Party Badge, which had been awarded to him and to all cabinet ministers on January 30, 1937, to celebrate the fourth anniversary of Hitler's appointment as chancellor.

From that moment on, Schacht was under constant surveillance by the Berlin Gestapo, so he moved to Gühlen, where the Gestapo agents were no longer in evidence. However, he was certain that his mail was being opened and that his phone was tapped.[273]

Since 1938 Schacht had been in touch with others who disagreed with the Nazis. This contact ranged from open and bold meetings to discreet and tenuous hints. The figure he most respected in the anti-Hitler resistance was still General Ludwig Beck, who had wanted to stop Hitler before Chamberlain came to Munich. He had become a center of opposition along with Carl Friedrich Goerdeler, a former mayor of Leipzig. Goerdeler even began to draw up plans for a post-Hitler German government. Goerdeler had resigned as mayor in a disagreement with National Socialism. He turned down a senior position at Krupp and launched himself into organizing opposition against Hitler.

273. Schacht, *76 Jahre meines Lebens*, p. 530.

Many of Schacht's contacts with the opposition came through the Mittwoch Gesellschaft, the Wednesday Club, a group of politicians, intellectuals, businessmen, journalists, and military men — part social, part political, not unlike New York's Century Association. The Mittwoch Gesellschaft put him in touch with Goerdeler; others whom he already knew were Ulrich von Hassell, former ambassador to Italy: Johannes Popitz, former state secretary of Prussia's minister of finance, a nationalist who never joined the Nazi Party and tried unsuccessfully to resign after the Kristallnacht debauch; Ferdinand Sauerbruch, Germany's most eminent surgeon; and Albrecht Haushofer, a professor of economics in Berlin, originally a mentor and then a protégé of Rudolf Hess. In the past Haushofer had also advised von Ribbentrop, who was at one time subordinate to Hess within the party structure. Haushofer needed patronage from up high because his mother was non-Aryan. With Hess in England and out of favor with the Führer, Haushofer walked a narrow and dangerous path.

They were all enemies of the Hitler regime, and most of them would become its victims before the final collapse.

Curiously, while he kept in contact with the Mittwoch group, Schacht, one of the most indiscreet men while in office, decided to withdraw from Goerdeler, whom he considered too indiscreet. Probably his most important source of information was his friend General Hans Oster, the right hand of Admiral Canaris, the Wehrmacht's chief of intelligence. Oster was a courageous enemy of the Nazis. Schacht also stayed friendly with Captain Hans Strünck, an intelligence officer, and his wife, Elisabeth; both were frequent visitors to Gühlen. Among his most interesting contacts was the lawyer Hans Bernd Gisevius, who was assigned to the Gestapo and then to the Abwehr (Intelligence), where he soon became a close friend of Oster's. Schacht stayed in close touch with Count von Helldorf, head of the Berlin police, and with Herbert Göring, a cousin but no friend of the *Reichsmarschall*. Arthur Nebe, a professional policeman and one of Gisevius's former Gestapo associates, was disillusioned with the Nazi leaders and became another source and ally.

All these men shared one goal: to get rid of the Hitler clique. Their plans were still vague. Hans von Dohnányi, a political specialist in the Abwehr, another of Oster's friends, drew a lengthy list of those who were to be prosecuted after Hitler was removed and others who would be chosen to govern Germany. Von Dohnányi, a legal expert, meant to structure the future before dealing with the present. When he read his outline to Schacht, it began with "Hitler is dead!" Schacht stopped him. He said, "Read me the outline after Hitler is dead!"[274] Von Dohnányi was eventually caught precisely because of his written plans and was executed in the Sachsenhausen concentration camp in April 1945, only a few days before Germany surrendered.

The preplanning of a future German government while Hitler was still in total command was also part of Goerdeler's thinking. While strolling in the gardens at Sans Souci, Frederick the Great's superb castle in Potsdam, von Hassell, speaking on Goerdeler's behalf, asked Schacht if he would serve under Goerdeler in a future government. Schacht refused to commit himself. He told von Hassell that the question was totally premature. In his memoirs Schacht mentioned somewhat acidly that von Hassell was probably afraid that Schacht might interfere with the old diplomat's desire to become foreign minister in the new regime.[275] In fact, Goerdeler was only planning a quasi-democratic form of government, with "special status" for "special groups" like the Jews. Goerdeler was eventually executed in Berlin's Plötzensee prison, a strange fate for a man who refused on moral grounds to consider the assassination of Hitler. The person who denounced him got a reward of 1 million marks.[276]

A telephone dispatch to the *New York Times* from Switzerland, printed on April 10, was headlined BERNE HEARS SCHACHT INCURS NAZI DISFAVOR.

274. Ibid., p. 532.
275. Ibid.
276. Christian Zentner and Friedemann Bedürftig, *Das Grosse Lexikon des Dritten Reiches,* pp. 220–21.

It stated that the "once financial dictator of Germany and influential factor in shaping early financial policies of the Nazi regime has retired to Lienzi, a quiet spot in the Tyrol, according to private advices [sic] from Berlin." The story further stated that "Dr. Schacht has been ousted from the Party and requested to return his golden membership badge, whereat [sic] the financier is alleged to have demanded the refunding of membership dues paid during the past year."[277]

The diaries of former Nazi diplomat Carl Prüfer show that on the morning of April 14, 1943, there were two air raids on Berlin and later that night he dined with friends where he "met Dr. Schacht and his wife. He is the same indiscreet Bramarbas he was in the past." *Bramarbas* is a term in a famous Spanish novel for a braggart. On the same day Prüfer recorded that the German government published the news about Katyn Forest, where Russian troops murdered thousands of Polish officers. Prüfer went on to write, "The effect of this announcement would be monstrous, were it not for the atrocities against the Jews," obviously indicating that the existence of extermination camps was widely known outside of the inner SS circles.[278]

Schacht's self-confidence remained indomitable. He kept thinking that he might still be able to influence events through the power of his logic. By the summer of 1943 he felt reasonably sure that he would not be arrested or worse, so once more he wrote to Hitler's faithful man Lammers. He pointed out that despite the treatment he had received, he "felt duty bound to submit to the Führer a short resume of my thoughts about the political situation." He wanted to do so, "since the fate of Germany, National Socialism and Adolf Hitler are totally intertwined." He asked if Hitler was prepared to receive his written views. Lammers's delayed answer finally came on August 19, 1943: "I have forwarded your request to the Führer and he wishes you to refrain from contacting him."

277. *New York Times* (April 10, 1943), p. 2:2.
278. Carl Prüfer, *Diaries*, pp. 73 –74.

Only then did he finally realize it was over. Nothing remained but total opposition.

In 1943 a new, important ally was introduced to Schacht by an old friend and fellow officer of Jens Schacht's, Luftwaffe Lieutenant Colonel Hans Gronau, an economics officer for the Berlin district army command. As early as 1939, while visiting Gühlen, Gronau had read a twenty-page anti-Nazi memorandum of Schacht's. Gronau was amazed at Schacht's openness, but Schacht told him, "Let the swine read it and then hang me!"[279] In 1943 Gronau introduced Schacht to General Fritz Lindemann, a friend of Goerdeler's and one of the few generals who decided that the time for draconian measures had come. As chief procurement officer for the artillery, Lindemann had easy access to the General Staff, where several other senior officers were ready for a coup d'état. Lindemann, who was stationed in the east, visited Berlin frequently. He was the sort of military ally Schacht had been looking for; so he finally committed himself to join the plot to assassinate Adolf Hitler.

In April 1943, because they were deemed either unreliable or incompetent, both Canaris and Oster were relieved of their positions. It was a great blow to Schacht and the others who had depended on them as sources of information. Berlin was under attack by Allied bombers both in the daytime and during the night. Sleeplessness was the norm, and ghostly people shuttled between their bomb-scarred places of business, their damaged homes, and the bomb shelters. The streets were filled with rubble. It became increasingly difficult and dangerous to conduct daily lives. When Abwehr intelligence officer Hans Strünck and his wife were bombed out, the Schachts offered them the basement of their Berlin villa.[280] Despite his chief's dismissal, Strünck, a friend of Oster's and one of the anti-Hitler group, had kept his post at Abwehr headquarters, and it was he who managed to keep Schacht informed. (Strünck's main source of infor-

279. Peterson, *Hjalmar Schacht,* p. 320.
280. Gisevius, *BIS ZUM BITTEREN ENDE,* p. 556.

mation was a Colonel Hansen, who was assigned to take Oster's place.) By the beginning of 1944 a feasible plan for the assassination of Adolf Hitler was finally in place. Schacht urged Lindemann and his associates to hurry, but they had to abandon date after date because of Hitler's uncertain and unplanned daily habits and travel plans. Unwilling to live the harried existence of others in the government, Hitler retreated into the vast, gloomy complex of cement bunkers deep in the woods in Rastenburg, East Prussia. It was romantically named the *Wolfsschanze* (Wolf's Lair). The official explanation was that it was "nearer to the troops on the eastern front," although Berlin would have been just as suitable, geographically.

Meanwhile, Hitler was still scheming. On January 6, 1944, the United Press reported from Berlin that Schacht was slated to replace von Ribbentrop as foreign minister.[281] On January 10, writing for the North American Newspaper Alliance, Dr. Max Immanuel, who had worked for Schacht before emigrating to the United States, pointed out in an article from Washington that the rumor was a trial balloon, floated by Hitler specifically to see whether, in case of any peace feelers, Schacht's vaunted connections in America were still usable.[282] The isolated Schacht was unaware of the report.

On the stormy morning of June 6, 1944, German troops manning the coastal fortifications of Normandy could not believe their eyes when a vast armada emerged from the hazy horizon to their west. The long-expected Allied invasion had begun. British and American airborne troops dropped from the sky behind the coastal defenses, and others stormed ashore from landing barges on a wide front.

The Normandy invasion took place during the final weeks of the long-planned military rebellion against the Hitler regime. The invasion came just in time. The anti-Hitler rebellion was too

281. *New York Times* (January 7, 1944), p. 4:4.
282. *New York Times* (January 10, 1944), p. 2:4.

late and also strangely amateurish, though it was launched by some of the best military men of the time.

Some leading officers who should have been at the forefront of the rebellion refused to participate. Several were probably too cowardly to confront the executioner's axe. Others felt bound by the oath they had given to obey Adolf Hitler "as Reich chancellor and Führer" following the Blomberg and Fritsch dismissals. No amount of proof that they had been deceived and misled by their commander in chief could sway them. One of these was General Franz Halder, who took over Beck's post as chief of staff in 1938 after Beck's resignation because of Chamberlain's act of appeasement. Halder had actually been in touch with the resistance people since 1938. He knew about Goerdeler, Schacht, Canaris, Beck. When he was first approached to join the group, he said, "Let Canaris do the assassinating."[283] He eventually found himself in forceful opposition to Hitler, but for professional rather than political reasons. He refused to go along with his amateurish commander in chief in matters of strategy and tactics. He insisted that troops be withdrawn from every other sector to relieve the Wehrmacht at Stalingrad, but Hitler refused. Halder was then dismissed, but he would not "compromise his oath as a Prussian officer" by joining the plotters. Nevertheless, he later was sent to a concentration camp by his suspicious Führer.

Marshal Erich von Manstein, an irascible cockspur but a brilliant soldier and Hitler's only remaining hope in Russia, was approached by the plotters. He refused, proclaiming that "German marshals do not mutiny!"[284] He had no idea that he would be fired by Hitler only weeks later. When he reported to the Berghof in Bavaria to get his final decoration and pro forma thanks-and-good-bye, he was quartered in a nearby vacation hotel. Several senior SS officers were raucously ill-behaved in the dining room, but von Manstein was so cowed that he did not even complain.

---

283. Joachim Fest, *Staatsstreich,* p. 131.
284. Ibid, p. 203.

So much for what remained of an irascible Prussian field marshal under the thumb of Adolf Hitler.

Others believed that assassinating the commander in chief in the midst of Germany's life-and-death struggle in Russia would undermine the troops' determination to resist the Soviets and would throw German defenses into complete disarray. For some, nothing could justify killing. Count Helmuth James von Moltke, one of Hitler's early enemies, and his "Kreisau" (the name of his estate) circle of civilian comrades objected on moral and religious grounds, as did Goerdeler.

Not all the plotters were longtime enemies of the regime. Many of the younger officers had been devoted Hitler Youth and willing recipients of quick promotions as the army expanded. They were aware of SS atrocities but shrugged. Then Stalingrad, Leningrad, Moscow, the Soviet army, Allied bombers over Germany, and finally the invasion of Normandy had combined to dim their enthusiasm. They were on the losing side, and their friends were dying while their families were being bombed out of their estates. "Time to get rid of the incompetent Austrian corporal and his riffraff and to sue for terms with the Western Allies, before the Russians overrun Germany."[285]

Some of the plotters were opportunists, but many others were religious and patriotic men and women. For instance, Axel von dem Bussche, an officer in Germany's most traditional Prussian unit, the elite Ninth Infantry Regiment, was driving back to the front to rejoin his regiment when he arrived at a clearing and watched an SS unit conduct the mass execution of naked Jewish men, women, and children. His immediate instinct was to undress and join the line of victims. In his eyes, it would have helped him save a vestige of German honor. He also realized that had he done so, he would have been arrested by the SS and sent to an asylum. So he returned to his regiment and told his fellow officers what he had witnessed. They all came to the conclusion that this

285. Frequent statement to author, 1944–45.

had to stop. Von dem Bussche, a handsome man, got himself assigned temporarily to Berlin to "model" a new winter uniform for the Führer. He then planned to step forward, embrace Hitler, and explode two primed grenades he carried in his pockets.

The plan was foiled by an Allied air raid. The new uniform was burned in a freight car at a Berlin railway station, and Hitler never appeared.

Another officer, Fabian von Schlabrendorff, placed a bottle of "cognac" filled with high explosives on Hitler's private plane under the guise of "sending a gift to a fellow officer at Berlin headquarters." The bomb's barometric fuse failed, and the bomb never exploded. A fellow plotter in Berlin had the less-than-enviable task of collecting it after the plane had landed safely. "Oh," said the plotter to the pilot, who thought he had done him a favor, "there it is! So kind of you to bring it!" He then quickly disappeared with his dangerous and temperamental burden. Several of these attempts were planned during 1942 and 1943 by individuals or small groups — whenever the opportunity seemed to present itself — but they had all failed.

On April 15, 1944, news came from Stockholm that delivered a blow to the Schacht family. The Gestapo had arrested Hilger van Scherpenberg, Inge's husband, now a Foreign Service officer at the German embassy in Sweden. He was accused of loose talk about Germany's lack of critical war matériel.[286]

Then, finally, came the most serious effort to conduct a coup d'état, which involved even officers in German army headquarters abroad, including the Paris garrison.

The man who took personal responsibility for the actual assassination was a much-wounded and -decorated young colonel, a devout Catholic named Claus, Count Schenk von Stauffenberg. The colonel was the hub of the plot, the man who had convinced, cajoled, and sometimes demanded that those who had not shown the courage must face the inevitable. He and his close associates

286. *New York Times* (April 16, 1944), p. 6:1.

had reached out courageously to officers of all ranks, from field marshals to lieutenants. He finally decided that since he had done most of the talking, it now was his duty to do the deed.

Everything seemed to fall into place for July 20, 1944, when he had an appointment to report to Hitler. Early that morning in Berlin, he met with his priest, who strengthened his resolve. He then immediately left by air for the Wolf's Lair. His official mission was to report to the Führer as Wehrmacht recruitment chief for foreign volunteers.

Armed with his written orders, he had no trouble passing the three tight SS security cordons of the Wolf's Lair. He was greatly handicapped by his wounds, which had left him with only one usable hand and its three remaining fingers. Firing a pistol was out of the question, so he carried a bomb that was concealed in a briefcase. He was scheduled to report to Hitler and his staff during the daily situation conference, and he placed the briefcase-bomb under the map table during a military conference, primed the bomb, and then excused himself, supposedly to make a phone call. Then a series of coincidences saved Hitler's life. The powerful bomb exploded, but the meeting was held in an aboveground wood barracks instead of the usual underground concrete shelter. The barracks could not contain the concussive force of the bomb, thereby diminishing the explosion. Also, someone had moved the briefcase aside with his foot, which diverted the explosion instead of vertically blowing up the heavy map table over which Hitler was leaning. After hearing the devastating noise of the bomb from outside, von Stauffenberg assumed that everyone at the conference was dead. He rushed back to the airstrip through the three SS cordons and had taken off for Berlin before anyone was aware of the nature of the explosion and the survival of the Führer. He did not know that he had failed until after he landed in the capital.

There was an immediate news blackout. Eventually, reports mentioned a failed coup by three generals, all "incompetent." They were Beck, Höpner, and Olbricht, who was actually in charge of the technical details of the plot. Von Stauffenberg was not mentioned. One New York newspaper said that Schacht had been arrested by the Gestapo and shot.[287]

Schacht was quite aware of the plot and of the plotters' identities. For safety's sake, he had taken his and Manci's two young daughters to southern Bavaria, where Inge van Scherpenberg lived, and had put them into her charge. Inge's husband was in Gestapo custody, and she now had to care for her two young stepsisters. But like her father, she could handle things. Schacht was back in the Hotel Regina in Munich when he heard through Colonel Gronau that the attempt had failed and that Hitler was only superficially wounded and still alive.[288] The hotel's concierge then discreetly pointed out two Gestapo men in the lobby who were obviously shadowing him, so on July 21 he left Munich and returned to Manci at Gühlen on the twenty-second. They spent the day listening to radio reports about the arrests and executions of the plotters. The coup itself was portrayed as "limited to a few ambitious and treacherous officers." Once more, "destiny had protected the Führer" for the German people. There were newspaper pictures of the ambulant Hitler, showing the scene of the explosion to a shaky and gray-faced Mussolini, who had just been saved by SS Colonel Otto Skorzeny and some commandos from being prosecuted by his own people. By coincidence, Mussolini had been scheduled to arrive at the Wolf's Lair to express his thanks to his patron and protector.

At 7 A.M. the next morning, on July 23, Schacht was awakened by the family cook. The frightened woman told him that two plain-clothes policemen had arrived at Gühlen. Still in his pajamas, he met with the agents. They informed him that he was under arrest. As he recalled, "I dressed calmly and informed my wife, who then also got dressed. I handed her our most important keys in the presence of the police, who then took me out to the road, where several cars were waiting near the gate. I bid my wife good-bye and called

287. *New York Times* (July 28, 1944), p. 4:1.
288. Schacht, *Abrechnung mit Hitler,* p. 99.

out to her that I would be back in a few days, but I could tell from her very pale face that she was not very convinced."[289]

Neither Kaltenbrunner, the national secret police chief, nor Otto Ohlendorf, a top Gestapo SS man, knew the detailed reasons for the arrest. Kaltenbrunner said later that only Hitler or Himmler could have ordered it and that only Hitler could have ordered Schacht's execution. Speer testified later that Hitler was infuriated by Schacht's final unwillingness to underwrite armaments for war. He quoted Hitler as saying, "Such men should be shot!"[290] The first reports in the Western press of Schacht's arrest came through Reuters in London on August 11. A tiny dispatch on page 4 of the New York Times claimed that Radio Moscow had made the announcement during a program for the Red Army. On October 11 Dagens Nyheter reported from Stockholm that Schacht's niece, Sigrid Schacht, who was working at the German legation, told the Swedish government that her uncle had been imprisoned by the Gestapo. That week Sigrid Schacht asked for and received Swedish citizenship.

New York congressman Emanuel Celler saw things differently. He warned in a statement to the press that the Nazis were actually grooming Schacht as a front man for future peace offerings and that Schacht was by no means anti-Nazi. He was being used by Goebbels.[291] "What keener choice than manipulator Schacht?" Celler "did not mean to impugn" the character of Americans who had dealt with Schacht, such as Herbert Hoover, John Foster Dulles, Allen Dulles, and Robert Murphy (an aide to Eisenhower).

From a completely different viewpoint, U.S. secretary of war Henry Stimson was no more generous. He warned people not to trust the "Junker rebellion."[292]

289. Schacht, 76 Jahre meines Lebens, p. 534.
290. Peterson, Hjalmar Schacht, p. 337.
291. New York Times (October 11, 1944), p. 6:1.
292. New York Times (July 28, 1944), p. 4:2.

19

PRISONS

HJALMAR SCHACHT spent the next four years in a succession of thirty-two different prisons or concentration camps, two of those years in solitary confinement. Schacht was a man in fine physical condition — tall, slim, and energetic — but the sixty-seven-year-old now had to face a complete change from his previous comfortable existence. As a wealthy banker, senior government official, and cabinet minister, he had lived in luxury, attended by chauffeurs and household servants. He had always traveled in first-class accommodations on trains and ships and descended at the grandest of international hotels. Beyond the loss of physical comforts, the complete loss of the privileges of rank outraged a man who began life without money, had created his own wealth and lofty reputation and had always ardently protected his place in society. He had always insisted on courtesy and formality and deemed himself the equal of any man, no matter how highly ranked. To Adolf Hitler's fury and expressed annoyance, Schacht rarely addressed the German leader as "Mein Führer," expecting that Hitler would address him as "Herr Doktor," which was his own due.[293] Now he found himself at the mercy of minor police officials and crude prison guards.

293. Picker, *Hitler's Tischgespräche*, p. 234.

He realized that he could no longer expect respectful treatment, and he accepted the boorishness and occasional cruelties without complaint or personal anguish. The tiny prison cells were often without sanitary facilities. If a commode was in his cell, he had to face the indignity of being observed through a peephole while he relieved himself. If the latrine was outside and communal, he had to call for a guard and be accompanied and supervised each time nature called. Since he had no access to reading matter, he had to use his imagination to provide his own intellectual entertainment. The man who once moved out of the Hotel Royal Monceau in Paris during a major international conference because the food "was inedible" now lived on the sparse and ill-prepared prison fare of a bombed and battered nation in economic distress. Finally, the man who loved women and had a fresh new marriage with two young children had to forgo even those comforts.

He faced his imprisonment with complete calm and a disdainful refusal to be disheartened, discouraged, or intimidated by his predicament. He was first confined in Ravensbrück, a concentration camp originally meant for female prisoners but now the grim accommodation for any "enemy of the state." Always the banker, the trader, the *débrouillard,* he managed to achieve some small special privileges from his Teuto-Lithuanian head guard, a man named Moschkus, by bribing him with some of the cigars he had managed to bring along from Gühlen.[294]

There were many rumors about his arrest and whereabouts. Victor Klemperer, whose recently published diaries document daily life in Hitler's Germany during the war, wrote on August 8 that "the Americans are on their way to Paris" and that "Schacht, Neurath and Nebe [the Gestapo man associated with Gisevius] were executed." Later that month Klemperer repeated the execution rumor about Schacht but added that Germany's most famous surgeon, Professor Ferdinand Sauerbruch, was also a victim.

Bomb-weary Berliners still kept some of their usual gallows

294. Peterson, *Hjalmar Schacht,* p. 536.

humor. They said that the thousands of signs that said LSR (*Luftschutzraum,* or air-raid shelter) actually meant *Lernt schnell Russisch!* (Quickly, learn Russian!)[295]

In Ravensbrück Schacht, though kept in isolation, spotted the reluctant General Halder and also former Weimar war minister Gustav Noske, who had once suppressed the left-wing Spartacus rebellion after World War I. Schacht bribed a guard into finding him a copy of the previous day's party newspaper, the *Völkischer Beobachter,* and he searched in vain through the list of arrested officers for the name of General Lindemann. Where, he wondered, was General Lindemann? Had he escaped? Lindemann was the only one who could have testified that Schacht was fully informed about the plot.

Schacht went through the first of the innumerable interrogations at a nearby police installation. His interrogator, a Lieutenant John, instructed him to dictate the story of his life to a typist. After being told to go into great detail, Schacht calmly proceeded to do as he was bid. It took hours. Ever the journalist, he probably remembered his old Berlin editor's admonition to write "what they want to read." He edited as he went along, with a clear eye toward the eventual readership, the Gestapo. He presented a politically sanitized version of Hjalmar Horace Greeley Schacht's curriculum vitae.

The following day's interrogation began on a more ominous note. Lieutenant John asked Schacht to "give us the names of your friends."

Schacht's answer, "I won't do that!" brought threats from the interrogator. Schacht finally calmed him and explained, "I must refuse, because I may mention some name first, and then you will assume that this person is particularly important to me. Or I may forget to mention someone, and when you find out that I know the person, you will think I was purposely withholding information." Then he showed his usual negotiating genius. "Why don't you call my wife in Gühlen and tell her that I have given you per-

295. Victor Klemperer, *Tagebücher,* pp. 559, 575.

mission to use our guestbook." Only overnight guests were asked to inscribe their names, and his anti-Hitler coconspirators invariably paid only hasty daytime visits. Besides, before Schacht's dismissal, there were leading Nazi figures among the overnight guests. Lieutenant John promptly visited Gühlen; was treated to coffee, cake, and charm by Manci Schacht; and returned, guestbook in hand, a much more benevolent inquisitor.

One day Schacht had to give his guard a special bribe to receive his *Völkischer Beobachter*. It had been withheld because it named twenty-eight officers who had been shot summarily. There was also a list of wanted persons, among them General Lindemann, which relieved Schacht. Lindemann was still free. Beck was dead. The night after the attempt had failed, sitting at his desk in his old office in the Berlin army headquarters, Beck had tried to shoot himself but succeeded only in blinding himself. He was finally helped by a compassionate sergeant who finished the job, supposedly on orders from army High Command. Compared with many others who fell into Gestapo hands later, the luckiest of the plotters were Stauffenberg and some of his close associates. Pinpointed by the headlights of SS vehicles in the courtyard of Berlin's army command, they were shot that very night. He shouted, "God preserve our holy Germany!" just before the volley was fired. Others were eventually put on public drumhead trials, condemned after listening to days of the prosecution's insults. The government's chief prosecutor, a hate-filled former Communist named Roland Freisler, conducted show trials in what was known as the People's Court (*Volksgericht*). His attacks on the men in the dock were so strident and vitriolic that Goebbels could not use all of them for propaganda purposes. The accused were the bearers of some of Germany's most historical names, like Moltke, Dohna, Witzleben, Hassell, Schulenburg, and Schwerin. Then the conspirators were executed in the most inhuman and cruel manner at Berlin's Plötzensee prison, hanged from meathooks. A film team was ordered to record their agony so that Hitler could see it for himself at the end of each day, but the film crew had to give up, the scene was so gruesome.

Justice was served only when an air-raid warning sounded during the trial of Fabian von Schlabrendorff, the officer who once tried to blow up Hitler's plane with a cognac bottle of high explosives. Both prosecutor and accused were rushed to the basement of the court building. Then an American bomb pierced the roof and sliced through floor after floor until it found the cellar, where it dislodged a ceiling beam, which then killed Freisler. Von Schlabrendorff, the accused, watched with some delight from only a few yards away. He survived both the People's Court and the war.

While these men were being tortured, the Allies were pushing across Holland, France, and Belgium. The Russians were bearing down on Germany's eastern border. Night after night, the RAF pulverized Germany's cities, and by day, the U.S. Air Force crushed what was left. The Wehrmacht was running out of fuel. The same problem also grounded the Luftwaffe. Hitler's threatened mystery weapons, the V-1 self-propelled bombs and the V-2 rocket missiles, failed to slow down the pace of the Allied effort. A final German offensive in December, which gambled everything on an attack in the snow-choked Ardennes mountains, was brought to a halt on Christmas Day 1944, when the skies cleared and Allied fighter planes went to work. His war was clearly lost, but Hitler's barbarism increased. The extermination camps ran twenty-four-hour shifts.

For Schacht, Ravensbrück was only the beginning.

On August 28, 1944, came the first real challenge to Schacht's usual equilibrium. He was ordered to don blue-and-white-striped prison gear with wooden shoes. He did not obey easily, but there was no swaying the warden, a Gestapo man named Lange. Wearing prison stripes plunged Schacht into unaccustomed feelings of inferiority. In his own words, he found it nearly unbearable that no degree of opposition or anger or insistence could protect him from having to wear the hated garb. He was equally aghast that guards immediately began to treat him like a criminal. Again in his words, "Who could blame them? A uniform identifies the man, the way an army officer's uniform often rewards an inferior man with the treatment of a gentle-man."[296] It gave him a sense of solidarity with others in prison stripes. For the first time he, who had never worn a uniform, re-alized how difficult it was for any uniformed man to maintain a sense of independence.

Worse, he was also handcuffed and loaded into the backseat of a car, with the Ravensbrück warden in front. They took him to the cells in the basement of Gestapo headquarters at 9 Prinz Al-brecht Strasse, in Berlin, the most feared address in Nazi Ger-many. He was kept waiting for hours without food or drink in a holding pen, until it was established that there was no cell free in the Gestapo basement. They then transported him to the Moabit prison, an old jail for criminals. His toilet kit had been lost in transit. For the first time he felt "like a postal package," being shipped to and fro.[297] It would happen constantly during the prison years to follow. He got used to sleeping on hard, louse-infested bunks and to hunting vermin. Unable to resist, he sug-gested to the prison staff that they should paint cell walls in light colors, to ease the hunt for bedbugs and lice. Like the others, he relieved himself into a bucket, which he put out to be collected each morning. His toilet kit never arrived.

Fortunately, he stayed in Moabit for only three days. Then it was back to the Gestapo. A cell was now free. Another unkempt four days later he finally got his personal gear. The underground cell had only a tiny grating to the fresh air above. He stayed there for the next four months.

Some things became a little easier. He was permitted to wear his civilian clothes and to receive some gifts of food and books from Manci, but none of his beloved cigars.

He suffered through more interrogations, which he felt were as foolish and pointless as the ones at Ravensbrück. He gathered through the interrogation that he was transferred into Gestapo

296. Schacht, *76 Jahre meines Lebens,* p. 539.
297. Ibid., p. 540.

custody because of something Goerdeler must have said during his inquisition. Schacht was asked about political discussions in the Wednesday Club, but he denied that the society was political. He insisted that it was primarily a fraternal group that covered all subjects. The interrogator insisted that Goerdeler had described it as political, so Schacht said, "Ask the others of the group whom you have arrested. They will confirm what I said." They changed the subject.

"You had a meeting with Gisevius on July thirteenth?"

"No."

"We have proof."

"Show me the proof."

"We have no intention of doing that."[298]

Schacht was certain that Gisevius was in Switzerland during the days before the von Stauffenberg attempt. He persisted. "Why don't you put me face-to-face with both of them, with Goerdeler and Gisevius? That will prove that you are wrong."

It was impossible. Gisevius was still in hiding.

The interrogator, a plainclothes police inspector, grew increasingly more angry, but he was not Gestapo, so he could not do much while they were on Gestapo ground.

The interrogation room was on the third floor of the building. When Schacht asked one of the guards why they used the back stairs instead of the main stairway, he found out that another prisoner had committed suicide by crashing through a window on the way upstairs. They took the windowless back stairs to avoid another suicide.

On December 6 he was informed he would be returned to Ravensbrück. Manci had just received permission to visit him at Gestapo headquarters. To Schacht's great joy, Jens, who was on leave, had received permission to visit him as well. In a food package he found an egg, which was wrapped in a newspaper clipping of "the deserter" General Lindemann's arrest, during which he

298. Ibid., p. 542ff.

had tried to use his weapon and was shot in the abdomen. He was in the hospital. Schacht was deeply worried but managed to ask Jens in a whisper if the general had survived. Jens told him Lindemann had died.

Because Gronau had still not been arrested, Jens told him to deny that Lindemann had ever known Schacht. That denial, and Lindemann's death, saved Schacht's life. A connection to Lindemann would have sent Schacht to the gallows.

Gronau was eventually arrested, and Schacht was interrogated about him. Was it not true that Gronau had been full of criticism of the regime in his presence?

"Indeed. We criticized the German fighter planes, which were not equipped to hold off enemy bombers." After all, Gronau was a Luftwaffe officer.

"Did he not criticize National Socialism while he was at your home?"

"If he had done that," said Schacht, "I would have thrown him out at once."[299]

The only contact with fellow prisoners was in the air-raid shelter, where they assembled frequently. He saw, among others, Goerdeler, von Schlabrendorff, Canaris, Herbert Göring, Strünck, and General Thomas. No talking was allowed. Their faces were composed, except for Goerdeler and Canaris, who seemed completely distraught.

Christmas 1944 in Ravensbrück cells meant listening to SS guards singing "Holy Night" to their rudimentary Christmas tree as the sounds of Berlin being bombed could be heard in the distance. Manci came to visit on February 3, loaded with supplies she had carried for miles; but in the middle of their reunion Schacht was ordered to his cell. The Russians were closing in, and most of Ravensbrück's prisoners, among them some of Germany's most distinguished names, were to be moved. Berlin was in flames when they arrived at Gestapo headquarters on Prinz Albrecht Strasse. They found most of it in ruins and burning. Nev-

299. Ibid., p. 546.

ertheless, some prisoners were taken to the cellar, but Schacht stayed in the police truck, which then found its way through the burning city to an overcrowded jail in the nearby town of Potsdam.

Schacht shared a small cell with State Secretary Hermann Pünder, a high Weimar official, and General Alexander von Falkenhausen, the former commander of occupied Belgium.

The next morning marked another radical change. A police lieutenant colonel appeared and informed them most courteously that he had been instructed by the head of the Gestapo, SS General Heinrich Müller, that from here on they would be treated as "honor prisoners" (*Ehrenhäftlinge*), although this new status remained undefined. At least they could now take a walk in the prison courtyard.

The next day it was back to a night in the shambles of the Gestapo basement, and from there into a bus with Generals Oster, Halder, and Thomas; Captain Strünck; and former Austrian chancellor von Schuschnigg, his wife, and daughter through bomb-cratered Berlin streets, out of town, heading south. That night they arrived behind the barbed wire and guard towers of Flossenbürg, one of the most feared of all the concentration camps. It was located alongside a rock quarry; populated by Russian, Polish, and Jewish prisoners from the eastern territories, Flossenbürg had a six-year history of unrelenting overwork in the quarry, ill treatment, brutality, and death through exhaustion, illness, or execution.

Schacht and the others had better accommodations than the rest of the prisoners, but they had no illusions about the frightening place. They heard nightly shouting and shots. The commandant of the camp turned out to be the same police officer who had become furious with Schacht during his Gestapo interrogation. Schacht fully expected to die in Flossenbürg, not far from Bayreuth, where Adolf Hitler had once offered him the Ministry of Economics.

He was wrong. After two months in the ugly installation, on April 9, 1945, Schacht, the von Schuschniggs, two captured British intelligence officers, and a nephew of Russian foreign minister

Molotov were transported to Dachau concentration camp, near
Munich. Those who stayed behind in Flossenbürg — Canaris,
Oster, and Strünck — all died. They were hanged.

Schacht noticed that during the transfer, the guards were unsure and jumpy; he assumed (correctly) that Allied troops must
have been quite near.

In Dachau they were quartered in open cells and received the
apologies of the camp commandant for their poor accommodations. Schacht met Martin Niemöller (his old Berlin pastor), industrialist Fritz Thyssen, former French premier Léon Blum and
his wife, and many others he knew, mainly foreigners. The guards
tried hard to make a good impression, probably in case the Allies
captured the camp. Two weeks later the "special" prisoners were
again on the move. A long convoy of buses took them farther
south, up into the mountains, until they arrived in the small
town of Niederndorf. The group had swelled to more than 130,
collected from various places of internment and imprisonment,
including one on the island of Capri. They were a formidable
bargaining chip for the SS. Among the French prisoners were a
former prime minister, a bishop, and a Bourbon prince. The
Dutch included a cabinet minister, and there was the former
Greek commander in chief. There were two Hungarian cabinet
ministers and an ambassador; a distinguished Italian general; a
large number of German generals, ambassadors, and government
officials; and a Prussian prince.

The SS mania for destruction seemed to continue. Colonel
Bogislav von Bonin, a German prisoner, overheard two SS guards
discussing their orders to shoot and "dispose of" certain prisoners and to bomb the others while they were still in their stopped
buses.

There are various accounts of what happened next. According
to Fey von Hassell, the daughter of the executed ambassador Ulrich von Hassell and herself a prisoner, when they reached a small
mountain village called Oberndorf, the SS commanders left the
convoy to get further instructions. Colonel von Bonin spotted a
group of German army officers standing not far from the convoy
in the village square; one of them was General Heinrich von

Vietinghoff, the commander of the southern region and a close friend. Alerted by what he had overheard and because he was still in full uniform although a prisoner, von Bonin bullied an SS guard into letting him leave the bus. He rushed over to the general, who was delighted to see him. Von Bonin begged for urgent help. The general immediately sent two army officers with drawn pistols in search of the convoy's two SS commanders, whom they found in a nearby tavern. They were ordered to hand over the prisoners and to leave with their men, which they did. Army men took over from the eighty SS guards.

Many others took credit for freeing the prisoners, among them Captain Payne Best, one of the captive British intelligence officers, who claimed he was the one who alerted the German army. There was even a senior SS defector, Himmler's former aide General Karl Wolff, who was the temporary German commander in Italy. He claimed that he authorized army troops from Italy to liberate the "specials."

Few people knew what had happened to Schacht over the past months, not even Manci. On April 13, 1945, Hjalmar Schacht's brother, Dr. Eddy, had told the AP that he thought his brother Hjalmar was dead. The doctor's wife said, "My brother-in-law was a victim of his tremendous ambition; he should have kept his fingers off Nazism."

For the Nazis, the game ended when Hitler and Goebbels committed suicide in Berlin on April 30, 1945.

The small contingent of German soldiers who had been left behind by General von Vietinghoff to protect the prisoners in the event that the SS returned was finally taken prisoner by an advance American unit led by Lieutenant Melvin Asche of General Leonard Gerow's Eighty-fifth Division.

This time U.S. Army vehicles took the "specials" across the Italian border to Verona, where they were quartered in a hotel. They were free to roam the town for a day. Then they traveled south by air to Naples and the Hotel Terminus.

To their bitter shock, it was then made clear to certain of the "special prisoners," Schacht among them, that they were no longer to consider themselves free. Schacht was informed that he was accused of a long collaboration with Adolf Hitler, despite the obvious fact that in the recent past he had become a prisoner of the Reich. His explanation for his falling-out with the Führer was considered suspect.

Schacht reacted with fury and indignation. He was outraged for himself and others who were being held by the Americans. "We were treated abruptly and even rudely. We definitely felt an attitude which reflected the influence of German emigrants." He could not grasp why "we, who had fought Hitler at the risk of our lives, were thrown into the same pot as those who were part of the Hitler regime."[300] He thought he had been given his complete freedom by General Gerow, but he had miscalculated. He was once more a prisoner, this time of the U.S. Army.

300. Ibid., p. 560.

20

TO NUREMBERG

Schacht was taken to a crowded POW holding camp at Anacapri in Aversa, near Naples, along with several of the captive German generals, like Thomas and Halder. Twenty of them were crammed into a barracks, which was separated from the rest of the camp by barbed wire. As usual, their personal baggage was missing, and some prisoners complained that their money had been stolen. They were kept incommunicado. Schacht could not let Manci know that he was alive and well or where he was. His conclusion that "one imprisonment was as bad as the other" was true only because he had never really been subjected to the steel fist of Hitler's jailers. Photographs of the conspirators of July 20 in the dock at Roland Freisler's People's Court show what the Gestapo could do to courageous men. The accused, many of them coolheaded professional officers whose sangfroid was legendary, looked wan and ghostly after the beatings, manipulation, and mental torture that followed their arrest.

Conditions in Allied custody were not unlike those he had encountered during his detention by the Nazis. Though it was hard on a man in his late sixties to be locked up in the crude Gestapo cellar, Schacht was there for only a few weeks. He wore prison stripes for only a few days and was never subjected to any of the infamous Gestapo "treatment." Having suffered no more than indignities, discomforts, poor food, and occasional boorishness under the Nazis, Schacht would now have to face similar discomfort, indignities, and boorishness from the Allies. However, the food certainly was an improvement.

He was interrogated by American intelligence officers. Some of them were exiles from Germany, now naturalized U.S. citizens. They recalled how he had come to the Harzburg rally in 1932 and legitimized Hitler. They knew that Schacht had tried to intercede for Hitler with heavy industry. They could prove that Schacht had made pro-Hitler speeches. They could document his early Nazi collaboration through hundreds of newspaper and magazine pictures and miles of newsreels of the tall banker with the tubular collar at Nazi functions, side by side with the uniformed dictator.

Schacht had been in Hitler's prisons and camps for ten months. Though he could not have imagined it at the time, seventeen months of Allied imprisonment lay ahead. The way he saw things, he had been righteous, honorable, and courageous by admitting his earlier political errors and by opposing the man he had trusted and who had then betrayed his trust. Instead of receiving the Allies' thanks and respect that he expected, he was rewarded with imprisonment and badgered and harassed by German Jewish exiles, who, in his view, should have been grateful for what he tried to do for the Jews. Worse, he was being forced against his will into close contact with Nazis whom he had always snubbed and detested. Surely, the Americans, of all people, were aware of his anti-Nazi feelings and his open criticism and opposition. Why, he asked, were they now forcing him to be a "Nazi war criminal"? Was it that they needed as many well-known names as they could get for their war-crimes trials?

His mood changed abruptly. His usual acid sense of humor deserted him, as did much of his stoicism. He showed bursts of temper.

At Anacapri he expressed his outrage in petitions, letters, and demands for hearings. He was ignored. The only good thing he could see was the brilliant Italian weather.

Meanwhile, the newly formed United Nations War Crimes

Commission drew lists of those who were to be indicted for war crimes and invited nations formerly occupied by Germany (such as Greece, Czechoslovakia, and Poland) to participate. Eisenhower invited six-man teams from each of these countries to fly to the former extermination camps and then asked them to add their list of accused war criminals. The first time Hjalmar Schacht's name appeared as a criminal was on the Czechoslovak list, where it was flanked by Göring's and Funk's. A *New York Times* dispatch of May 15, 1945, reported that "the War Crimes Commission has recognized in principle *that every member of the German Government, not merely the German War Cabinet, must be held personally responsible for crimes in Allied countries* [italics added]."[301]

The actual categories for indictment were defined three months later:

> *Crimes against peace* Conspiracy to prepare for war, conspiracy to launch war
> *Crimes against humanity*
> *War Crimes*

Schacht's indictment fell into the first category. He was designated "one of the Germans who surrounded Hitler and helped him to press the program which led to the Second World War."[302] This charge was the cause of Schacht's confinement, but from the beginning he absolutely refused to acknowledge that he was in any way culpable.

Early in June Schacht, Halder, Thomas, and Fritz Thyssen were put aboard a U.S. Air Force plane. After a wild flight through a large thunderstorm over the Mediterranean and the south of France, they landed at Orly Airport, near Paris. The next few days were spent in a deserted and neglected private mansion, where they were joined by Albert Speer, Hitler's former architect and

301. *New York Times* (May 15, 1945), p. 4:2.
302. *New York Times* (August 30, 1945), p. 1:7.

protégé, who became his minister of war production; Ernst Heinkel, the aircraft manufacturer; and, as Schacht put it, "various gentlemen of the leadership of I. G. Farben." A few days later, joined by women prisoners who had been held nearby, they were trucked east, and Schacht temporarily regained his good spirits. He spent a beautiful night outdoors on a camp bed under the stars, surrounded by rambling roses, with campfires crackling, and had a "splendid breakfast" in the old garrison town of Metz.[303] Then they went on the bombed autobahn toward Frankfurt and into the Taunus mountains to a Hessian castle called Kransberg. During the war it had been expanded and expensively renovated by Speer for Göring as a sort of Luftwaffe command post. Schacht compared Kransberg with a well-run hotel. The accommodations were excellent, as was the food (courtesy of the U.S. Army's Quartermaster Corps). Days were spent with cards, lectures, discussions, and long walks in the castle's park.

He would remain there for three months, while the population of forty or fifty prisoners changed constantly. Schacht described them as "prominent men I had known from the world of business or academics."[304] He could not know that Kransberg was an Allied internment area for German business, technical, and governmental experts who were of possible future use. To take the edge off their confinement, they were given deluxe treatment. Rocket expert Wernher von Braun was one of the internees.

Schacht could not convince the commander of Kransberg to allow him to contact Manci, but in August his daughter Inge van Scherpenberg did manage to smuggle a message to her father. One of the castle's cleaning women slipped him a box of cigars and a letter, both brought to Kransberg by a friend of Inge's. The two younger girls were safe with their old nurse, who lived on the Lüneburg Heath.[305] There was no news of Manci, but he assumed

---

303. Schacht, *76 Jahre meines Lebens,* pp. 564–65.

304. Ibid., p. 565.

305. Heinz Pentzlin, *Hjalmar Schacht,* p. 265.

she had stayed in Gühlen as he had advised her to do. He did get word later in August from Hitler's physician, Dr. Karl Brandt, who had spoken to Manci just before his own arrest by the Americans. Manci was alive.

Brandt was eventually executed as an SS physician who was deeply involved with the Nazis' euthanasia program and also in experiments using helpless concentration camp prisoners to test human endurance under emergency conditions.

21

ACCUSED

WAR-CRIMES TRIALS were scheduled to begin late in September of 1945. Schacht was still in Kransberg when he heard on the radio that he was an indicted war criminal. He was interrogated repeatedly by British and American officers and complained only about the rude treatment handed to him by a "Jewish American officer." By contrast, he praised a "tough but fair" British major named Tilley, who admitted that he had distrusted Schacht but asked him to write down his views about Hitler. He then told Schacht that "he had changed course 180 degrees" after reading Schacht's essay. The British major seemed easier to convince that Schacht hated Hitler than the "Jewish American officer."[306] No wonder Schacht was pleased with him.

On September 15 Schacht was transferred to a camp near Oberursel. Like a lot of U.S. Army disciplinary installations, it was described as a "cage." Prisoner "cages" were usually temporary installations for American service personnel accused of crimes.

An indignant Schacht chose to accept the term "cage" as fact. For the first time since he entered Allied custody, he was confronted with a harsh disciplinary regime. Prisoners were quartered in small cells surrounded by barbed wire and slept on

306. Schacht, *76 Jahre meines Lebens*, p. 569.

wooden bunks with a wool blanket. There were only two sparse meals per day and ten minutes of exercise. He was visited by a Berlin reporter who wanted to do a story, but Schacht got rid of him. Then a former U.S. Foreign Service officer named Pool paid a visit to find out how Schacht was faring. They had known each other in Berlin, and Pool was sympathetic. Schacht soon received a real bed and mattress and was permitted some walks in the nearby mountains, accompanied by two American officers.

On October 7, just before he was taken to Nuremberg, the Associated Press ran the following syndicated story:

ALLIES WERE "SUCKERS" TO ASSIST PRE-WAR REICH, SCHACHT IMPLIES

OBERURSEL, Germany, October 7 — Dr. Hjalmar Horace Greeley Schacht, master-mind of German finances, accused as a major war criminal, in fact described the Allies as suckers today for giving Germany credits after World War I.

"Germany has always been bankrupt from the outside since Versailles," he declared. "Foreign creditors lost. I am sorry to say they did not hear my warnings from 1924 to 1930 to keep their money and let Germany do by her own [sic]."

Schacht, one of twenty-four top Germans slated for trial in Nuremberg, is kept separate from other prisoners because of his violent tantrums. Day and night he shouts, "I'm no criminal," launches into repeated tirades against Adolf Hitler and other Nazis, denies he adhered to the Nazi Party and complains against his present treatment.

Calling Hitler and former Marshal Hermann Goering "nothing but gangsters," he shouted that if the Americans would give him a gun, "I'd gladly shoot Goering myself — kill him." Asked whether he thought that Hitler was dead, Schacht snapped, "Certainly; if I thought he wasn't, I would kill him personally."

Three weeks after he arrived in the "cage" at Oberursel, Schacht was loaded into a car with former Panzer General Walter Warlimont and Franz Xaver Schwarz, the former treasurer of the Nazi Party. They arrived in Nuremberg's Palace of Justice on the afternoon of October 9, 1945.

It was fitting that Nuremberg, the medieval gingerbread town in south Germany, was chosen by the Allies to conduct the International Military Tribunal.

Historic Nuremberg represented the best and worst of Germany. It was the home of the great Albrecht Dürer, but its name was also attached to the Nazis' infamous racial laws. It was the setting for Wagner's *Meistersinger,* which was why Hitler chose it for his massive annual Nazi Party rallies. They were neo-operatic events. For a week each September, hundreds of thousands of the Nazi uniformed faithful were drawn up before Hitler on a vast parade ground. Standing alone on a small high platform beneath a vast stucco swastika, he announced to the rest of the world what he had planned for the year to follow. These bombastic speeches were usually a cluster of threats followed by a hypocritical olive branch.

Those outside Germany who had barely heard of the town of Nuremberg had been forced to learn the name. The city known for toys and crunchy pastries became a rumbling volcano ready to spew danger. Newsreels, magazines, and newspapers trumpeted each of Hitler's latest annual messages from Nuremberg with its very real threats. In the time of Adolf Hitler, each year that lay ahead seemed to depend on the German Führer's messages from Nuremberg.

By 1945 the nightmare voice from Nuremberg was finally stilled, but the opening of the extermination camps made it a grim victory. The victors realized that this was like no other war in history and that the surviving Nazi leaders had to be held accountable for their acts. The shattered old streets, gates, and towers of Nuremberg then housed the biggest criminal trials in history. It seemed right that the Nazis would face their sins in Adolf Hitler's holiest of holies.

Nuremberg's central courthouse, the Palace of Justice, one of the few buildings not destroyed by Allied bombers, was renovated and made ready. Its holding cells were patched and painted, and the actual courtroom was redesigned for the multilingual, multinational events. First came the "major" war criminals. It was strange how many of them had surrendered without a fight.

Perhaps they thought they would be judged as "men who had only done their duty and followed orders," or perhaps they were too cowardly to fall on their swords. It was equally astonishing that many of the lower-ranking Nazis, the functionaries who ran the Gestapo, the concentration camps, and the extermination battalions — the dry bureaucracy that administered denunciations, arbitrary arrests, and mass executions — were also in custody. Their trials came later. First it was the turn of their masters. The courtroom was jammed with the accused; the multinational staffs of judges, prosecutors, and defense attorneys; interpreters; and the representatives of the world press.

Less than a year after the Germans had surrendered, Göring, Hess, von Ribbentrop, Keitel, Kaltenbrunner, Streicher, Rosenberg, Speer, and the others were tried in the Anglo-Saxon tradition, which presumed their innocence until they were found guilty. The French jurists, who traditionally assigned guilt before the proof of innocence, were willing to compromise, but the Soviets preferred the swift judgment meted out in Moscow's Lubyanka prison.

The leading criminal was not in the dock. Adolf Hitler and his new bride, Eva, had committed suicide. Their bodies were hastily cremated and buried in a shallow grave in what remained of the Chancellery garden. Nearby lay the charred corpses of Joseph Goebbels, his wife, and their six children (all poisoned by their parents). Goebbels was the only paladin who had stayed with his master. The others all tried to distance themselves from their irrational demigod and his last bombproof underground dwelling.

Three of the defendants had already escaped judgment. Robert Ley, formerly the Nazi labor leader, a flabby alcoholic, had hanged himself in his cell before he could be sentenced. Martin Bormann, Hitler's closest assistant, tried to escape under heavy artillery fire across a bridge near the Führer's bunker during the Soviets' final assault on Berlin. He was never seen again. Bormann was tried in absentia and found guilty.

Heinrich Himmler never made it to Nuremberg. The SS overlord was discovered hiding among some German POWs dressed as an SS private. In his view, mass killing was sickening and ugly, but "a courageous act for the preservation of our race." Those who did these deeds "were the true heroes of the Reich." He identified himself to his British captors but showed little heroism. He tried to negotiate a special arrangement for himself but soon realized that he was daydreaming, so he chewed down hard on a poison capsule that lay hidden in a hollow back tooth.[307]

The most prominent prisoner to be tried was *Reichsmarschall* Hermann Göring, once Hitler's heir apparent. When Berlin was ready to fall to the Soviets, Göring removed himself, his family, and twenty-four Luftwaffe trucks filled with paintings, objets d'art, and jewelry to Bavaria. On April 22, 1945, while Berlin was in the final days of the Soviet siege, he sent a cable from the security of Bavaria to Adolf Hitler in the Berlin Führer-bunker. Göring offered to assume leadership, unless Hitler notified him that he was still in charge. Hitler immediately ordered that "this traitor Göring" be stripped of all rank and party membership. The SS men with Göring were then assigned to kill him, but they did not do so.[308] Perhaps the nearby sounds of American tanks and planes helped them make their decision. The sweating, drug-addicted *Reichsmarschall* then surrendered himself, his wife, and daughter to the Seventh U.S. Army. He thought he was acting with knightly grace and expected respectful treatment. He did not surrender his cache of art. He wanted to "preserve it for Germany." Aware that Göring had been condemned by Hitler, the senior officers of the Seventh U.S. Army were unsure of his status. At first, they treated him as an honorable prisoner of war and even began to lionize him. Göring felt that this was his due. A Seventh Army intelligence officer arranged to present the captured number two Nazi to the international press. He organized a conference in the sunny garden of a requisitioned Augsburg villa. At 3 P.M. on May 11, 1945, the blubbery Göring, dressed in Luftwaffe light blue, with his *Reichsmarschall* insignia in place, slumped in a gilt armchair while dutiful Allied journalists squatted

307. Author's interview with eyewitness (former British major) Mark Lynton.
308. William Quinn, *Wild Bill Remembers*, pp. 192–93.

in front of him on the lawn and newsreel cameras whirred. The interplay of questions and answers implied that Göring, the great statesman, was willing to explain himself to the plebs. It all seemed like a grand publicity coup.[309] The next day Eisenhower was shown the filmed footage. He was furious. He immediately ordered Göring stripped of his marshal's insignia. The fat peacock was swiftly plucked from pomposity to prisoner and transformed from a gracious loser into an accused war criminal. There were some red faces at Seventh Army headquarters.

Schacht, as a new prisoner at Nuremberg, did not stray far from his usual style. He immediately complained bitterly that he was "not treated as a suspect, but as a convicted criminal." He found Colonel Burton Andrus, the prison commander, unpleasant and objectionable. He described the prison's bureaucratic narrow-mindedness as "worse than in any of Hitler's concentration camps."[310] Anyone who ever existed in the grinding horror of life as a true concentration camp inmate would have brushed away Schacht's comparison as ridiculous. Colonel Andrus, a former cavalry officer, was indeed a stiff-necked bespectacled disciplinarian, a poor replica of General George Patton. The colonel must have either hated his assignment as prison warden or relished the power it gave him over the world-famous personalities in his charge. Very few people, German or Allied, had much good to say about him. In a typical contretemps with Schacht, he punished him for throwing hot coffee at a pesky and persistent American reporter. Schacht's "coffee privileges" were withdrawn for a week, but he was offered unending free coffee by several of the colonel's men.

Andrus accused him of insulting the American uniform by throwing the coffee. Schacht calmly pointed out that the correspondent was wearing a "similar suit" to the colonel's, but without any insignia. It was therefore not an American army uniform. It was always hard to argue with Schacht.

Schacht was also infuriated when an MP insisted that he sleep

309. Author was eyewitness.
310. Schacht, *76 Jahre meines Lebens*, p. 568.

with his face toward the cell door so he could be observed. He yelled at the man in his most imperious manner to produce his officer. The officer then came and told the guard to leave Schacht alone.

Despite his many trips to America, he had never dealt with working-class Americans like the MPs, whose offhanded familiarity often bordered on rudeness. To his surprise, most of the black soldiers were more easygoing than their white comrades.

To the wily old financier's amusement, he was asked to undergo Rorschach and IQ tests. He was not a believer in the inkblot technique, but it did not surprise him that he scored the highest IQ (143) of any prisoner. The lowest was Julius Streicher, the Franconian Jew-baiter, a crude man and one of Hitler's earliest comrades; he was shunned by the others. The psychological tests were administered by Captain Gustave Gilbert, the prison psychologist, whom Schacht snidely described as "of Viennese birth," his way of calling Gilbert a naturalized American, probably not born with the Anglican name of Gilbert. Schacht also chose to make similar broad hints about some of the American army interrogators, both officers and noncoms, many of whom were naturalized U.S. citizens. It amused Schacht that an American-born interrogator praised his English. "You speak it better than some of my colleagues."

During the IQ tests, Schacht told Gilbert that he had always been a poor arithmetician. "But," he went on, "show me a financial man who is good at arithmetic and I'll show you a swindler." [311]

Hermann Göring became the most contentious and difficult of the prisoners. He tried hard to squelch any sign of regret or guilt shown by the others. Some of them were cowed by him. The *Reichsmarschall* was now detoxified and thirty pounds lighter, but Schacht remained unimpressed. He was more upset by the flood of visiting Allied VIPs, and he complained to Colonel Andrus that he hated being stared at. It was not a zoo!

311. Joseph E. Persico, *Nuremberg,* p. 117.

Dr. Gilbert tried to frustrate Göring's machinations, outbursts in court, and coaching of the others during meals He split up the seating during lunch. There was the "youth room" (with architect Speer, broadcaster Fritzsche, *Gautleiter* von Schirach, and Funk), and the "elders" (Schacht, von Papen, von Neurath, and Dönitz) were in another room.

Schacht had to choose defense attorneys, and he aimed high.

Manci convinced one of Berlin's leading trial lawyers, Dr. Rudolf Dix, to represent her husband. Dix was the former head of Germany's legal association. Schacht approached Professor Herbert Kraus, head of the law faculty of the University of Göttingen, to back up Dix. Kraus had taught at American universities and understood international law. Both men shared Schacht's own political views, which he described as democratic conservatism.[312] Dix was described as effective but slow, exact, and ponderous. Kraus worked mainly on preparing the case.

312. Schacht, *76 Jahre meines Lebens*, p. 581.

22

ON TRIAL

Franz von Sonnleithner, a former Foreign Ministry officer and a fellow prisoner, spoke of the high regard in which Schacht was held by some of his fellow accused.[313] Schacht's past obstreperous behavior toward Hitler and his equally unyielding attitude toward the Allied authorities did not go unrewarded.

On April 30, 1946, Schacht finally took the stand. He found himself in what he described as an artificially lit anthill in constant activity. He made special mention of the gum-chewing American stenographers. ("As if they were chewing each word they typed into their steno machines.") German journalists in the courtroom, the only spectators in civilian clothes, were very subdued.

As always, Schacht was easily irritated. Gum chewing was not the only American annoyance. In the cellblocks, loudspeakers boomed out popular American tunes. Ironically, the song of the moment was "Don't Fence Me In," probably Bing Crosby's version. A British officer said to Schacht, "It's not a trial. It's a circus." Between pretrial preparation and time on the stand, he spent a year in the strange chamber, which was shaped like the dining room of a transatlantic liner, with long raked galleries flanking a

---

313. Franz von Sonnleithner, *Als Diplomat im "Führerhauptquartier,"* p. 261.

lower "dance floor." The unusual size and shape was a matter of necessity. It was probably the first time in history that so many prisoners, defense attorneys, interpreters, judges, and their staffs had been assembled for one mass trial.

As usual, no matter what the occasion, Hjalmar Schacht was ready for battle. Although the atmosphere was not at all to his liking, he got hold of himself, overcame his feelings of pique and aversion, and faced his accusers. He testified on his own behalf to this strange assembly of multinational inquisitors and did so in English. He felt it was his duty to make the true events and influences that had brought on the Nazis clear to the members of the court. He would clarify his own decision to be of help to Hitler. Then, from the moment he knew that Hitler was deceiving Germany, Schacht had fought against him.

To the indictment he pleaded that he was "not guilty in any respect."

His inquisitors were primarily American since the British had not planned to categorize him as a war criminal in the sense of the indictment. The American prosecutor, Robert H. Jackson, was a major juristic figure, an associate justice of the U.S. Supreme Court. The thrust of his attack on Schacht's claim of innocence was contained in a three-and-a-half-hour general summation about all the defendants on July 26, 1946. When he got to Schacht, he singled him out as one who was at the forefront of mobilizing the economy for war. He then became specific.

He spoke scathingly about "the defendant who, if pressed, would concede that he is the most intelligent, honorable and innocent man in the dock. . . . When we ask why he remained a member of the criminal regime, he tells us that by sticking on, he expected to moderate its program. Like a Brahmin among the untouchables, he could not bear to mingle with the Nazis socially, but never could he afford to separate from them politically. . . . Having armed Hitler to blackmail a continent, his answer now is to blame England and France for yielding. . . . Schacht always fought for his position in a regime he now affects to despise. He sometimes disagreed with his Nazi confederates about what was expedient in reaching their goal, but he never dissented from the goal itself. When he did break with them in the twilight of the regime, it was over tactics, not principle."[314]

The direct examination by defense attorney Dix was slow and exacting. He had Schacht on the stand for two days. Schacht would not deny his total disdain for the Versailles Dictate and his early help to Hitler's regime, which he attributed to patriotism. He remained at Hitler's side until he found he had been deceived and that Germany had been betrayed. He then openly disagreed with Hitler and was eventually jailed for his opposition. He had never even become a member of the Nazi Party. When Jackson asked him about the Golden Party Badge, which Schacht had often worn on other-than-formal party occasions, Schacht said quite airily that it helped him get good seats in restaurants, at theaters, and on trains.

At one point Dix gestured toward former Gestapo head Kaltenbrunner. He then pointed at Schacht. "Here we have the grotesque situation of jailer and prisoner sharing the same bench in the dock." Dix had defended Schacht as an "enemy of the people" before the vicious Roland Freisler of the Nazis' People's Court. Now he was defending Schacht in front of a democratic court.

Wilhelm Vocke, a banker who had been on Schacht's Reichsbank board and was not a Nazi, confirmed Schacht's defense about the need to rebuild Germany's armed forces for the sake of peace, not war.

"Schacht said that foreign policy without armaments was impossible. Neutrality must be armed neutrality. Without armaments, Germany would always be defenseless among armed nations. He also saw rearmament as one way of reviving Germany's industry and unemployment."[315]

314. Werner Maser, *Nuremberg: A Nation on Trial*, pp. 222–23.
315. Telford Taylor, *The Anatomy of the Nuremberg Trials*, p. 390.

As part of Schacht's testimony, Dix referred to a well-known incident, a stormy face-to-face dispute between Hitler and Schacht on August 11, 1937, at the Berghof. He asked Schacht what had caused the argument with Hitler. The Führer's angry shouts and Schacht's forceful and unyielding replies were heard by other guests, including Albert Speer, through a window opening onto a terrace. Hitler finally came to join his guests, ranting about "the disobliging and narrow-minded minister who was holding up the armaments process."[316] Speer was quoted as saying that Hitler also told the group, "I have had a grave disagreement with Schacht. I cannot work with him any longer. He upsets my financial plans."[317]

"Why," Dix asked Schacht, "was Adolf Hitler so angry?"

"Because," said Schacht, "I refused him any more of the Reichsbank's money."

"What if you had explained to him that you refused him the money because you thought he wanted to make war?"

"Then," said Schacht, "I could not have the pleasure of this verbal exchange. I would be dead. I would need a preacher, not a lawyer."[318]

In the Schacht case, Jackson was not very effective. He had been given more than a duel by Hermann Göring, whom he had cross-examined earlier and who had made him look inept. He did not want to be made to look foolish, and so he interrupted Dix a total of twelve times

The final blow to Jackson's prosecutorial efforts came through Hans Bernd Gisevius, the former Gestapo and Abwehr officer who had worked closely with Schacht during the assassination attempt of July 20, 1944. In earlier testimony, Jackson had described Gisevius as "the one representative of democratic

316. Albert Speer, *Inside the Third Reich*, p. 97.
317. Schacht, *76 Jahre meines Lebens,* p. 600.
318. Ibid., p. 601.

forces in Germany" and had spoken of him admiringly. When called by Dix as a witness for Schacht, Gisevius stated:

> I would like to emphasize that the problem of Schacht was confusing, not only to me but to my friends as well. Schacht was always a puzzle to us. Perhaps it was due to the contradictory nature of this man that he kept his position in the Hitler government so long. He undoubtedly entered the Hitler regime for patriotic reasons, and I would like to testify here that the moment his disappointment became obvious, he decided for the same patriotic reasons to join the opposition. Despite Schacht's many contradictions and the puzzles he gave us to solve, my friends and I were strongly attracted to Schacht because of his exceptional personal courage and the fact that he was undoubtedly a man of strong moral character, and he did not think only of Germany but also of the ideals of humanity. That is why we went with him, why we considered him one of us; and if you ask me personally, I can say that the doubts I often had about him were completely dispelled during the dramatic events of 1938 and 1939. At that time he really fought and I will never forget that. It is a pleasure for me to be able to testify to this here.[319]

Jackson's case was falling apart under the narrow definition of "conspiracies to prepare for and to wage war." His case against Schacht was also hurt by his refusing the help of General William Donovan, former chief of the OSS and a lawyer of great international range. Donovan attended the trials on a voluntary basis. After his views on how to prosecute Schacht were ignored by Jackson, the general left for the United States. With him went Colonel Murray Gurfein, who had interrogated Schacht and knew the details better than the men who helped Jackson prepare his brief. Jackson's research was so slipshod that after Schacht's many interrogations, he was charged with "being a member of the Nazi Party," even though this was easily disproved. It was one of the opening counterattacks of Dix's defense.

---

319. Taylor, *The Anatomy of the Nuremberg Trials*, p. 386.

While Jackson failed to make his case against Schacht based on the specifics of the indictment, he used a part of Schacht's pivotal and controversial Königsberg speech in August 1935 to show that Schacht was an anti-Semite. As Otto Tolischus of the *New York Times* had reported, Schacht, after chiding Germans who were mindlessly led into various anti-Jewish acts, then stated that "the Jews must know that their influence is over." He then outlined some anti-Jewish measures that were parallel to those of the Nazis.

As usual, Schacht acknowledged his own words, this time as reflecting his personal views in 1935. He never denied his attitude toward Germany's Jews and his advocacy of steps to limit their cultural and official influence, but he had always insisted that they had the right to live unharmed among their neighbors. Again, while it failed to present him in a sympathetic light, it did not prove that he had conspired to make war.

On the subject of the *Anschluss* with Austria, Schacht objected to the manner of the takeover but stated that in principle, it was a natural union and bound to be consummated sooner or later. Schacht had arranged the takeover of Austria's reserve bank and had also incorporated the federal Czechoslovak banking system into the Reichsbank. He saw nothing wrong in that.

Jackson asked Schacht if he had approved of the law threatening the death penalty for Germans who smuggled German property (currency) abroad or kept German property there, instead of repatriating it. Schacht said he agreed with the law. Jackson then pointed out that this would hit mostly those German Jews who wanted to leave the country and wanted to assure themselves of having some money abroad.

Schacht smugly stated his amazement that Jackson would assume that Jews cheated more frequently than Christians.

Jackson tried to prove that Schacht had conspired to make war. He asked Schacht, "Did you consider the attack on Poland as an unprovoked aggressive act?"

"Absolutely."

"And Luxembourg?"

"Absolutely."

"And Holland?"

"Absolutely."

"And Denmark?"

"Absolutely."

"And Norway ?"

"Absolutely."

"And Yugoslavia?"

"Absolutely."

"And Russia?"

"Absolutely, sir, and you forgot Belgium."[320]

Jackson then pointed out that all these attacks were committed with an army that Schacht had financed. Was he aware of that?

Schacht said, "Unfortunately." From the beginning of the trials, he had contended that he helped finance the army, but not for making war. His testimony did nothing to negate that.

About the Nazi theories that there is a German master race, Schacht said that he had always found it disagreeable that anyone could speak of things like the "chosen people" or "God's own country." "As for the idealized types touted by the Nazis, their leaders were not exactly fine Nordic examples. Goebbels, particularly, was known as the pre-shrunk Teuton [*Schrumpfgermane*]. One thing united them, alcoholism, which was one of the main components of Nazi ideology."[321]

Schacht parried all accusations that he condoned anti-Semitic atrocities. He did not hesitate to state his long-held view that Jewish cultural influence must be contained, and he quoted his reasoning, which involved religion. To prove that he held no personal animus against Jews, he offered his Königsberg and Reichsbank speeches in evidence. Both were protective of Jewish rights and were delivered at some risk to himself.

Describing Hitler, Schacht spoke of his lack of education, his wide reading, his impressive use of half-facts, his diabolical abil-

---

320. Schacht, *76 Jahre meines Lebens,* p. 615.

321. Ibid., p. 589.

ity to gauge the psychology of the masses. While Göring, who was sitting in the dock, ostentatiously turned his back, Schacht continued. "No doubt Hitler thought he was doing good things at the beginning, but soon he deluded himself while he was deluding others. He fell for his own magic."[322]

Schacht spoke of the young SS men who considered themselves an elite but who were only being used, and of there being some decent people in the Nazi Party, but everyone lived in a totally controlled police state, without chance to disagree or complain. Between Dix and Schacht, they pointed out the inaccuracies in the indictment, such as his supposed Nazi Party membership. He rebutted the accusation that while he was a cabinet minister Germany's birth rate went up by saying that he really could not take responsibility for that.

It brought a frosty smile from the French judge.

No matter how ill-smelling the tar with which Schacht was painted by Jackson, none of it made him guilty in the sense of the indictment. Jackson should have expected the acquittal. Schacht and his defense attorneys had checkmated him every step of the way. Unable to appeal, Jackson had to accept his defeat, but his doubts persisted until the end of his life. How could Sir Geoffrey Lawrence, the British judge, have called Schacht "innocent, a man of character"? Foster Adams, an investigator on Jackson's staff, claimed that Sir Montagu Norman, governor of the Bank of England, had somehow "reached" Sir Geoffrey.[323] Francis Biddle, the American judge, had favored conviction but had to admit that Schacht and his attorneys had presented a solid case. He had no choice but to go along with the British and French judges.

It had all gone with surprising efficiency and even a degree of decency. The tribunal of American, British, French, and Russian judges had made strenuous efforts to give the accused a fair hearing, despite the differences between the Western judges and their Soviet colleagues.

322. Ibid.
323. Tom Bower, *The Pledge Betrayed: America and Britain and the Denazification of Postwar Germany,* p. 324.

The prosecutors for both factions were more in accord. They had all asked for death sentences for each and every prisoner. When Schacht was acquitted, General Alexandrov, the Russian prosecutor, was apoplectic. For once, Robert Jackson was in full and unusual agreement with his Soviet colleague.

On the morning of sentencing, the prisoners were escorted from their cells to a hall on the main floor of the court and then into the courtroom. Each one in his turn then stood to hear his fate.

Three men were freed: Schacht, Hans Fritzsche, and Franz von Papen.

Fritzsche was the official chief announcer of Radio Germany, the *Deutschlandsender*. As a broadcaster, his tone was often overbearing and filled with irony, which could be expected from the domain of Dr. Joseph Goebbels. Fritzsche had developed a new and breathlessly sensationalist style, which was widely copied among German announcers. Every statement was written in present tense to heighten the effect. ("The Führer steps onto the podium. The great bodyguard braces to attention. He is as one with the people!")

But despite his wide identification among German and foreign listeners as the voice of Hitler's Germany, he merely read scripts prepared by the Propaganda Ministry's broadcast section.

Franz von Papen, the former chancellor, vice chancellor, and intimate of President von Hindenburg, was deeply involved and instrumental in the negotiations that made Hitler chancellor. A year later von Papen had suddenly located von Hindenburg's supposed testament, in which the old marshal had put the care of Germany into the hands of Adolf Hitler. As a Catholic noble, von Papen had even eased the way for the agreement (*Concordat*) between Hitler's Nazis and the Vatican. Then in 1934 he suddenly and unexpectedly seemed to turn on Hitler. His speech at Marburg University criticized nearly every aspect of Hitler's regime. Days later, during the purge of Röhm and his storm troopers, his speech writer Jung and another of von Papen's closest assistants were executed by the SS.

Thoroughly frightened, von Papen quickly left for his country estate. From that moment on, he became Hitler's marionette, filling important but messenger-boy posts, such as ambassador to Austria before the *Anschluss,* a touchy stopgap assignment. His last posting was as ambassador to Turkey, where he had once served. He was expected to use his connections to help Germany. Evidently, von Papen was distasteful, but was he guilty as charged?

Sir David Maxwell-Fyfe of Great Britain had the task of prosecuting the aristocratic von Papen. He quickly proved that the man was vain, ambitious, cowardly, and caddish; he had betrayed his dead assistants and never raised a word of protest against their murder. Sir David showed that von Papen was a man who did the Nazis' bidding even though he had come to detest them. But Maxwell-Fyfe did not manage to nail von Papen to the wall as a conspirator to prepare for and commit war. Like Schacht, von Papen had been indicted on the first two counts only, and like his fellow prosecutor Jackson, Sir David failed to prove that his man was guilty of these charges beyond a reasonable doubt.

Late in the day on October 1, 1946, after the acquittal of the three, there was a press conference. Allied reporters wanted to meet these "sanitized Nazis." It was a raucous event. Fritzsche smoked and drank wine. Von Papen, ever the grand seigneur, was aloof. Schacht, dressed in the old fur-collared overcoat he had worn at many winter conferences all over the world, traded his autographs for chocolates. Ever the deal-maker, it was the best he could do for Manci and their two girls. He also bargained for cigarettes and, according to reporters at the conference, finally had one lit cigarette in each hand.

He complained to the journalists that his wife and daughters had been expelled from Gühlen by German Communists, who then looted the house. Manci and the girls had to walk forty miles to Berlin. Actually, Manci had stayed in Gühlen until the Russians came. There was a firefight on the estate between Russian and German troops, and sixteen German *Landser* lost their lives and were buried on the property. During the search for mines, the Russians came across a steel case of anti-Nazi material, buried there by Schacht. It helped Manci after she was arrested and detained in various nearby Red Army headquarters for six weeks. After she addressed a letter to Marshal Zhukov, she was returned to Gühlen along with the important documents and given a telephone so she could call Russian headquarters in case she was molested. When the new East German government took charge, she had to trek from Gühlen to Berlin. Far from being "expelled," she fled the estate to avoid being deported to Moscow by the new East German overlords. In Berlin she was barred from moving into their old Berlin apartment, so she finally made her way with the children to the Lüneburg home of their old nanny, in a village called Hollenstedt.

The British then arrested her and interned her in a guesthouse, where they asked the landlady to keep a suicide watch over Manci. Only after they finally were convinced that she was not about to kill herself could she return to Hollenstedt and the children, where she spent two winters and a summer. She had no money but somehow managed, although shopping for whatever she could get meant a daily two-mile hike each way.

To the leaders of the new democratic Germany, von Papen's acquittal was perhaps the most unacceptable and least justifiable. The democratic heads of the newly founded Federal Republic of Germany (West Germany) were also appalled by Schacht's acquittal, but ever the realist and cynic, he had expected their anger. After all, he understood that it was politically to their advantage to display violent opposition to anyone who had ever been associated with the Nazis. He wanted to join Manci and the girls. Carrying a bag and a bedroll, he got as far as one of the gates of the Nuremberg prison but stopped when he saw the mass of German police, so he accepted a suggestion by Colonel Andrus to remain in his cell for a few more days as a guest of the International Military Tribunal.

Dana Adams Schmidt reported to the *New York Times* on October 4, 1946, from Nuremberg, that

GERMAN POLICE FAIL TO JAIL FREED NAZIS

CLAY BARS REARREST PENDING RULING ON STATUS

HE IS SAID TO ORDER SAFE-CONDUCTS

In the hope of arresting Dr. Hjalmar Schacht, Franz von Papen and Hans Fritzsche as they left prison, German police surrounded the Nuremberg court house at 8 o'clock this morning, but were called off at 1:30 P.M. by order of Lieut. General Lucius Clay, Deputy Military Governor.

The three men, whom the International Military Tribunal ordered discharged last Tuesday morning, remained in jail, however, and tonight began their third night in prison cells that were unlocked and unwatched in token of their technical liberty.

General Clay explained by telephone from Berlin what had happened:

He had ordered the German police to withdraw because their action was not necessary or in good taste. The three would have to stay where they were while the Military Government's legal division decided whether Germans who were involuntarily in the United States zone were subject to the zone's denazification law and consequently subject to arrest under its provisions.

In Berlin, 20 000 transport workers went on strike for one day to protest the acquittal of the three.

The new Federal Republic of Germany was divided into states (*Länder*), each with its own prime minister. Schacht, after being freed from war-crimes trials, fell under the jurisdiction of the state of Bavaria. The Bavarian prime minster, Dr. Wilhelm Hoegner, and Anton Pfeiffer, Bavaria's chief of denazification, knew that the matter was by no means over. The order that prevented them from arresting Schacht would be only temporary. The new German federalists were not about to remain silent spectators. They would not repeat the mistakes of the 1933 Weimar Republic and its impotent Reichstag.

After three days in an open cell, shortly after midnight, Schacht finally left the Palace of Justice on a truck that delivered him to the room Manci had rented for herself and little Cordula and Konstanze. It could barely be called a reunion. In the early morning hours Schacht, while drinking a cup of tea, was arrested by Nuremberg police chief Leo Stahl. When Stahl barged in, Schacht pulled out Captain Andrus's *laissez-passer* letter, which was ignored. He was taken to Nuremberg police headquarters and booked, despite his vehement protests. He was then released on the orders of an American army captain but not without a lengthy argument. The captain told the police that they might be able to arrest Schacht the next day, but for the time being he would stay with his wife and consider himself in the U.S. Army's protective custody.

But not for long. The U.S. military government soon handed him over to the German authorities. In the Americans' view, "the future liability of any of the men under German laws to the people of Germany for crimes within Germany must be determined by the German courts."

23

THE NEW GERMANY

HE WAS A PRISONER once more. Over the next years he was a pawn, handed from jurisdiction to jurisdiction, from state to state. Each one wished to have its chance to tackle this seemingly invulnerable former Nazi cabinet member.

This continued the process that began when Hitler's Gestapo arrested him on July 23, 1944. His main complaint to the German prison doctor about his years of multinational imprisonment was that he "had put on some weight."[324]

He was certain, time and again, that he would find a way to prove they were wrong to arrest him. It was yet another battle, another chance to measure his ideas against those of others. He had been let down by all of them: by the monarchy, by the democratic men of Weimar, and by the deceitful and strange Adolf Hitler. How did this new Federal Republic of Germany measure up? Not too well, in his view. His immediate reaction was that they were toadies for the U.S. military governors, whose only aim was to remove Germany once and for all from world competition. Behind everything, he thought he saw the revengeful hand of the German Jewish exile community. He was unfairly victimized "after all he had done for the Jews." He was furious.

---

324. Maser, *Nuremberg*, p. 240.

There were attacks on him in the New York press. Doubts were cast that he was "the man who found the way to end inflation in 1923." Expert witnesses pointed out that the cure had originally been found by Emil Helfferich, the kaiser's former minister of finance, and that Schacht had only implemented it.[325] His original West German postwar prosecutor was "a Jew named Marx who had never suffered a day under Hitler." A request for leave from prison to be with his wife when one of their girls was being operated on was denied by "an American official named Friedmann." He was sure he had become a worldwide Jewish target. At the end of March 1947 he had an operation for a hernia in the Ludwigsburg prison hospital. Then he found himself back on a roller-coaster ride of several years of legal triumphs and setbacks. Few men of his age and recent prison history could have survived with their emotions and determination intact.

The newspaper headlines over the next three years tell the story best:

SCHACHT BOASTS OF 4 PLOTS AGAINST HITLER, DEFIES COURT TO PROVE HIM A "MAJOR NAZI" (*New York Times,* April 10, 1947)

SCHACHT TELLS COURT HE FOUGHT NAZIS IN '36 (UP, April 21, 1947)

8-YEAR TERM FOR SCHACHT URGED (AP, April 30, 1947)

SCHACHT MAKES PLEA AS TRIAL IS ENDED (AP, May 4, 1947)

SCHACHT CONVICTED BY GERMAN COURT (AP, May 13, 1947)

END OF THE ROAD (*New York Times,* May 14, 1947)

SCHACHT WILL ASK FOR A THIRD TRIAL (*New York Times,* May 14, 1947)

SCHACHT IN PRISON CAMP (AP, May 15, 1947)

U.S. AIDES TO QUESTION SCHACHT (UP, June 14, 1947)

Hjalmar Schacht arrived at Nuremberg today to testify in the trial of twenty-four members of the I.G. Farben Cartel . . . (UP, July 8, 1947)

SCHACHT RELEASE TURNED DOWN (AP, May 27, 1948)

325. *New York Times,* "Letters" (June 28, July 2, July 21, 1947).

SCHACHT HEARING IS BEGUN (AP, August 2, 1948)

SCHACHT IS FREED BY GERMAN COURT

    DECISION MUST BE APPROVED BY U.S.(AP, September 1, 1948)

SCHACHT IS RELEASED FROM GERMAN CAMP (AP, September 1, 1948)

SCHACHT FEARS "ALMS" IN GERMAN ECONOMY (*Reuters*, September 17, 1948)

A RETURN BY SCHACHT TO STATE JOB IS STUDIED (*New York Times*, October 4, 1948)

GERMANS CANCEL SCHACHT RELEASE PENDING NEW STUDY OF NAZI TIES (*New York Times*, November 5, 1948)

SCHACHT ELUDES SEARCH (UP, November 8, 1948)

SCHACHT FOUND BY POLICE (UP, November 10, 1948)

THIRD SCHACHT TRIAL AS TOP NAZI ORDERED (UPI, December 7, 1948)

Calm as ever, he told the press on December 30, 1948, that while he was on trial at Nuremberg, he had written an operetta about a love affair between an American GI and a German girl. [326]

Then back into battle:

SCHACHT WON'T ATTEND TRIAL (AP, January 29, 1949)

SCHACHT DEFIES GERMAN COURT (AP, January 31, 1949)

SCHACHT LIABLE TO JAIL

    BUT NAZI MINISTER REFUSES TO RETURN FROM BRITISH ZONE (*New York Times*, February 14, 1949)

GERMAN BOARD NULLIFIES 8-YEAR TERM OF SCHACHT (AP, February 25, 1949)

RUHR UNIONS OBJECT TO SCHACHT (AP, May 12, 1949)

SCHACHT DENIES QUITTING GERMANY (UP, May 29, 1949)

SCHACHT IS CLEARED AGAIN (Reuters, June 13, 1949)

U.S. OFFICIAL HOLDS SCHACHT ELIGIBLE TO TAKE OFFICIAL POST IN A WEST GERMAN GOVERNMENT (*New York Times*, June 15, 1949)

SCHACHT FACES NEW TRIAL (AP, August 9, 1949)

GERMAN POLICE SAVE SCHACHT FROM A MOB (AP, October 14, 1949)

TRIAL OF SCHACHT CALLED OFF (Reuters, November 15, 1949)

---

326. UPI, ex *New York Times* (December 31, 1948), p. 5:5.

SCHACHT RIDICULES GERMAN DEMOCRACY (Reuters, February 1, 1950)

GERMAN MINISTER ACCUSED OF MAKING DEAL TO CLEAR SCHACHT (*New York Times,* February 2, 1950)

SCHACHT ON TRIAL FIFTH TIME (AP, August 21, 1950)

FIFTH TRIAL FREES SCHACHT ON CHARGE OF BEING A NAZI (AP, September 13, 1950)

It was finally over.

He persisted in blaming General Lucius Clay, deputy military governor of Germany, for his persecution by the German authorities, fully believing that Clay was influenced by Jewish exiles in the occupation administration as well as in the United States.

He used his time in prison for drafting a book.

His attitude toward the German prosecutors is illustrated by a piece of repartee. In one of the innumerable German trials at Lüneburg, the cross-examiner asked him, "How could a little lion like you hope to survive when you entered the cage of the big lions?"

Schacht answered, "You forget that I entered the cage as a lion tamer, not as a little lion."[327]

---

327. Schacht, *76 Jahre meines Lebens,* p. 645.

24

ONCE A BANKER . . .

IN SEPTEMBER 1948 the penniless Schacht was fighting his legal battles with only two and a half marks to his name. Gühlen had been confiscated by the East Germans. His Berlin houses were bombed out or requisitioned. He owed a small fortune to his lawyers. Hjalmar, Manci, and Konstanze lived in a tiny house near Hamburg. Cordula was in Bavaria with her stepsister.

Luckily, an enterprising publisher bought the book he had outlined in jail, thereby saving him. *Abrechnung mit Hitler (Settling Accounts with Hitler)* sold 250,000 copies. Finally, some cash! Cordula in Bavaria had hurt her leg, and it was slow to heal. The doctors were suspicious that it might be tubercular, so the three Schachts decided to move south to be near her. Schacht got word that he would be arrested if he crossed into Bavaria. The Bavarians were not ready to forgive and forget. Once more, Schacht's lawyers went into battle. They stalled the proceedings, and after endless wrangles, he was finally acquitted. His small new hoard of cash shriveled under a new assault of legal costs, living expenses, and doctors' fees. Then he received his second offer to write, this time from a Hamburg publisher, who also offered to provide living and working quarters for the Schachts. Saved again.

Two factors were in his favor. His reputation as a financial wizard had not dimmed, and many of the world's newest countries were desperate for financial advice. The end of the war had given them independence but had saddled them with new problems. They were in need of economic doctoring, and within the surprisingly inbred world of international finance, there were few names to rival Schacht's when it came to economic therapy.

The first of several governments to approach him was Indonesia's. The new republic, finally free of Dutch colonial rule since 1950, found itself in dire financial straits. They called on Schacht to come to the rescue. He had no idea of the situation, so he agreed to come to Jakarta as an unpaid consultant, if the Indonesian government assumed his and Manci's travel expenses. His actual words were more Schachtian: "I felt in the mood to make my experience available to other countries."[328] Besides, his romantic attachment to the Orient and the exotic Pacific had not dimmed. After the bleak years, here was the chance for adventure.

He was ready, but the fates were not. He slipped and broke his arm near the shoulder, a bad fall and a complicated fracture. Shortly after surgery, he was informed that he would need weeks of therapy. But he would have none of it. To begin their trip to Indonesia, the Schachts drove a tiny Volkswagen south across the Brenner Pass to Merano, where they stayed for several weeks until he had recovered.

The AP signaled his plans to many newspapers:

POST FOR SCHACHT IS SEEN

TRENTO, Italy, July 5 — Dr. Hjalmar Schacht, former Nazi Finance Minister, is believed here to have accepted the task of trying to restore order to Indonesia's finances. Dr. Schacht, vacationing in nearby Merano, had a long meeting two days ago with S. Pamontyak, Indonesian Ambassador to Italy. Reports printed in Trento and Bolzano newspapers said the Ambassador had brought Dr. Schacht travel documents.

Schacht declined comment, but the reporters were ahead of him.

---

328. Ibid., p. 662.

Dr. Schacht was said to have taken inoculations necessary for a trip to the tropics.

They flew from Rome to Cairo. At the airport they were greeted by a delegation of Egyptian officials and invited to stay in Egypt as guests of the government, lodged at the luxurious Hotel Semiramis. Egypt's minister of finance "hoped that they would find time for him." Manci was surprised, but Schacht was probably not. Had news of his impending arrival been leaked by the press, by Egyptian government agents, or by Schacht himself? He played coy. "I never thought of myself as particularly prominent, so I could not hide my surprise and pleasure in accepting the kind invitation."[329]

Playboy King Farouk was still on the throne, though he was traveling abroad, as usual. The coup to dethrone him was near. Within a year Egypt would be headed by a group of military officers, and tubby King Farouk would be back on the Riviera spending his cached funds. Colonel Gamal Abdel Nasser eventually emerged as Egypt's *supremo,* though the man who greeted Schacht was another colonel, Mohammed Naguib. On this initial trip Schacht reported only the usual tourist sightseeing, but it is almost certain that the requested meeting with Egyptian government officials took place.

The next phase of the trip to Jakarta was sidetracked first by typhoons and then by Schacht's own stormy ways. They stopped in Calcutta, where he talked business with various Indian financial officials "at the request of Nehru," who was trying to guide India through its first five-year economic plan. Next the Schachts went to Bangkok, where they were greeted warmly. On the final leg of the trip, they had scheduled a short stop in Singapore, but Schacht canceled it in a fit of pique. He had read an unpleasant article in the *Singapore Straights Times,* which doubted that he should be allowed a visitor's visa, considering his Nazi history. To the touchy Schacht, it "reeked of 'Dogs and Germans not desired.'" He refused to set foot in Singapore, so they continued straight on to Indonesia.

British journalist-writer William Stevenson, who was in Jakarta, described a chance meeting with Schacht:

> Djakarta was in utter chaos when the fastidious figure of Dr. Schacht appeared on the scene. The economy suffered from galloping inflation, which reminded him of 1923. His remedies were less easily applied in Indonesia. I wondered how Schacht could survive five minutes of discussion with [President] Sukarno. They were totally different. Sukarno was a sex symbol to millions of followers. Schacht was a frosty old man who had always looked at life through spectacles he adjusted to reflect the light back into the eyes of his interlocutors. The banker was reluctant to be seen at all by a reporter.
>
> I met Schacht at the Hotel Capitol, overlooking the filthiest of Djakarta's canals. There was no protection from swarms of malarial mosquitoes and the stench of sluggish chocolate brown waters sprinkled with garbage and human excrement. His narrow head balanced on a scrawny neck, his thin mouth pulled down at the corners, he regarded me warily. Below the open-sided hotel restaurant, women loosened their batik sarongs and splashed their firm breasts in gestures that deepened his expression of disapproval. Further along the banks, men and boys urinated in graceful arcs. I quoted an Indonesian saying that applied to the clogged canal: "Good germs eat up bad germs, if you leave things alone." He smiled faintly.[330]

Schacht's frostiness was probably deliberate. He knew how to deal with journalists, and it was not his moment to banter with the press. Besides, Stevenson started asking him about the Brotherhood, a subject Schacht either did not recognize or chose to ignore. Stevenson was working on an exposé of an underground organization, supposedly founded by former SS members and Hitler secretary Martin Bormann. There were rumors of many such groups, and some were true. A substantial number of SS

---

330. William Stevenson, *The Bormann Brotherhood*, pp. 130–31.

were ferried to Spain and South America by groups such as the *Odessa,* an acronym for Organization for Former Members of the SS. However, nothing could have been further from Schacht's range of interest or involvement.

The Schachts had planned to stay in Jakarta from July to September 1951. His stated purpose was that he was "making a survey" of Indonesia's economy rather than acting as an advisor. Shortly before leaving Jakarta he announced that he would visit Iran in October.[331] He also clarified on Radio Jakarta, as reported by the AP, that he had been invited by the Iranian government. Yet, two days later he told the *New York Times* man in Jakarta that he had no intention of being an economic advisor or making an economic survey in Iran. He was only going to lecture at the university. His trip had nothing to do with the Iranian government. Vintage Schacht!

His actual date of departure from Jakarta was November 3, and he left on an optimistic note because the Indonesian economy was in much better condition than he had assumed. He planned to postpone his Iran visit until spring 1952.[332]

In case anyone had forgotten his reputation for provocation, he raised eyebrows during a stopover in Calcutta on November 6. His depth charge for the reporters was that "[postwar] West Germany is suffering from the control of foreign powers!" When he was asked how quickly these so-called controls should be removed, he said, "Yesterday afternoon — at the latest, tomorrow morning." The reporters must have loved it. Every press story about Schacht still identified him as "the former Nazi financial wizard," "former Nazi financial guide," "formerly Hitler's financial genius," or "Hitler's economics minister." He was never free of the past, and his acquittals did not matter to the press.

On the way home to Germany, his plane landed at Lydda Airport in Israel. A few days later, after the Schachts had left the country, a furious member of the Israeli Knesset asked his gov-

331. Reuters (September 13, 1951), quoting Radio Jakarta.
332. *New York Times* (November 4, 1951), p. 3:2.

ernment to explain why Israel had allowed "one of the architects of the massacre of our people" to stand on Israeli soil without being arrested under an Israeli law that provided the death penalty for war criminals.

The actual event was much less dramatic. On landing, the Schachts had left their passports with Israeli police and had eaten breakfast in the airport. Walking to the cafeteria, they were photographed by reporters.[333] According to Schacht, he was surprised when he found out the plane would stop in Israel and fully expected trouble. Since his last release from jail, he had been the subject of much Jewish enmity. To avoid problems, he and Manci wanted to stay aboard the plane but were not allowed to do so. Instead, they were ushered into the airport to have breakfast. Manci was too nervous to eat, so he ate both their meals. After he finished, a cafeteria employee asked in perfect German, "Was it all right, Herr [Reichsbank] President?" Schacht said yes, and the waiter asked Herr President for an autograph and a few minutes later asked for several more for his colleagues. The exile said he was from Frankfurt and missed it. "If one could only go back!" Several other strangers introduced themselves, among them a man and his wife who said that they could get nowhere "in this country" and were on their way to Chile. Schacht was rather gleeful about these meetings, but a nervous Manci urged him to hurry and get their passports back. Her instincts were right. Although the Schachts had no trouble leaving Israel, David Ben-Gurion's eventual answer to the angry Knesset deputy was "If I had known that Schacht was at the airport, I would have had him arrested at once." Schacht was glad to have escaped another arrest, this time in what he described rather archly as "the Blessed Land."[334]

The eventual advice he gave Indonesia was to overcome its reluctance to import foreign capital. It was clearly difficult for

333. *New York Times* (November 27, 1951), p. 10:4.
334. Schacht, *76 Jahre meines Lebens*, p. 669.

former colonies like Indonesia to borrow money from their former Western overlords, but the fact that Schacht was planning to open an export bank in Hamburg seemed convenient.

His reputation with new governments that were suffering from fiscal pains was growing. In January 1952, following the reports of his work in Indonesia, the Egyptian consulate in Frankfurt made a formal inquiry as to whether Schacht would work for the Egyptians as an economics expert. At the same time the Egyptian government told the press that it was also looking for expertise in the military field.[335]

By June 1952 Schacht was ready to open shop as a banker. He applied to the Central Bank of Hamburg for a license to found an export bank in partnership with Waldemar Ludwig, a former Reichsbank director. Proposed opening capitalization was a paltry million deutsche marks (the equivalent of about $235,000), but Schacht felt certain that when people heard he was back in business, his bank would be oversubscribed.[336]

Iran soon followed Egypt's lead. On July 14, 1952, *Ettelaat,* Iran's leading newspaper, reported that Schacht would come to Iran to help the government correct financial and economic problems. Iranian prime minister Mohammed Mossadegh had already asked the Shah for full dictatorial powers to carry out any plan of Schacht's. So much for Schacht's earlier explanation that he was only going to Iran to lecture at the university.

Then came a typical setback of the sort Schacht had almost come to relish. On July 16 the Hamburg senate refused him a license to open his bank. He realized that accepting foreign financial consultancies while applying to open a bank for export was a red flag for the Central Bank of Hamburg. To calm things, he promptly told the press that he had "declined offers from Egypt and Iran."[337] He was back in court September 2 to force the sen-

---

335. AP (January 16, 1952).
336. *New York Times* (June 25, 1952), p. 5:2.
337. Reuters (July 18, 1952).

ate to reverse the prohibition. On September 6 a Hamburg administrative court overruled the senate, allowing him to open his doors. The very next day it was announced from Tehran that he was on the way to Iran. So much for "declining the offer." He arrived there on September 9, as a guest of the Iranian government and Prime Minister Mossadegh.

Schacht promptly managed to get into the middle of a fracas with both Britain and the United States. Both governments had been trying to finalize some arrangements with Iran to assure themselves a supply of oil. These talks were being conducted at the highest level, involving both the American president and the British prime minister. Now Iran postponed the negotiations in order to wait for Schacht's findings. It was a time when the incumbent Washington Democratic administration, facing a presidential election year, was mired in seemingly hopeless truce talks in Korea. Eisenhower, the Republican candidate for the presidency, must have relished the government's problems with Iran.

For a short time, Schacht was once more swimming with the big fish.

Strangely, his eventual advice to Mossadegh was inflationary. He felt that more currency could be printed by the Iranian government, probably banking on the outcome of the Anglo-American oil negotiations to back up Iran's currency. Mossadegh followed Schacht's advice, but failed to carry out the rest of his own plans, which included turning Iran into a republic. The Shah dismissed him on August 18, 1952, thereby costing Schacht a new client.

The Schachts returned to Egypt. On September 22, 1952, they arrived in Cairo. He was to act as a consultant to Egypt's minister of finance, Abdel Guelil. After all, Schacht's Hamburg bank was now open, a fait accompli, and in democratic West Germany it was not so easy to withdraw a license. His specific task in Egypt was to advise on how to float bonds to compensate Egyptian landowners who had lost their holdings under Colonel Nasser's sweeping agrarian-reform program. While Schacht was in Cairo, the press asked him about the skirmish between Iran and the

United States over oil. He benignly suggested direct negotiations between the United States and Iran, but of course "taking into account the British point of view."[338] He must have been delighted. Suddenly, he was once more a player on the international scene. In his memoirs Schacht talked with great admiration of (now) General Naguib, one of the new Egyptian leaders: "a gentle and charming man." Too gentle, it seemed. He was soon elbowed aside by the more martial Nasser, who eventually took Egypt into the desultory Six-Day War against Israel.

The publicity surrounding his time in Iran and Egypt could not fail to bring its reaction in Hamburg. His banking permit came under review — a costly and complicated procedure for the Hamburg senate, clearly politically motivated. No elected Hamburg official wanted to be accused of "Nazi coddling."

Not surprisingly, Schacht still had supporters in West Germany. On November 21 Dr. Wilhelm Vocke, who now ran the Bank Deutscher Länder, a quasi–national reserve bank and the closest thing to the old Reichsbank, testified at the hearing in Hamburg that Schacht was "a superior expert of incontestable quality."[339] The AP reported that he finally retained his full bank permit on December 19, 1952. He was seventy-five years old and was described in the report as the man who once "juggled figures for Adolph [sic] Hitler."

He returned to the Near East. On December 7, he and Manci were in Damascus to help the Syrians. They needed his help in financing a development and reclamation project.[340] He was successful and was hired to handle various other Syrian projects.

The lean years were over, once and for all. He always liked to do things around New Year's, so he opened a second bank in Düsseldorf on January 15, 1953. Schacht & Co. was now in full swing. There seemed to be no end to its projects. In 1959 the eighty-two-

338. UPI (September 25, 1952).
339. *New York Times* (November 22, 1952).
340. AP (December 9, 1952).

year-old Schacht was invited to survey the Philippine economy for the Philippine National Bank. In 1963 he advised Algeria, and in 1964, at eighty-seven, he was on his way to Lima with Manci. (He was in Peru only "as a tourist.")[341] He also planned to build a palm oil plant in Indonesia.

On rare occasions, there were setbacks. Novelist Robert Daley, then a roving sports correspondent for the *New York Times*, reported in 1959 that Schacht & Co. had offered to finance a 100,000-seat football stadium in Marseilles, at an interest rate of 6 percent, but Schacht's bank was turned down because the Marseille government resented his history. [342]

In 1960 the Catholic church dedicated a chapel at the site of the old Dachau concentration camp, and as a former inmate Schacht was invited by Munich's Bishop Neuhäusler to attend the memorial. Among the others present were former prisoners Edmond Michelet, the French minister of justice, and former Austrian chancellor Leopold Figl. It should have served to rehabilitate him with some of those who still thought of him as a Nazi, but some Brown stain always remained. The Ruhr newspaper *Esscher Tageblatt* reported on June 17, 1952, that along with other former government officials of the Nazi era like State Secretaries Meissner and Lammers, Vice Chancellor and Ambassador Franz von Papen, and Postal Minister Wilhelm Ohnesorge, Schacht was still drawing a substantial governmental pension.[343] It raised eyebrows and complaints. On a return trip from Cairo, his plane made an overnight stop in Geneva, and he was prohibited from leaving the airport because he was still not welcome in Switzerland. He had to sit up most of the night in the airport waiting room, until a policeman came to drive him to a hotel. His complaints were loud and bitter, but he made his connection.

341. AP (June 4, 1964).
342. *New York Times*, (October 26, 1959), p. 44:4.
343. T. H. Tetens, *The New Germany and the Old Nazis*, p. 218.

25

FINAL BALANCE

SCHACHT CAREFULLY CHRONICLED the details of his life in his widely read autobiography, *My First Seventy-Six Years*. Thereafter, many authors wrote strange accounts of his doings. Two books accuse him of having collaborated with the well-known Nazi thug and "liberator of Mussolini," SS Colonel Otto Skorzeny, who was living in Spain and had supposedly married a niece of Schacht's. Schacht was said to have earned a fortune in Madrid, where Skorzeny had created an ex-Nazi, ex-SS center of sorts. Schacht was said to have helped Skorzeny locate hidden German funds in Spain and to have helped Skorzeny obtain orders for military equipment and German military experts for Egypt. The so-called niece, a Nazi sympathizer named Ilse von Finkenstein, did indeed marry Otto Skorzeny, but she was not Schacht's niece. She was vaguely related to the family doctor with whom young Hjalmar Schacht had lived as an upper school student in Hamburg. When Hjalmar and Manci Schacht first arrived in Madrid on a business trip, the woman attached herself to them and represented herself as their "niece" to Madrid's ex-Nazis, like former Luftwaffe fighter ace Hans-Ulrich Rudel and Belgium's former Nazi chief Léon Degrelle.[344] Perhaps she wanted to as-

---

344. Author's interview with Manci Schacht, October 24, 1996.

sume the dubious prestige of being related to a former minister of the Third Reich. Since Ilse Skorzeny was widely involved in helping former SS men escape Germany and emigrate to South America, she probably had much contact with organizations of former SS members like the Brotherhood and *Odessa*. Schacht was accused of indirectly helping these organizations through the Skorzenys. This was probably the reason why William Stevenson, the British journalist who met Schacht in Indonesia, had asked Schacht what he knew about the Brotherhood. The rumor was persistent but patently untrue. Skorzeny died of cancer in Madrid in 1975, ending these accusations.

The emerging Cold War called for the return of German pragmatism. Konrad Adenauer, the towering figure at the helm of the new West Germany, was the right man for the time and the task. Adenauer managed to battle the Allied victors while holding off certain devotedly democratic and liberal Germans. Under Adenauer, West Germany faced old debts, such as monetary compensation for former German citizens of the Jewish faith and made forceful efforts to support the new state of Israel. Yet, his state secretary (chief of staff) was the politically tainted Dr. Hans Globke, who in 1934 had provided a legal commentary for the racial laws, the so-called Nuremberg Laws, which became the Nazis' definition for the status of Germany's Jewish citizens. These were the laws that legalized all eventual Nazi excesses against German Jews, including the infamous Final Solution.

In 1952 Globke had held high office. In the new Germany, in September 1968, the president of West Germany, Heinrich Lübke, and Chancellor Kurt Kiesinger gave a retirement dinner to honor Globke.

Trying to restabilize a shattered nation frequently called for awkward and distasteful compromises. The Federal Republic made use of General Reinhard Gehlen, an anti-Russian intelligence specialist who had received his training as an important functionary in Hitler's German army. Nor did the victorious American government set a shining example when they recruited Wernher von Braun, whose V-2 rockets had rained death on

Britain's civilian population. (The *V* stood for *Vergeltungswaffe,* or "revenge weapon.")

Adenauer understood how to balance the external and internal demands of the fierce Cold War with the long-term democratic goals of "his" new Germany. No one could accuse him of fascist sympathies or of a lack of principle, but he was a political professional with a keen eye for the persuasive power of good results, even if the solution involved some short-term compromise. Men like Globke and Gehlen were part of short-term solutions. Other prominent but sullied Germans were found newly acceptable by the former Western Allies in the hasty bedfellowship of the Cold War, but not Schacht.

Schacht was once again a prominent international banker, but Adenauer and his associates had no intention of offering him a role in the Federal Republic. They seemed more than leery of turning to the ambitious, unaccountable and obstreperous curmudgeon Hjalmar Horace Greeley Schacht for opinions and assistance. He had fought against every previous regime, and the new Federal Republic needed help, not outrage.

Schacht's export bank remained open until 1963. He became comfortably wealthy but by no means contented.

Second-rank countries still begged and cajoled him to help solve their financial crises, but the great nations of the world, just like his own, ignored him, as did the great bankers. According to Ron Chernow's history of the distinguished Jewish Warburg banking family, sometime during the fifties Siegmund Warburg was asked by Schacht to meet with him in Munich. Siegmund accepted the invitation and found "a servile and groveling Schacht rambling on about some investments in the Philippines." Warburg was not interested but, as a courteous gesture, offered to take the proposition under advisement. He never pursued it. His attitude seemed typical of the international banking community.

The Schachts lived in a pleasant apartment in an upper-class residential section of Munich. He bought a summerhouse on the Chiemsee, a lake near Munich, and tried to draw his family around him. His eldest daughter, Inge van Scherpenberg, whose husband was once more in Germany's postwar Foreign Service, gave him four grandchildren. Konstanze married Michaele Spadafora, an Italian of prominent family, but their marriage came apart when Konstanze left her husband for another man. Cordula became a lawyer in Munich but became somewhat estranged from Manci, who faced her ninetieth birthday in 1997.

Schacht's energy lasted until the day of his death. After 1963 Schacht lectured frequently and answered unending requests by the news media and individual authors for commentary and opinions. He appeared on television in Washington, D.C., in the spring of 1963. Cordula accompanied her father to America, while Manci stayed in Munich because there were only tickets for two. Cordula would have enjoyed the trip, had her father desisted from lecturing her and instructing her without respite. The octogenarian Hjalmar Schacht was not an easy man. Only Manci seemed able to deal with him, and she was the only person he would listen to.

During the 1960s many producers of film and television documentaries had their final chance to tap the knowledge of the last aging survivors of Hitler's court, and like Speer, Schacht was among those who were interviewed. He was busy, but not in the manner and at the level he wished. Interviews and the lecture circuit are never a satisfactory final chapter for any man who has participated in the Sturm und Drang of major international events.

He increasingly turned toward Manci.

They now lived alone, in the apartment on the residential square on the suburban side of the Isar River. The building was pleasant and quite modern, almost functional, with four stories and a self-service elevator. There was a row of bell buttons near the front door, and one of them simply said "Dr. Schacht." None of the honorary titular preambles that had once preceded his name. The apartment's decor was definitely Manci's, with many touches of her favorite pink. They spent less time at their country place on the Chiemsee and settled for the company of a few remaining friends in Munich. Increasingly, Schacht was unwilling to mingle, to chat, to make small talk.

One evening in 1970 the Schachts were to join old friends for dinner. It was their host's eightieth birthday. Hjalmar complained. He did not feel like going out and making dinner conversation. Even worse, it was black tie! Manci chided her ninety-three-year-old husband that they could not disappoint their host. "After all," she said, "he's eighty!" A grumbling Schacht started to put on his dinner suit, or as the Germans call it, his *Smoking*. As he climbed into his trousers, he lost his balance and fell. Manci helped him into an armchair, but he had obviously hurt himself seriously and was soon in great pain. They called their family doctor, Dr. Hans Huber, who rushed over and knew at once that Schacht had cracked his hipbone and probably more. He had to be rushed to the hospital. After Huber had telephoned for an ambulance, he told his patient, "For heaven's sake, Dr. Schacht, why not sit down when you put on your trousers?" Then, before he was carried out of the apartment, Schacht, as usual, had the last word. Clearly angry, he said to the doctor, "Why the devil didn't you tell me to sit down whenever I put on my pants?"

He was taken to the hospital, where he died not long after being admitted. The man who escaped Hitler's wrath and the Allied hangman was killed by an embolism. The date was Thursday, June 4, 1970.

He was buried at Munich's Ostfriedhof cemetery. One hundred fifty mourners were graveside, including the president of the Bundesbank and other prominent members of the new Germany's financial community. According to the *New York Times,* "The brown wooden coffin was piled high with flowers." One card said, "To a companion in hard times — 20 July Foundation."

On July 20, 1944, the late Count von Stauffenberg had tried unsuccessfully to assassinate Adolf Hitler.

QUESTIONS

I STILL HAD thirty minutes until my rendezvous with the ninety-year-old Manci Schacht. I wanted some time to think before I faced her in the Schacht apartment. I found a small *Konditorei,* a coffee shop, around the corner. It served magnificent Bavarian pastries and strong coffee. The place was quite empty except for an elderly, well-dressed couple, obviously at their *Stammtisch,* their usual table. They spoke in the slightly nasal accent of the north and were most courteous to the young girl who served them their coffee and cake. Noblesse oblige. They were sure to know Manci Schacht. This residential section of Munich, across the Isar River from the main part of town, is home to many wealthy retirees, and they all know one another. Coincidentally, at the end of the war, a group of us, all American military intelligence people, had a villa nearby.

Enough stalling. Soon I would ring the bell marked "Dr. Schacht," and then I would have to ask questions. I tried to assemble the list.

When you write biography, you put the facts into chronological order and then place them into context with the events of the time. You also try to reconstruct the way people thought. Not easy, that. Even recent history seems hard to swallow.

It is hard to believe that forty short years ago U.S. Senator Joseph McCarthy caused decent Americans to compromise their principles by making other Americans into outcasts because they refused to "think the way they were supposed to." McCarthy was a hero to many.

Okay, the questions.

I would ask about his admitted prejudices — or would I?

I could never accept Schacht's view of the Jews, nor could my father. Schacht's insistence on designating Christianity as the only cultural basis for German, and probably European, culture would have robbed us of so much great painting, theater, music, architecture, and literature. No sense then, asking the question. It would never be understood.

Schacht's view of democracy was also flawed, but so was the American version until women's suffrage and civil rights legislation.

What about his towering ambition? He freely admitted it and considered it a laudable trait. He was born into an educated environment but was haunted by a constant lack of money. He could probably be forgiven for swearing that it would never happen to him. Also, did he want to prove himself equal to his mother's titled family? Was he trying to remove the taint of a mésalliance? All understandable, but his youthful ambition became a lifelong obsession. The Germans have a word for it, *Geltungsbedürftnis*, the need to be recognized. He would do anything for recognition. He was even furious when his achievements were not listed by a Nazi newspaper he detested.

Was he a genius?

He made his international reputation in 1923 by insisting on dictatorial powers to deal with runaway inflation, a national emergency. How he became currency commissioner is still an open question. Some feel that it was Jakob Goldschmidt's way of ridding himself of Schacht while creating a powerful government contact. It was Goldschmidt who persuaded the government to hire Schacht.

Was he inventive?

No doubt, but behind all the razzledazzle he remained a deeply conservative banker who believed in the gold standard, in export, in profit, and in solid collateral. His impoverished beginnings, his time as a journalist and a lobbyist, taught him that if you do not own a suit of tails, you have to borrow one. What matter if illusion is the basis for a deal, so long as the deal succeeds?

What of his patriotism?

It became his justification for almost all his personal and public decisions, and he based his Nuremberg defense on it. In the kaiser's Germany, patriotism was usually proven in blood on the field of battle, but Schacht never wore a uniform. His high collar was his battle armor, but he was never part of the parade ground fraternity. Did he decide he would show them it took more than a uniform to serve your country? Patriotism became his obsession. International financial machinations, battles with foreign statesmen, fights with the Weimar leaders, his early support of Hitler, his breach with Hitler — whatever he did was done for his personal definition of patriotism.

Was he guilty of helping Hitler haunt the world?

He was freed by the International Military Tribunal at Nuremberg by defending himself against the narrowest of accusations. The tribunal's credibility depended on the validity, the enforceability, of its indictments. They could not prosecute a man for loving the devil. They could only accuse him of helping the devil to do a specific criminal thing. The real crime was admiring him.

Was he ever a Nazi?

There was a time when he admired Hitler. Surely, he had to have known from the very beginning that Hitler stood for murder, brutality, and arrogance. The viciousness of the original Nazi program, the earliest demonstrations of brutality, the Röhm affair, the murder of the von Schleichers and other conservatives, the open street beatings and arbitrary arrests, could have left him no doubt. He even voiced his complaints directly to Hitler as early as 1934. He knew he was dealing with a thug and his henchmen. He made sure never to join their party. He detested war and extralegal excesses like Kristallnacht because they interfered with international commerce. He loved trade — everywhere, anytime, and with anyone. It was his language, his music, his religion. Hitler's *Lumpen* anti-Semitism interfered with trade. Hitler's military buildup after the necessary rearmament interfered with trade. Autark and Göring interfered with trade, as did Goebbels's propaganda. Schacht helped some Jews because their persecution might have caused international boycotts. He tried to block Hitler's demands on the Reichsbank because his war preparations were inflationary and ruined exports. Eventually, he broke with Hitler, but he had also broken with the monarchists and with the Weimar Republic. He simply could not believe that any German government was smart enough, clever enough, worldly enough to run the country.

In his view, only international commerce backed by military might could keep Germany great, and it seemed eminently clear that only he, Hjalmar Horace Greeley Schacht, understood that formula. Even after he was dismissed, he could not bear to think that the man in the Chancellery would be so foolish as to ignore the views of his wisest minister.

Would I ask her any of these questions? Never! Besides, by now I think I know the answers. So I paid for my *Kaffee und Kuchen* and left the nice little *Konditorei* and its seductive smells. On the way out, the old couple silently gestured a courteous greeting.

A few minutes later I rang the bell marked "Dr. Schacht." Manci Schacht was still tall, beautiful, gracious, and filled with charm. She had brewed excellent tea and served delicious pastries. We chatted awhile at random and then I asked her a few details about their travels, their homes, their children, and the circumstances of her husband's death.

It was easy to see why Hjalmar Schacht had fallen in love with her.

BIBLIOGRAPHY

Bower, Tom. *The Pledge Betrayed: America and Britain and the Denazi-fication of Postwar Germany.* Garden City, N.Y.: Doubleday, 1982.

Chernow, Ron. *The Warburgs.* New York: Random House, 1993.

Classen, Werner. *Fourier.* Zurich, 1977.

Dawes, Rufus C. *The Dawes Plan in the Making.* Indianapolis: Bobbs Merrill, 1925.

Dodd, Martha. *Through Embassy Eyes.* New York: Harcourt Brace, 1939.

Duggan, Steven. *A Professor at Large.* New York: Macmillan, 1943.

Eckhardt Wolf von, and Sander L. Gilman *Bertolt Brecht's Berlin: A Scrapbook of the Twenties.* New York: Anchor/Doubleday, 1975.

Engelmann, Bernt. *Germany without Jews.* Trans., D. J. Beer. New York: Bantam, 1984.

Feis, Herbert, *1933: Character in Crisis.* Boston: Little, Brown, 1966.

Fest, Joachim C. *Das Gesicht des Dritten Reiches.* Munich: R. Piper, 1988.

———. *Hitler.* Trans., Richard and Clara Winston. New York: Vintage, 1975.

———. *Staatsstreich.* Berlin: Siedler, 1994.

Fischer, Albert. *Hjalmar Schacht und die Deutsche Judenfrage.* Cologne: Bohlau, 1995.

Fromm, Bella. *Blood and Banquets.* New York: Birchlane Press, 1990.

Gisevius, Hans Bernd. *BIS ZUM BITTEREN ENDE.* Zurich: Fretz & Wasmuth, 1946.

Hassell, Ulrich von. *Die Hassell-Tagebücher 1938–1944: Deutscher Widerstand 1937–1945.* Berlin: Siedler, 1988.

Hemingway, Ernest. *By-Line: Ernest Hemingway.* New York: Scribner, 1967.

Higham, Charles. *Trading with the Enemy: An Exposé.* New York: Delacorte, 1983.

Höhne, Heinz. *Canaris: Patriot im Zwielich.* Munich: Bertelsmann, 1984.

———. *Die Machtergriefung: Deutschland's Weg in die Hitler-Diktatur.* Hamburg: Spiegel-Buch, 1983.

———. *The Order of the Death's Head: The Story of Hitler's SS.* Trans. Richard Barry. London: Pan, 1972.

Huddleston, Sisley. *In My Time: An Observer's Record of War and Peace.* New York: Dutton, 1938.

Hull, Cordell. *Memoirs.* New York: Macmillan, 1948.

Klein, Ernst. *Road to Disaster.* London: George Allen, 1940.

Klemperer, Victor. *Tagebücher.* Berlin: Aufbau, 1995.

von Krockow, Christian. *Die Deutschen in Ihrem Jahrhundert 1890–1990.* Hamburg: Rowohlt, 1994.

Lange, Annemarie. *Berlin in der Weimarer Republik.* Berlin: Dietz, 1987.

Mann, Golo. *Deutsche Geschichte des 19 und 20 Jahrhunderts.* Frankfurt: Fischer, 1992.

Maser, Werner. *Nuremberg: A Nation on Trial.* Trans. Richard Barry. New York: Scribner, 1979.

Metcalfe, Philip. *1933.* Sag Harbor, N.Y.: Permanent Press, 1988.

Moffat, J. P. *The Moffat Papers.* Cambridge: Harvard University Press, 1995.

Mühlen, Norbert. *Schacht: Hitler's Magician.* New York: Alliance Book Corp., 1939.

Papen, Franz von. *Der Wahrheit eine Gasse.* Munich: Paul List, 1952.

Pentzlin, Heinz. *Hjalmar Schacht.* Berlin: Ullstein, 1980.

Persico, Joseph E. *Nuremberg.* New York: Viking, 1994.

Peterson, Edward N. *Hjalmar Schacht: For and Against Hitler.* Boston: Christopher Publishing House, 1954.

Picker, Henry. *Hitler's Tischgespräche.* Frankfurt: Ullstein, 1989.

Prüfer, Carl. *Diaries.* Kent, Ohio: Kent State University Press, 1988.

Przybski, Peter. *Täter neben Hitler.* Berlin: Brandenburgisches, 1990.

Quinn, William. *Wild Bill Remembers.* Fowlerville, Mich.: Wilderness Press, 1991.

Schacht, Hjalmar. *Abrechnung mit Hitler.* Hamburg: Rowohlt, 1949.

———. *Grundsätze Deutscher Wirtschaftspolitik* (2 vols.). Oldenburg: Stalling, 1932.

———. *Interest or Dividend?* Speech delivered before the German Chamber of Commerce in Basel, Switzerland, December 11, 1933. Trans. and printed by the Reichsbank, Berlin, 1933.

———. *[Das Jahr] 1933: Wie eine Demokratie Stirbt.* Düsseldorf: Econ., 1968.

———. *76 Jahre meines Lebens.* Bad Wörishofen: Kindler & Schiermeyer, 1953.

Schmidt, Paul. *Statist auf der Diplomatischer Bühne 1923–1945.* Bonn: Athenaeum, 1951.

Simpson, Amos E. *Hjalmar Schacht in Perspective.* New York: Humanities Press, 1969.

Snowden, Philip. *Autobiography.* London: Nicolson & Watson, 1934.

Sonnleithner, Franz von. *Als Diplomat im Führerhauptquartier.* Munich: Langen-Müller, 1989.

Speer, Albert, *Inside the Third Reich.* Trans. Richard and Clara Winston. New York: Macmillan, 1970.

Stahlberg, Alexander. *Die Verdammte Pflicht: Erinnerungen 1932 bis 1945.* Berlin: Ullstein, 1987.

Stevenson, William. *The Bormann Brotherhood.* New York: Harcourt Brace, 1973.

Tansill, Charles Callan. *Back Door to War.* Chicago: Henry Regnery, 1952.

Taylor, Telford. *The Anatomy of the Nuremberg Trials.* New York: Knopf, 1992.

Tetens, Tete Harens. *The New Germany and the Old Nazis.* New York: Random House, 1961.

Weitz, John. *Hitler's Diplomat.* New York: Ticknor & Fields, 1992.

Zentner, Christian, and Friedemann Bedürftig. *Das Grosse Lexikon des Dritten Reiches.* Munich: Südwest, 1985.

INDEX